Complexities of Researching with Young People

Currently, most books on youth research available on the market focus on 'how to' conduct youth research or the research process itself. This edited collection proposes to take this process a step further and discuss the complexities of youth research from a practical and theoretical context.

In total, five themes are examined – conceptualising young people, ethics and consent, the digital, voice, participation and unexpected tensions. In this book, authors from six countries explore the complexities of researching with young people across disciplines and national contexts.

Offering a closeup examination of their own research experiences, the authors address the complexities of researching with young people beyond simple questions of protection from harm and coercion by problematising notions of 'resilience', 'participation', 'risk' and 'voice'. This edited collection takes the reader through an exploration of its key themes and, in doing so, presents a cast of candid and insightful accounts from youth researchers situated within the humanities and social sciences.

Paulina Billett is a lecturer in sociology at La Trobe University, Victoria. Her research explores questions of wellbeing, identity formation and lived experience with a focus on women and young people.

Matt Hart is a lecturer in digital society at the University of Leicester. His research interest is the sociology of youth and digital culture.

Dona Martin is an adjunct researcher at La Trobe University, Bendigo, Victoria. Dona's portfolio includes a broad area of research in education.

Youth, Young Adulthood and Society

Tracy Shildrick
Newcastle University, UK

John Goodwin
University of Leicester,

UK Henrietta O'Connor
University of Leicester, UK

The Youth, Young Adulthood and Society series approaches youth as a distinct area, bringing together social scientists from many disciplines to present cutting-edge research monographs and collections on young people in societies around the world today. The books present original, exciting research, with strongly theoretically and empirically grounded analysis, advancing the field of youth studies. Originally set up and edited by Andy Furlong, the series presents interdisciplinary and truly international, comparative research monographs.

Rethinking Young People's Marginalisation
Beyond Neo-Liberal Futures?
Perri Campbell, Lyn Harrison, Chris Hickey and Peter Kelly

Youth in the Digital Age
Paradox, Promise, Predicament
Edited by Kate C. Tilleczek and Valerie M. Campbell

Modernization as Lived Experiences
Three Generations of Young Men and Women in China
Fengshu Liu

Italian Youth in International Context
Belonging, Constraints and Opportunities
Edited by Valentina Cuzzocrea, Barbara G Bello, Yuri Kazepov

Brazilian Youth
Global trends, local perspectives
Edited by Cláudia Pereira

Complexities of Researching with Young People
Edited by Paulina Billett, Matt Hart and Dona Martin

For more information about this series, please visit www.routledge.com/Youth-Young-Adulthood-and-Society/book-series/YYAS

Complexities of Researching with Young People

Edited by Paulina Billett, Matt Hart and Dona Martin

Routledge
Taylor & Francis Group

LONDON AND NEW YORK

First published 2020
by Routledge
2 Park Square, Milton Park, Abingdon, Oxon OX14 4RN

and by Routledge
52 Vanderbilt Avenue, New York, NY 10017

Routledge is an imprint of the Taylor & Francis Group, an informa business

British Library Cataloguing-in-Publication Data
A catalogue record for this book is available from the British Library

Library of Congress Cataloging-in-Publication Data
Names: Billett, Paulina, editor. | Hart, Matt (Sociologist), editor. |
    Martin, Dona, editor.
Title: Complexities of researching with young people / edited by
    Paulina Billett, Matt Hart, and Dona Martin.
Description: Abingdon, Oxon ; New York, NY : Routledge,
    2020. | Series: Youth, young adulthood and society | Includes
    bibliographical references and index.
Identifiers: LCCN 2019035533 (print) | LCCN 2019035534
    (ebook) | ISBN 9781138388611 (hardback) | ISBN
    9780429424489 (ebook)
Subjects: LCSH: Youth—Research—Methodology. | Participant
    observation.
Classification: LCC HQ796 .C729 2020 (print) | LCC HQ796
    (ebook) | DDC 305.235072/1—dc23
LC record available at https://lccn.loc.gov/2019035533
LC ebook record available at https://lccn.loc.gov/2019035534

ISBN: 978-1-138-38861-1 (hbk)
ISBN: 978-0-429-42448-9 (ebk)

Typeset in Times New Roman
by Apex CoVantage, LLC

For our families, who have given us so much.

Contents

Tables

Contributors

Shain Akhtar is a children's commissioner working for Dudley Metropolitan Borough Council in the UK. Her research interests are the participation and engagement of young people in decision-making processes and influencing social change. She is currently working on preventative work streams for children and young people.

Loretta Anthony-Okeke is a senior tutor in education at the Manchester Institute of Education, University of Manchester, UK. Her latest publication is *Ethically engaging international students: student generated material in an active blended learning model* (Lomer & Anthony-Okeke, 2019).

Tea Torbenfeldt Bengtsson is a senior researcher at VIVE – The Danish Center for Social Science Research, Denmark. Her research focuses on youth in out-of-home care, youth crime, marginalisation and social interventions. She has recently published articles on experiences of belonging and silence in qualitative interviewing and is the coauthor of the book *Youth, Risk, Routine* (2019), together with Signe Ravn.

Moshoula Capous-Desyllas is an associate professor in the sociology department at California State University–Northridge. Her areas of interest and expertise are in arts-based and anti-oppressive approaches to research. Her passion lies in utilising the arts as a form of activism for social justice and change.

Marilyn Chetty is a doctoral candidate in criminology at the University of Auckland. Her research has looked at faith-based interventions in the corrections sector and culturally responsive probation work, and her undergraduate teaching is in penology and criminological theory.

Louisa Choe is currently undertaking a mixed methods PhD, examining why and how the poor pay more in relation to adolescents' experience of unstable housing in New Zealand. Her study seeks to conceptualise and operationalise the different financial, social, opportunity and emotional costs that adolescents are challenged with in situations of unstable housing. In 2018, her paper, 'Evicting my childhood: Adolescents' survival of unstable housing', won the Graduate Essay Prize from the Sociological Association of Aotearoa New Zealand.

Philippa Collin is an associate professor and principal research fellow at the Institute for Culture and Society, University of Western Sydney, and a stream leader in the Wellbeing, Health and Youth Centre of Research Excellence (www.why.org.au). Her publications include *Young Citizens and Political Participation in a Digital Society: Addressing the Democratic Disconnect* and *Young People in Digital Society: Control Shift* (with Amanda Third, Rosalyn Black and Lucas Walsh).

Julia Cook is a lecturer in sociology at the University of Newcastle, Australia. Her research interests are the sociology of youth, time and housing. Her first book is *Imagined Futures: Hope, Risk and Uncertainty*, published in 2018. Follow Julia on Twitter: @julia_anne_cook.

Lucy Cowie (Ngāti Ranginui) is completing a Doctorate of Clinical Psychology at the University of Auckland, which explores LGBTQIA+ young people's understandings of psychological distress with a focus on improving outcomes for LGBTQIA+ young people.

David Farrugia is a senior lecturer in sociology at the University of Newcastle, Australia. His major publications include *Spaces of youth: Work, citizenship and culture in a global context* and *Youth homelessness in late modernity: reflexive identities and moral worth*. Follow David on Twitter: @DavidFarrugiaAU.

Alan France is a professor of sociology at the University of Auckland. His previous publications include *Youth and Social Class: Enduring inequality in the UK, Australia and New Zealand* and *Understanding Youth in the Global Economic Crisis*. Follow Alan on Twitter: @AlanFrance4.

Rimi Khan is a senior research fellow at the University of Melbourne. Her work is broadly concerned with creativity, citizenship and cultural economy. She has published on migrant youth participation and belonging in the context of unstable economic contexts and shifting institutional settings. Her book, *Art in Community: The Provisional Citizen*, was published in 2015.

Fiona MacDonald is a research fellow in the Institute for Sustainable Industries and Liveable Cities (ISILC), Victoria University. Her research is positioned at the intersection of education, belonging and identity for children and young people. Fiona was Chief Investigator on the Victorian Government's School Breakfast Clubs and is currently a chief investigator on the Educational Transition from Custody Project and the BNHCRC Diversity and Inclusion: Building Strength and Capability Project.

Arianna Mainardi is a postdoctoral research fellow at the Department of Sociology and Social Research at the University of Milano-Bicocca. Her research deals with political participation and gender issues, digital culture, youth and social change. Follow Arianna on Academia: https://unimb.academia.edu/AriannaMainardi

David Mayeda is a senior lecturer at the University of Auckland in sociology and criminology. His research interests lie in ethnic minority student success in higher education and youth violence prevention. Follow David on Twitter: @davemayeda.

Aslihan McCarthy is a lecturer at Chisholm Institute and an honorary research fellow at La Trobe University in Australia. She teaches community development and social policy alongside her research on immigrant women.

Joel Robert McGregor is an associate lecturer at the University of Newcastle, Australia. Joel's research interests are on youth, crime and desistance. His PhD examined case management in youth reintegration programs. Follow Joel on Twitter @joelmcgregor.

Sarah Mountz is an assistant professor of social work at the State University of New York at Albany. Her previous research focused on the experiences of LGBTQ youth and young adults who had been incarcerated in girls' facilities in the juvenile justice system in New York. Sarah is especially interested in youth organising and activism and social justice in social work education.

Althea Pestine-Stevens is a PhD student in the School of Social Welfare at the State University of New York at Albany. Her background includes researching and evaluating projects related to kinship families and trauma-informed care in residential treatment centers for youth.

Tepora Pukepuke is a Māori doctoral student at the University of Auckland. Her research interests and publishing cover transforming communities through Maori education success and wellbeing. Follow Tepora on Twitter @TeporaTeach.

Signe Ravn is a senior lecturer in sociology in the School of Social and Political Sciences at Melbourne University. Signe's research centres on the sociology of youth, with a particular focus on drug use and risk, youth cultures and gender, vulnerable youth and processes of marginalisation in youth transitions to adulthood. Signe has published her research in a number of high-ranking international journals, and in 2019, she published her coauthored book *Youth, Risk, Routine*, a new perspective on risk taking in young lives, with Tea Torbenfeldt Bengtsson.

Cosimo Marco Scarcelli is a lecturer in sociology and digital media at Istituto Universitario Salesiano Venezia (IUSVE) and an adjunct professor at the University of Padova. His research deals with youth studies, digital media, the social construction of gender and sexuality. Follow Marco on Twitter: @CMScarcelli.

Darren Sharpe is a senior research fellow at the University of East London. His research interests are in children and young people's health, social care, education and citizenship. Darren has provided academic consultation for the UK Government and EU.

Barbara Spears is an associate professor of education at the University of South Australia. She is widely published and has led many projects, including a review of the National Safe Schools Framework; A Public Health Approach to Sexting; Youth Exposure to and Management of Cyber-Bullying Incidents in Australia; and the Safe and Well Online Study: Young and Well Cooperative Research Centre, in partnership with Western Sydney University.

Spyros Spyrou is a professor of anthropology at European University Cyprus. His research interests include children and identity, nationalism, borders and qualitative research. He is the author of *Disclosing Childhoods: Research and Knowledge Production for a Critical Childhood Studies*.

Teresa Swist is a research fellow at the Institute for Culture and Society, Western Sydney University. Her work has been published in *Journal of Youth Studies*, *New Media and Society*, *Communication and the Public*, and *Continuum: Journal of Media & Cultural Studies*.

Carmel Taddeo is a lecturer in the School of Education at the University of South Australia, and she was postdoctoral research fellow on the Young and Well CRC: Safe and Well Online Project. Her research interests include online research methods and design, change processes, ethics, wellbeing of young people and the potential of technology to facilitate positive outcomes, both in learning settings and broader life contexts.

Dan Woodman is TR Ashworth Associate Professor of Sociology in the School of Social and Political Sciences at the University of Melbourne. Dan's research areas are the sociology of youth, young adulthood and generations. Follow Dan on Twitter: @DrDanWoodman.

Acknowledgement

We wish to thank our families, friends and colleagues for their support and encouragement in putting this edited collection together. We would also like to thank the many wonderful contributors for their candour in sharing the complexity of the research process and the lessons that have been learned.

Most importantly, on behalf of the editorial team and all the contributors to this book, our deepest thanks go out to all the young people we have researched with over the years who have shared their incredible stories with us, from which we have all learnt so very much.

Abbreviations

ABS	Australian Bureau of Statistics
AIFS	Australian Institute of Family Studies
AOIR	Association of Internet Researchers
ARC	Australian Research Council
ARACY	Australian Research Alliance for Children and Youth
CAB	Community Advisory Boards
CALD	Culturally and Linguistically Diverse
CBPR	Community-Based, Participatory Research
CMY	Centre for Multicultural Youth
DECRA	Discovery Early Career Researcher Award
DIMA	Department of Immigration and Multicultural Affairs
ECCV	IRB Institutional Review Boards
EU	European Union
HREC	Human Research Ethics Committee
IRB	Institutional Review Board
LGBTQ	Lesbian Gay Bisexual Transgender Queer/Questioning
LA	Los Angeles
MoNE	Ministry of National Education
NESB'	Non-English Speaking Background
NSW	New South Wales, Australia
PTSD	Post-Traumatic Stress Disorder
PISA	Programme for International Student Assessment
OCN	Open College Network
OHCHR	Office of the United Nations High Commissioner for Human Rights
SEERC	South-East European Research Centre
SNS	Social Network Site
SWO	Safe and Well Online
TEC	Temporary Education Centre
UEB	University Ethics Board
UNCRC	United Nations Convention on the Rights of the Child
WHO	World Health Organisation
YLS/CMI	Youth Level of Services/Case Management Inventory

Chapter 1

Complexities of researching with young people

Conceptualising key issues

Paulina Billett

Conceptualising complexity

The reason that drew us to write this book is a simple one: we, like many others before us, have grappled with the complexity of researching with young people (For example see Bennett, Cieslik and Miles, 2003; Greene and Hogan, 2005; Clark, Flewitt, Hammersley and Robb, 2014). Researching with young people is often as difficult as it is rewarding. Not only are researchers tasked with balancing their own interests against the competing needs of institutions, funding bodies and ethics committees, as well as those of young people, but they also face complexities including ethical, conceptual and design, which they must address if they are to create a successful project.

For most researchers, these complexities centre on how to define who a young person is (particularly since this is not the same across all cultural contexts), ethical issues such as protection from harm and coercion, 'participation', 'risk' and 'voice'. The works presented here provide accounts of young people's lives and experiences by illustrating the reality of their lives. A reality that, as the chapters in this edited collection demonstrate, includes many challenges young people face such as forced migration, homelessness, poverty, interrupted educational pathways and incarceration. Thinking through how we conceptualise position and represent young people as subjects of research allows us as researchers to create an understanding of not only what leads us to researching particular aspects of young people's lives but also the changes and challenges experienced by young people in the 21st century and beyond.

Opportunity to consider a broad perspective of complexities, before undertaking research, is of great benefit to researchers, as it is not uncommon for early career researchers, even those further along the research journey, to feel uncertain about a project and to agonise over ethical question and procedural matters. We therefore suggest that in thinking about why we are conducting the research in the first place, or how our research structure other's thinking about young people, we can come to deeply question our motivations as well as the assumptions we may hold about those who fall within the category of youth. In turn, this introspection allows us to both lay bare the ways in which we construct or personify those we are researching while simultaneously helping us to uncover how society thinks about young people. While instruments, theories and concepts provide a lens which both makes visible and 'shapes' what it means to be a young person (Wyn and White, 2015), it is only with deep reflection on how we think about young people, why we have chosen to use one particular lens over others or why we accept or challenge stablished thinking on the conceptualisation, representation and participation of young people, which help us to understand how we, as researchers overlay, position and construct meaning. Not surprisingly, we felt that questions about how we think about, rather than how to research with young people as central to this book.

In putting this book together it became clear that there are five main, at times overlapping, themes, which presented the largest complexities – how we define young people; ethical issues in researching with young people; the pressures of researching with young people; and young people's voices and participation. What is more, youth research, once seen as a 'soft science' (Heath and Walker, 2011), led us to the push for new and innovative social research as a way to bolster its credibility. While these innovations are derived from older paradigms, for example feminist discussions about voice, others explore areas such as digital youth research, which 20 or so years ago would have been impossible to imagine.

The category of youth

Youth is not a natural category but a relatively recent social construct which is used to define one specific group of society. Youth as a social concept only began to appear in the upper-class in the 17th century when young people were expected to pursue studies. As education became more prevalent, the separation between childhood, youth and adulthood grew. By the turn of the 19th century, with the increasing push for universal education, coupled with the growing alienation of young people from the workforce, the category of youth grew into other classes. However, youth as a life stage was not identified until the early part of the 20th century with the work undertaken by Granville Stanley Hall.

G. Stanley Hall was an American psychologist whose work focused on childhood development and evolutionary theory. In his two-volume work, *Adolescence: Its Psychology and Its Relations to Physiology, Anthropology, Sociology, Sex, Crime, Religion and Education*, originally published in *1904*, Hall examines adolescent development and concludes that adolescence was a psychological and physical stage in life, primarily determined by the onset of puberty and rapid biological changes and characterised by depressed mood. He called this a time of storm and stress. According to Hall, this stage began at around 13 years of age and concluded with full maturity at 24 (Arnett and Tanner, 2006). During this time, young people experienced several distrubances including decreased self-control and an increased sensitivity towards stressful situations. Problematically, the storm and stress models have led to the perception of young people as highly emotional, ready to explode at the least provocation. Hall's storm and stress model, while widely challenged, has also been highly influential. Developmental psychologists still adhere to many of Hall's assertions, including that adolescence is irreversibly linked to biological changes which affect a young person's psyche (see, for example, Reed and Ham, 1993; Arnett and Tanner, 2006; Spear, 2000; Casey et al., 2010).

Psychobiological explanations of adolescence have in turn informed both common societal ideology on youth as well as government policy on young people. In policy as well as 'common sense', young people are conceptualised in terms of qualities young people are believed to be 'lacking' when contrasted to adults – in particular, maturity (both physical and psychological) and responsibility. This outcome is contrasted with the qualities which young people are believed to possess which adults do not: boundless free time and a predilection for risk taking. Unsurprisingly, much focus is placed on the intersection between these qualities; that is what young people do during their leisure time.

Young people's leisure is often seen as a risky endeavour, and unsurprisingly much effort is devoted to regulating this space 'in the best interest' of young people. What young people do in their leisure time has become an object of intense concern for society and interest to those researching young people's lives. The work of youth researchers on young people's leisure time was sparked by the work of Robert Park and Ernest Burgess, who in the 1920s begun constructing ethnographic maps of the social and cultural territories of the Chicago population. Soon after, the work from the Chicago School refuted the dominant psychological theories of deviance which, in line with Stanley Hall's conceptualisation, claimed that youth delinquency was a psychological factor and borne out of young people's craving the thrill of risk taking. Instead the focus shifted to understand delinquency within its sociocultural context, with deviant behaviour being explained as a functional response by young people to their marginalised positions (Bennett and Kahn-Harris, 2004; Blackman, 2005). Rather than simply seeing it as a question of psychology or biology, youth researchers began to argue that the category of youth is highly complex, with social constructions playing a large role in how we define and conceptualise young people and their role in society. Work by the Centre for Contemporary Cultural Studies in Birmingham in the 1970s furthered this.

While accepting the basic premise of deviance as a process, theorists at the CCCS rejected one very important assumption made by earlier theorists: that youth was a homogenous and unified group with its own distinctive culture (Widdicombe and Wooffitt, 1995). The CCCS argued that even though youth appear superficially to be a homogenous entity, it was in fact driven by class divisions and underprivilege: 'unemployment, educational disadvantage, compulsory miseducation, dead end jobs, the routinization and specialisation of labour, low pay and the loss of skills' (Clarke, Hall, Jefferson and Roberts, 1976, p. 4). As a result, deviance was explained as a way in which [predominantly working-class youths] actively expressed their dissatisfaction with life in postwar Britain. Finally, postsubcultural theorists working in the 2000s have reconceptualised leisure time and deviance in a very different way. First seen in the work of Chamber (Muggleton and Weinzierl, 2003), the post-subcultural approach has shown how post-industrialisation and unstructured free time have resulted in a 'clubbing culture'. It is argued that young people's subcultures should not be seen in political terms but instead as a form of escapism or resistance, often afforded by drug use.

Youth transitions in the 21st century

While the work of cultural theorists has influenced much youth research, those examining young people's life trajectories in terms of transitions has been equally important. As has been discussed in the previous section, young people's lives have been primarily conceptualised in terms of an evolution from childhood to adulthood. These transitions are carefully monitored with parents, teachers, social workers and many others routinely 'recruited' to help curb risky behaviour which could pose a threat. As a result, sexual activity, drinking, drug taking, smoking and other 'dangerous' pastimes are highly controlled and regulated by the adult world. Instead young people are encouraged towards 'ideal' 'healthy' pursuits, including exercise (particularly in team and other controlled sports) education and wholesome (often same sex) friendships (Billett, 2014a). Young people who do not accept or conform to this narrow conception of behaviour risk being labelled 'at risk'.

Discourses on youth at risk are framed by the idea that adolescence should be a transition from normal childhood to normal adulthood (Kelly, 2001). There are three 'Traditional transitions' which are most widely recognised; the shift from school to work, from parental home to an independent household and from family of origin to family of destination (Coles, 1995). These pathways into adulthood have habitually been conceptualised as an uncomplicated linear progression, and while this may have been true at some point in the past, evidence suggests that they are harder to achieve in the 21st century.

The interest in understanding and in structuring transitions for young people emerged during the 20th century in response to the increasing failure of young people to achieve these traditional pathways. This is because, in the linear conceptualisation of transition, the failure to meet one key milestone can severely impact an individual's ability to achieve the next, placing the young person at risk of failing to transition. At risk discourses are centred on two key parameters – a 'humanistic concern', encompassing issues of harm, danger, care/support and an 'economic concern', focused on the benefits of identifying risk factors and at-risk populations and the costs of mobilising interventions on the basis of these (Withers and Batten, 1995). As a result, intense interest has been placed on enabling the timely transition through early milestones, particularly that of school to work.

Young people performing poorly or not engaged in education and training are seen as a danger to themselves and society. This outcome is because young people are constructed in terms of future resources, particularly in terms of social and economic capital (Billett, 2014b). Yet, the conditions which lead young people to perform badly or disengage from school are seldom acknowledged. Instead, the failure to perform in school is explained in terms of a young person's lack of future aspiration or other personal 'failing'. Rather than seeing the failure to transition as originating from personal choice or character flaws, youth theorists have sought a more complete explanation. Following theories of reproduction and class, youth researchers examined how different careers, life patterns and trajectories affect young people's ability to achieve adulthood. For example, studies, such as that of Paul Willis's (1977), in which he examined working class youth's rejection of formal education in favour of working-class jobs, have found that gender and socioeconomic background play a large part in the value young people place in education. What is more, as global forces shift the landscape of the workplace, transitioning from school to work may become increasingly more difficult for young people.

The rise of the gig economy, casualisation, under employment and soaring global youth unemployment rates have contributed to making young people's transition into employment harder than ever before. In post-industrial societies, the shift from manufacturing to a service-based economy has meant that young people are finding it increasingly harder to find adequate employment upon completing basic studies. While the promise of post-industrial service sector once appeared to be a concentration on exciting, highly skilled technologically based employment, it has instead delivered employment which is semi-skilled, repetitive and lacking autonomy (Strangleman and Warren, 2008). What is more, the post-industrial push also saw a call for greater flexibility, pushing workers to project-based, short-term, precarious types of contracts.

The gig economy is one of the latest results of the push into an ever more flexible sector. Enabled by the growth of digital platforms, the 'gig economy' 'is based on contracts that are individual rather than collective and irregular, both in terms of hours and duration and in terms of being poorly regulated' (Minter, 2017). Work in the gig economy usually relies on the poorly skilled and is precarious at best, with workers engaged as independent contractors rather than employees and not eligible for basic worker protections or other entitlements (penalty rates, sick leave and so on). Yet for many young school leavers, the reality is that until they are able to gain further qualifications, their employment choices may very well be limited to these more precarious markets.

Unsurprisingly the shifts in economics and social changes have raised uncertainty about the value of traditional conceptions of youth transitions. The once apparently simple linear transition from school to work, from parental home to independent household and from family of origin to family of destination no longer applies for many young people. Instead, youth theorists are challenging the notion of youth transitions as a linear process, and they instead argue that transitions may be fragmented, delayed, blocked or even broken (Chisholm, 1993, p. 30) and may include ambiguities and circularity.

Indeed, the 'scape' of work, education, home ownership has considerably shifted in the 21st century, making their achievement more difficult, but it has also delivered choices. Many young people are now choosing to marry later or not to marry at all, and birthing rates are in decline across most developed nations. Further, while the rise of digital platforms has led to the precariousness of the gig economy, for some, choosing temporary work may be made from a conscious decision rather than necessity. As a result, the choices now available to young people have become increasingly complex (Cieslik and Simpson, 2013).

Consequently, youth transition researchers, rather than seeing the changes to youth transitions purely in terms of structural factors such as social class or gender, have begun to focus more strongly on the role of young people themselves within this process. In short, youth research is attempting to understand how it is that individuals make sense of their lives as a dynamic process rather than simple destiny.

In this section I have overviewed how youth theorists have attempted to understand youth as more than just a question of psychology or biology but instead as a highly complex social construct which defines young people and their role in society. In the next section we turn our attention to the shape of the book and overview the themes and their importance.

Shape of the book

This book examines the complexities of researching with young people. To our knowledge, most books on youth research focus on 'how to' conduct youth research or the research process itself. This edited collection proposes to take this process a step further and discuss the complexities of youth research from a practical and theoretical context. In total five themes are examined – Conceptualising young people, digital research, ethical dilemas, voice and participation and the unexpected tensions of researching with young people. I unpack the aims of each of these themes later in this chapter.

Our aim for this edited collection is to create an offering which has 'self-cohesive' themes that create a 'conversation' between the thematic sections. In order to do this, we have selected works which we felt 'straddled' two or more thematic complexities (for example, digital research and ethics or participation and voice). Therefore, in this collection, we explore the complexities of researching with young people across disciplines and national contexts. As a result, we invite readers to read beyond the section of their main interest and thus begin to consider how the complexities which they may be facing in their research may in fact be the product of larger and far more complex conditions.

Theme 1 – Conceptualising young people

In **conceptualising young people**, readers are reminded that youth is not a stand-alone concept but a complex system of meanings and inferences about who young people are and their place in society. Our authors show that youth is a fluid concept which is constantly constructed, negotiated and reconstructed, and that the meaning of youth changes in different cultural and social settings and through time periods. Researchers are challenged to consider youth as a system of meaning making, one which is largely a Western construct that reproduces existing power imbalances and colonial history. This, we are reminded, are issues which must be considered when undertaking research in culturally diverse settings and in particular with indigenous young people.

Not surprisingly, under this theme it is argued that defining what is a young person is no simple task but rather a highly fraught procedure. In defining young people, our contributors explore the difficulties that arise from attempting to undertake research in settings which may include a multitude of definitions or rejection of youth as a category.

Opening this section is the work of Alan France, Lucy Cowie, Tepora Puke-puke, Marilyn Chetty and David Mayeda. In their work, **Researching the lives of young Māori in Aotearoa, New Zealand: creating culturally sensitive methods and theory**, they neatly conceptualise the complex, methodological and ethical dilemmas encountered in culturally diverse research with young indigenous people. The authors construct an argument based on the juxtaposition of a sensitivity to colonial history, which has and continues to impact via an inherent imbalance of power in the life worlds of the indigenous population. Their work argues that colonising agents such as compulsory education, unified national identity and 'knowledge' enables an imperialistic 'ethnographic gaze' around how social science research is framed. In short, through the work undertaken in this chapter, the authors remind us of the importance of making use of research methodologies that not only recognises the continued impact of colonialism but also finds value in contributions from social science methods and theory when researching with indigenous young people.

Joel Robert McGregor and David Farrugia challenge the ongoing re/definition of youth within a case management program within the Australian juvenile justice system. In **Doing research in organisations: implications of the different definitions of youth**, McGregor and Farrugia argue that youth is a fluid concept that needs to go beyond the discursive construction of risk. They draw upon case managers' constructs of clients by exploring accounts of young people leaving juvenile justice. What emerges in these narratives is a relationally constructed and constantly negotiated fluid and heterogeneous concept of youth, one that requires new approaches to researching young people.

Finally, Matt Hart's chapter **They look before they leap: conceptualising young people as digitally competent risk takers and its implications for ethical internet research** closes this section with a discussion on the ethical complexities that arise when researching in online environments due to our legitimate necessity to address human research ethics committee (HREC) and institutional review board (IRB) rules and regulations. Hart explores in situ a researcher's requirement to ensure safety for participants, researchers and host institutions. While respecting the need to preserve the rights and dignity of young research participants within 'risk-averse' projects, he also highlights how restrictive current regulations are to researchers working in this space. The argument posed is of great interest to many, as the notion of youth as inherently 'at-risk' or 'vulnerable' is often easily challenged by young people employing informed knowledge and keen skills demonstrative of 'competent' online participants. In his chapter, Hart challenges researchers to explore current workarounds and to use them to build processes and structures to offer those involved in HREC/IRB work.

Theme II – Digital research

With the rise of digital media, we have seen the birth of digital research. The interest in the digital world, and how young people occupy and make use of this space, is an object of intense interest to academics and professionals. However, as research into the digital world grows, so do our experiences of the complexity of researching in this space. Digital environments call for researchers to develop sensitivity towards and awareness of how young people's lives are being performed, recorded and commodified.

As it is shown by the writers for this section, the digital is a minefield for researchers. The rise of digital research has brought into question the relevance and suitability of traditional research methodologies for the online environment, leading to new sets of challenges surrounding the best ways in which to adapt these methodologies successfully. It has also highlighted a number of ethical pitfalls which researchers must navigate, including issues of representation, data collection and participation.

How we may best interpret young people's intimacy in digital spaces may represent our greatest trial. Youth in the digital are often sources of public and social anxiety (Hasinoff, 2012). Researchers have contributed to this by being largely focused and reporting on the negative effects of young people's intimate engagement in these spaces. Yet, as the work presented in this section shows, some researchers are taking strides to demonstrate the potential benefits young people can leverage through the digital helping to redefine how we interpret young people's intimacy in this space. Further to this, the digital, like no other space, blurs the boundaries between ethical research and exploitation. While ethical concerns surrounding exploitation are largely centred on issues of data collection existing in the 'public' domain (such as posts or blogs), and its ethical use, there are other ways in which young people's digital presence may also lead to a subtler form of exploitation. Exploitation can occur in a number of ways, including the inability to accurately represent young people's works as they chose to present them (for example using pseudonyms or obscuring faces or other identifying markers on photos).

In short, our authors explore several aspects of digital research, including the theoretical complexities and challenges of digital youth research, particularly around the ethics of data capture and analysis, the convergence of 'new' and 'old' methods of research, trends in digital research, such as digital rights for young people and sexualities and the use of digital tools specifically created for use by young people, all of which are opening up new research opportunities.

In **Critical reflections: merits of using youth-centric technology in keeping young people safe across Europe**, Darren Sharpe, Spyros Spyrou and Shain Akhtar draw on the lessons learned from an EU funded project to produce a digital tool for young refugees to discuss participatory research leading to the successful coproduction of digitals tools for safeguarding young people in the 'real world'. In their work, they offer an illustration of the complexities and benefits, both theoretically and in practice, in coproducing research with young people. The work provides insights, for those keen to explore youth voice and engagement within settings of nonformal learning, as it demonstrates a way for young people to have their rights as citizens acknowledged, respected and safeguarded and to have their perspectives made visible

In sharing their successes and challenges, the authors not only broaden perspectives for those exploring digital coproduction and research participation but also present valuable insights for those keen to explore issues of voice and participation.

In **Digital modes of data collection in a mixed-method longitudinal youth research**, Julia Cook and Dan Woodman's share their insights into the recent integration of digital data collection within a long-running, large-scale, mixed-methods study of two generations of Australian young adults as part of a Life Patterns study. In their work, Cook and Woodman invite us to explore new challenges and opportunities offered by digital data collection in contemporary youth research and explore the potential of digital data to produce valuable insights into the complexities that characterise young lives.

Finally, in **Revealing intimacy through digital media: young people, digital culture and new research perspectives,** Cosimo Marco Scarcelli and Arianna Mainardi encourage the reader to consider the ways in which young people's intimacy is 'imagined' and constructed in these spaces, as well as the impact this can have for our understanding of young people's digital engagement. Scarcelli and Mainardi skilfully demonstrate how we must employ a complex understanding of youth intimacy in the digital space which moves beyond deterministic explanations to conduct effective digital research. Scarcelli and Mainardi's work also speaks to the themes of voice, participation and conceptualisation of young people.

Theme III – Ethical dilemmas

Issues of consent and ethics are key aspects of creating sound youth research. Consent is intrinsically tied to issues of justice, stemming from society's preoccupation with issues of protection, the likelihood of conflicts of interest and potential harm to young people from unethical research practices. This work has led to a standardisation of administrative aspects that influence the research process. Yet little attention is paid to how ethical requirements may impact the populations who we research with.

Under this theme, authors explore the complexity of ethics on and off the field and in a multiplicity of contexts. We are reminded that ethics, while essential in creating sound research, can also hamper the research process. This is particularly true when researching with vulnerable young people and non-Western cultural settings.

Opening this section is the work of Loretta Anthony-Okeke. Her work, **Researching young people's experiences: an African-centred perspective of consent and ethics**, brings to attention the need to broaden Anglo-Western universities' ethical review boards' understanding of ethics to include non-Western parameters. Her argument focuses attention on added challenges and complexities when applying Anglo/Euro-Western-based hegemonic ethics, in particular the principle of informed consent, to research young Africans' academic experiences. She adeptly argues that an Afrocentric paradigm, emerging from an African knowledge and value system about lived experience, is hindered by postcolonial deficit literature and theories.

Loretta articulates a strong argument for change through a critical analysis of ethical frameworks and an incorporation of particular cultural elements and nuances that influence the worldview of the researcher/researched in terms of how they *know* and *see* consent in the research process. Loretta's contribution offers researchers ways to broaden postcolonial frameworks and to embrace marginalised groups into sharing in the privilege of knowledge and the value systems of the researched.

In **Working with complexity: between control and care in digital research ethics**, Philippa Collin, Teresa Swist, Carmel Taddeo and Barbara Spears highlight wide disparities between the collection and treatment of data across digital platforms and services. In this chapter, the reader's attention is drawn to some of the unintended consequences and limitations of current ethical conventions in the context of digital research with young people. This work connects a historical account of the development of ethics with deficit-based notions of youth and challenges current parameters of privacy, consent and risk within rapidly transforming processes of data collection, analysis and application. Researchers are encouraged towards a receptive and responsive approach to ethics, a deliberate turn away from risk management approaches with regard to digital cultures and data and encourages adoption of an integrated approach to research ethics. An approach that recognises novel entanglements of people, platforms and places and promotes young people's agency.

In the concluding chapter for this theme, **Informed consent as a situated research process in an ethnography of incarcerated youth in Denmark**, Tea Torbenfeldt Bengtsson adds depth to discussions around securing informed consent by taking us into the world of ethnographic research with incarcerated youth. Bengtsson's analysis of lived experiences heightens our awareness of the complexities in connecting with young people in vulnerable situations and encourages discussion of what actually constitutes informed consent in practice. Bengtsson connects informed consent with perhaps the greatest engagement issue with similar cohorts that of pushback, often the only way such a cohort has to fight the system or have any control over the circumstance of their involvement. In exploring workarounds and reflexivity when gaining informed consent, Bengtsson shares ways for researchers to establish access, build connections and contextualise methods – all points of great value in studies where the power imbalance is clear and where there is a denial of access to the researcher.

Theme IV – Voice and participation

There are a number of issues which are explored under this theme; there are the complexities which arise from trying to understand what social, economic, cultural or political participation means for young people; the need to balance young people's participation in research with the needs of the researchers, compliance with ethics committees and timelines; and how young people's voices are 'made' and 'heard' through participatory practices.

Within this theme, readers are reminded that in researching with young people it is important to ensure that those we research with do not become mere objects of research, but instead they become partners in the research process whose voices are genuinely represented and heard (Billett, 2012). However, as can be seen from the contributions to this section, this outcome is often not easy to achieve.

Those who research with youth faced many hurdles which must be overcome, including engaging young people in research, satisfying the requirements of ethics committees and engaging vulnerable or difficult to reach groups of young people in the research process. The choice of where and who to research with is usually guided by practical aims of the research design and scope can also be problematic. As is ensuring that we continue to work with 'difficult to engage' or 'vulnerable' to avoid the 'invisibility' and 'muteness' of these groups. In short, in this section, readers are invited to consider who they will research with and how we can ensure genuine participation and representation.

Opening this theme is the work of Fiona MacDonald, **The undue burden of methodological warrant on the collective voice of disengaged young people**. Macdonald takes us through an exploration of the burden of methodological warrant research using the collective voice of young people. Her work focuses our attention on research in school reform by having the reader consider the affordances provided to the self-narratives of young people reengaged with education as a way of allowing them to speak for the passively disengaged. Macdonald's work highlights that while some participants share a narrative of difference, the participants we most need to give voice to have an inability to conform. In short, her work is a timely reminder to researchers working with young people who have disengaged with education that in doing so, we need to build targeted insights into how the process of disengagement begins and progresses before we work to discern the most appropriate intervention stages.

In the work presented in this chapter, the reader is challenged to reflect on the point, that while the subjective voices heard must be recognised for the valuable insights they provide into the 'inequalities associated with learning', we as researchers must be alert to the point that these voices are those of the direct beneficiaries of any end product/service and therefore cannot be used directly as a key argument for school reform.

Critically examining participation, power, ethics and the co-construction of knowledge in a community-based photovoice research project with LGBTQ former foster youth shares individual and collective transformative aspects of research that used photovoice to overcome complex ethical issues encountered in a community-based, arts-informed research program with LGBTQ former foster youth in Los Angeles, California. In their research, Moshoula Capous-Desyllas, Sarah Mountz and Althea Pestine-Stevens highlight the voices of LGBTQ former foster youth and demonstrate how to share power in the research process. This research focuses our attention on empowering marginalised individuals to represent themselves, to be participants and to have a voice. In their work, the team explores outcomes collected through critical reflections with various stakeholders and foster youth via a community-based photography exhibit, a community-informed dialogue session, a graffiti board and an interactive website.

Their work highlights important issues/pitfalls researchers should consider when preparing an arts-based research project for institutional ethics approval. They share details of a participatory method that both enabled them to engage stakeholders in the planning process of the research and to facilitate community investment in the research. Their work offers researchers a strong account of recruitment, and outcomes of participant interaction. Through their discussion, they offer insights into participatory research as a way to transform and expand access within other institutional research settings.

In a shift of perspective, Signe Ravn's ethnographic work **Participation, positionality and power: critical moments in research with service-engaged youth,** reflects on recruitment as well as ethical challenges to research based on the participation of young women who are marginalised in the educational system and/or labour market and involved in drug treatment or criminal justice programmes in Victoria Australia. Her work is valued for broadening the research ethics perspective by including discussion on participation and constructive researcher-participant relationships. Ravn's work provides researchers with insight into a structure that considers recruitment and participation, researcher positionality and the management of relations with participants. By encouraging consideration of the broader social and symbolic hierarchies, unavoidably reflected in an interview/research encounter, Ravn also explores the frustration and challenges of participants not wanting to engage in research programs. In giving 'voice' to young people, Ravn discusses ways to alter power relations, establish rapport in the field, add value to reflecting on performative aspects of research, consider the power dynamics and offer us opportunities to shape our research so as to better understand and interpret resulting data. In providing this well-articulated insight into her research, Ravn provides us an opportunity to not only broaden our perspective but also to develop as researchers.

In her desk review of existing international research addressing the needs, concerns, attitudes and aspirations of young Syrian refugees in Turkey titled **Participatory research and political ecology: an evaluation of research with young Syrian refugees in Turkey**, Aslihan McCarthy challenges the accuracy or appropriateness of values placed on standardised research instruments and techniques. She situates this focus through a consideration of power asymmetries and/or cultural group and demographic differences, in work with young refugees involved in multidisciplinary research, and she draws attention to significant challenges to research in difficult situations such as the negotiation of appropriately informed consent. Overall, McCarthy's contribution draws attention to research complexities and issues that require focused consideration. For example, in drawing on the sociopolitical context of Turkey, shedding light on the sociocultural framework and the 'political ecology', we find we are challenged to consider if we as researchers are influenced by the Western ideal of democracy in any of our participatory research. In drawing attention to challenges faced by young Syrian refugees, McCarthy causes us to question how we engage in research on sensitive subjects, through an exploration of research hampered by bureaucratic barriers, political concerns and security issues.

The contribution of this desk review is significant, as it encourages all researchers to consider ethical concerns and/or language barriers in their research and because it provides researchers another's perspective into interpreting and understanding social justice issues.

Finally, following discussions in the educational context, Dona Martin's **Youth in voice: the concept of voice** offers quite a unique perspective of participants marginalised by a lack of voice. Her work in the discipline area of mathematics in teacher education explores influences in practice and targets exploration of the factors that contribute to or impact on a 'young voice'. Martin's work, just like that of researchers working on conceptualising young people, uses a fluid notion of youth, one not wedded to age but instead one that identifies 'youth' as individuals fixed in a culture of accepting external authority as opposed to having a more mature engagement. Her contribution to the text challenges us to explore how knowledge is developed or accumulated. Martin's work provides insight into the traits of those with little or no voice, which in turn offers interesting perspectives on the reasons for disengagement. Her work is valuable in its offer to have us consider research on 'voice' and 'participation' from educationally focused research perspectives.

Theme V – Unexpected tensions

This theme explores tensions in researching with young people which may not often be immediately apparent. Complex issues such as intimacy and proximity to research participants, how to build trust and reciprocity, finding suitable youth specific interview spaces and the suitability of tools used to yield data can add to the pressures experienced from more trivial issues, such as dealing with ethics committees and resource and timeline management. Not surprisingly, the reality of the research process can be a startling complex labyrinth, and seeking to resolve the issues faced can at times seem almost impossible.

Under this theme, we invite readers to consider the unexpected tensions which researchers face before and in the field. Authors engaging in this discussion demonstrate some of the strategies which they have employed in attempting to navigate these challenges.

Opening this thematic section is the work of Louisa Choe, **How contradictory friendships disrupted my study of working class girls' residential instability**. In her frank account of the challenges of creating rapport with participants, Choe reminds researchers that there is no handbook or manual to follow or 'one-size-fits-all' approach to engaging with participants so as to ensure a mutually beneficial outcome.

Choe did not intentionally nor specifically conceptualise her work as adopting friendship as a methodology, but as the research progressed and relationships were formed, she found that friendships with participants, while enhancing data collection, also created several pitfalls which needed to be carefully navigated. Her work demonstrates the emotional impact on a researcher via firsthand encounters in building rapport with young participants and raises ethical dimensions that extended beyond the obvious.

In the chapter, **The Multicultural Youth Australia Census: reading complexity and migrant youth citizenship into survey methods**, Rimi Khan discusses new approaches to engaging with census survey data via exploration of a partnership between university researchers and a number of institutions working with migrant youth. Khan's work draws close attention to the materiality of survey instruments and encourages broad consideration of their privileged tool status, gained from use in informing policies and shaping narratives in government decision making.

However, more than just questioning and searching for challenges and limitations, Khan's work proposes new approaches for engaging with census data by sharing outcomes of a study based on highlighting the relationships between the survey instrument itself and its research subjects. Khan's work explores ways to make the complexity of young refugee and migrant people's lives comprehensible to researchers, policymakers and to the young people themselves.

Closing this section is the work of Darren Sharpe, **The pressures of building reciprocal relationships in an intergenerational research team**. In his work, Sharpe faces up to the reality of working with some of the most disadvantaged and marginalised groups of young people in society and explores the building, maintenance and successful modelling of reciprocal relationships within an intergenerational research team. This offering encourages us to think critically about the concept of 'reciprocal relationships' in social research and ways of working, in terms of what can be offered to all participants when building trusting and empowering relationships. Sharp's work offers researchers a way to breathe new life and vitality into how we organise and undertake social research. It not only offers demonstrable, candid outcomes from involving young, geographically familiar contributors to the development of ethical frameworks and research but also explores the cultivation of competent coinquirers.

Conclusion

The authors of the chapters included in this edited collection have sought to offer new insights and strategies into contesting current research environments. In sharing their experiences of researching with young people in varied settings and global contexts, they advance new considerations for researchers building methodologies and those working to attain ethically sustainable workarounds within existing research paradigms. Furthermore, the works presented challenge the accuracy or appropriateness of values placed on standardised research instruments and techniques and encourage us as youth scholars to contest how knowledge is developed or accumulated. Indeed, each contribution offers something different, from sharing ethical concerns and offering ways to appropriately negotiate informed consent. They provide innovative perspectives into interpreting and understanding social justice issues, ways to engage in research on sensitive subjects and/or ways to overcome bureaucratic barriers or political concerns. These authors draw attention to ethical considerations prevalent in research with those who have linguistic and/or cultural differences and reflect on recruitment challenges as well as how to build constructive researcher-participant relationships.

Overall, the work presented in this edited collection provides clear insights into how to build recruitment and participant interaction, how to engage and involve stakeholders, as well as how to prepare for unanticipated ethical issues, ensure confidentiality, set boundaries, offer reimbursement and address participant anonymity, amongst other salient issues.

References

Arnett, J.J. and Tanner, J.L. (2006) *Emerging Adults in America: Coming of Age in the 21st Century* (Washington, DC: American Psychological Association).

Bennett, A., Cieslik, M. and Miles, S. (2003) *Researching With Youth* (Basingstoke, UK: Palgrave MacMillan).

Bennett, A. and Kahn-Harris, K. (2004) *After Subculture: Critical Studies in Contemporary Youth Culture* (New York: Palgrave Macmillan).

Billett, P. (2012) 'Lessons from the Field: Ethics in Youth Social Capital Research', *Youth Studies Australia*, 31(3), 43–50.

Billett, P. (2014a) 'Dark Cloud or Silver Lining? The Value of Bonding Networks During Youth', *Journal of Youth Studies*, 17(7), 847–856.

Billett, P. (2014b) 'Youth Social Capital Place and Space', in J. Westwood, C. Larkins, D. Moxon, Y. Perry and N. Thomas (eds.), *Participation, Citizenship and Intergenerational Relations in Children and Young People's Lives: Children and Adults in Conversation* (Hampshire, UK: Palgrave Pivot), 71–82.

Blackman, S. (2005) 'Youth Subcultural Theory: A Critical Engagement With the Concept, Its Origins and Politics, From the Chicago School to Postmodernism', *Journal of Youth Studies*, 8(1), 1–20.

Casey, B.J., Jones, R.M., Levita, L., Libby, V., Pattwell, S., Ruberry, E., Soliman, F. and Somerville, L.H. (2010) 'The Storm and Stress of Adolescence: Insights From Human Imaging and Mouse Genetics', *Developmental Psychobiology*, 52(3), 225–235.

Chisholm, L. (1993) 'Youth Transitions in Britain on the Threshold of a "New Europe"', *Journal of Education Policy*, 8(1), 29–41.

Cieslik, M. and Simpson, D. (2013) *Key Concepts in Youth Studies* (California: Sage).

Clark, A., Flewitt, R., Hammersley, M. and Robb, M. (2014) *Understanding Research With Children and Young People* (London: Sage).

Clarke, J., Hall, S., Jefferson, T. and Roberts, B. (1976) 'Subcultures, Cultures and Class', in S. Hall and T. Jefferson (eds.), *Resistance Through Rituals: Youth Subcultures in Post-War Britain* (London: Hutchinson).

Coles, B. (1995) *Youth and Social Policy: Youth, Citizenship and Young Careers* (London: UCL Press).

Greene, S. and Hogan, D. (2005) *Researching Children's Experience: Approaches and Methods* (California: Sage).

Hasinoff, A.A (2012) Sexting as Media Production: Rethinking Social Media and Sexuality, *New Media and Society*, 15(4), 449–465.

Heath, S. and Walker, C. (2011) *Innovations in Youth Research* (Basingstoke, UK: Palgrave MacMillan).

Kelly, P. (2001) 'Youth at Risk: Process of Individualisation and Responsibilisation in the At-Risk Society', *Discourse Studies in the Cultural Politics of Education*, 22(1), 23–33.

Minter, K. (2017) 'Negotiating Labour Standards in the Gig Economy: Airtasker and Unions New South Wales', *The Economic and Labour Relations Review*, 28(3), 438–454.

Muggleton, D. and Weinzierl, R. (2003) *The Post Subcultures Reader* (New York: Berg).

Reed, L. and Ham, M. (1993) 'Stress and "Storm and Stress" in Early Adolescence: The Relationship of Negative Events With Dysphoric Affect (Personality and Emotions)', *Developmental Psychology*, 29(1), 130–141.

Spear, L.P. (2000) 'The Adolescent Brain and Age-Related Behavioral Manifestations', *Neuroscience and Biobehavioral Reviews*, 24, 417–463.

Stanley Hall, G. (1908) *Adolescence: Its Psychology and Its Relations to Physiology, Anthropology, Sociology, Sex, Crime, Religion and Education* (New York: Appleton).

Strangleman, T. and Warren, T. (2008) *Work and Society: Sociological Approaches, Themes and Methods* (Oxford: Routledge).

Widdicombe, S. and Wooffitt, R. (1995) *The Language of Youth Subcultures: Social Identity in Action* (New York: Harvester Wheatsheaf).

Willis, P. (1977) *Learning to Labour: How Working-Class Kids Get Working Class Jobs* (Aldershot: Ashgate).

Withers, G. and Batten, M. (1995) *Programs for at Risk Youth: A Review of American Canadian and British Literature Since 1984* (Melbourne: Australian Council for Education Research Ltd).

Wyn, J. and White, R. (2015) *Youth and Society* (Melbourne: Oxford University Press).

Conceptualising young people

Chapter 2

Researching the lives of young Māori in Aotearoa, New Zealand

Creating culturally sensitive methods and theory

Alan France, Lucy Cowie, Tepora Pukepuke,
Marilyn Chetty and David Mayeda

Introduction

In this chapter we explore the challenges of researching the lives of young people in Aotearoa, New Zealand. In it we show that capturing the complex nature of what it means to be a New Zealander creates methodological and ethical dilemmas. By its very nature the homogenous term 'New Zealander' encompasses a number of distinct ethnic groups, including *tangata whenua* (the people of the land, Māori), Pākehā (New Zealand Europeans) and more recent migrants from a multitude of countries. Yet in researching this diversity amongst young people we argue it is necessary to create a methodology that is culturally sensitive to the colonial history of New Zealand, one that recognises the imbalance of power that has and continues to shape the life worlds of the indigenous population.

Contemporary New Zealand identity is complex and cannot be understood outside of the process of colonisation (Bell, 2017). The early contact period in the late 18th and early 19th century between Māori and Europeans was dominated by trade and missionary influence. However, early European settlers also brought lawlessness, muskets and disease to Aotearoa (Belich, 1996; King, 2003). As such, a number of *rangatira* Māori (Māori chiefs) signed a treaty with representatives of the British Crown in 1840, known as the Treaty of Waitangi, in an attempt to control the problematic behaviour of European migrants (Orange, 2011). Despite the Waitangi Tribunals ruling in 2014 that Māori never ceded sovereignty, the treaty was used to justify the imposition of British rule on New Zealand (Durie, 1998; Orange, 2011; Waitangi Tribunal, 2014). British rule led to the marginalisation of many Māori, through land confiscation (and consequent loss of food and resources), war and laws which actively suppressed *tikanga* (Māori customs) and *mātauranga* Māori (Māori knowledge; Belich, 1996; Mutu, 2012).

The education system was also used as a tool of assimilation and colonisation. The Native Schools Act (1867) created segregated schools for Māori, and has since been referred to as the 'Trojan horse of colonisation' (Pihama, 2001, p. 306). Māori land was confiscated for these schools, and *tikanga* and *mātauranga* were repressed. Māori students were punished for speaking *te reo* Māori (the Māori language) and were expected to adopt Pākehā names (Hoskins and McKinley, 2015; Macfarlane, Glynn, Cavanagh and Bateman, 2007; McKinley and Hoskins, 2011; Pihama, 2001; Smith, 1992). In the context of tertiary education, New Zealand universities were inaccessible for Māori for many years but were formed using funds derived from land confiscation and built on stolen land (Pihama, 2001; Smith, 1996). The University of Auckland, where the present research is based, for example, benefitted from lands stolen from Ngāti Awa, Tainui and Ngāpuhi (Pihama, 2001). Such a legacy of colonisation in schools and larger society has left its mark, creating a New Zealand which saw 'the impoverishment of Māori, marginalisation of elders and chiefly authority and a structural relationship of Pākehā dominance and Māori subjection' (Walker, 2004, p. 10).

Although the Treaty of Waitangi continues to be contested in many ways, it is now relatively accepted that the Treaty of Waitangi formalised a partnership between *tangata whenua* and the Crown. This has seen state legislation and legal practice make significant changes such as integrating the Treaty of Waitangi into New Zealand laws, making *te reo* Māori an official language of New Zealand and aiming to give *tikanga* Māori (the right cultural practice) equal status and correctness as non – Māori customary practices. How far these changes have addressed the imbalance of power remains to be seen as evidence indicates that much is still to be done (Bell, 2017), and the dominance of Western values and practices still operate in ways to disenfranchise and marginalise Māori. Researching 'being a New Zealander', therefore, can only be achieved when such power relationships are recognised and built into the method.

It is also important to acknowledge the role of social science in the processes of 'knowledge building' and its significant contribution in the colonising of countries such as New Zealand. Linda Tuhiwai Smith (1999) reminds us that the enlightenment period in Victorian England gave increased value to Western science as a part of the modernising project, suggesting it was creating 'true knowledge' about the world. In such a context 'indigenous peoples were ranked as, "'nearly human", "half human" or "sub human"' (Smith, 1999, p. 60). Such systems of categorising people were then constituted as research and became ways of legitimising various colonial practices. For example, anthropology set about studying the 'other' in places such as the Pacific, defining such groups as a form of 'primitivism'. In this context, the 'ethnographic gaze' was seen as both 'takers and users' becoming a science of imperialism that reinforced the idea of the need to civilise the savage (Kuper, 1988). As a result, scientific research became synonymous with colonialism, creating suspicion and criticism that reaffirmed the notion that Northern social science held the 'truth', and other belief systems are primitive. The use of power by colonial researchers reinforced these notions by adhering to particular methodological approaches. However, these imbalances within the research environments have been countered by scientists such as Tuhiwai Smith (1999) and other indigenous peoples to assert alternate research ways.

In keeping with the notions of colonial dominance in research over indigenous peoples is the similar argument of nonyouth working in the area of youth research. Privileging the voice of youth in authentic ways within research would include them as equal research partners, coauthors and project leaders. As we see in other chapters of this book achieving 'authentic voice' in research for the young is challenging as power dynamics between the adult and youth create significant imbalance of power (Spyrou, 2011). While youth may be seen to lack prerequisites for 'knowing the world' or 'having the necessary experience of older researchers', recent political events, such as the school strikes over global warming, show young leaders to be proactive in political affairs and recruiting for large interest group rallies.[1] This one example belies the many others around the world, and particularly with indigenous youth, on their ability to articulate their concerns for their future world and to harness their technological skills for enhanced community involvement. That said Spyrou (2011) highlights strategies such as using visual methods over the interview, using children and young people as coresearchers or primary researchers, although it has to be recognised that such strategies will never remove the imbalance completely.

It is within this context that the discussion in this chapter is framed. It emerges from our attempts, as social scientists, to create an approach to social research that captures the diversity in New Zealand. Two of the authors (Alan France and David Mayeda) are from Europe and America respectively and are themselves migrants to New Zealand, who have come from the Northern Hemisphere and have been trained in social science research methods that were developed in the West. Coming from primarily Northern contexts, therefore, creates challenges over how to capture the life worlds of Māori participants while not contributing to a form of research that is exploitative and judgmental and reinforces negative explanations of the indigenous population in New Zealand. The other three authors have local New Zealand roots. Cowie and Pukepuke are both from New Zealand and are Māori; Chetty is from Fiji. The first part of the chapter explains the growing influence of indigenous methodologies showing how Kaupapa Māori in New Zealand is offering new ways of capturing and understanding the life worlds of young people. We will also give two case study examples of how such an approach shapes the way a research project with young people can be undertaken. In the second part of the chapter we will show how it is possible for approaches from the Northern Hemisphere to have a role to play alongside approaches such as Kaupapa Māori. Third, we will show how such an approach combined with the work of Bourdieu can bring about new insights into our understandings of New Zealand youth.

Indigenous knowledge and Kaupapa Māori

As a result of concerns by indigenous populations over the way that the social sciences have constructed and portrayed indigenous populations, we have seen a growing interest in the development of theoretical and empirical approaches to social research that emerged out of indigenous struggles that gave central recognition to their life worlds and interpretations. Core to this approach is the belief that these approaches can and should make a significant contribution to the self-determination of indigenous populations:

> Indigenous Peoples must look to new anti-colonial epistemologies and methodologies to construct, rediscover, and/or reaffirm their knowledges and cultures. Such epistemologies must . . . carry within them the potential to strengthen the struggle for emancipation and the liberation from oppression.
>
> (Rigney, 1999, p. 114)

In sociology there has also been a growing recognition that 'Northern theory' contributes to creating a world vision that reflects and justifies the dominance of Western thought and explanations, creating a 'truth' that is Eurocentric and Americanised. Not only does this form of social science contribute to the process of colonialism by helping impose Western interpretations, but it also marginalises and undervalues other world views that exist in the Southern Hemisphere, suggesting they are inferior to Northern knowledge and built upon superstition and myth. Connell (2007) suggests that by giving recognition to indigenous methods we not only get fresh insights but also create new understandings. For example, land is often positioned as central, not only to indigenous economic positioning but also to their world views, spirituality and relationships with the broader ecological aspects of their lives. Aboriginal peoples, for example, in their fight in the Northern Territories of Australia shows, 'in the European system people own land, while in the Aboriginal system the land owns the people' (p. 201). Likewise, Māori consider a fluid relationship between the corporeal self and the land, interchanging the notion of the body not as something that exists on the land; rather, it is the land. Such collective concepts of the land concurrently being part of the body links the physical with the spiritual. Stories about spirit journeys then constitute social relationships and the groups that practice them. It is therefore impossible to understand the social structure of many indigenous peoples without recognising the importance of land and place in their lives.

In terms of New Zealand, there has been a strong movement that argues for the centralising of Kaupapa Māori as a method of understanding and researching the lives of Māori. Such an approach is underpinned by a philosophical orientation that expresses a Māori worldview. Smith (1999) suggests this is a form of 'localised critical theory' that shares the particular notions of critique, resistance, struggle and emancipation not dissimilar to theorists such as Gramsci and Freire and those who helped establish the feminist movement in the 1960s. At the heart of Kaupapa Māori theory and methodology is *tino rangatiratanga*, which translates to sovereignty, self-determination, governance, autonomy and independence (Pihama, Cram and Walker, 2002). It emerged partly as a part of a global movement amongst indigenous peoples for self-determinism but also as the New Zealand state increased its commitment to the Treaty of Waitangi; it developed new initiatives such as Kōhanga *reo* (Māori language preschools) and Kura Kaupapa schools (where Māori language and tikanga – culture and customs- are taught); alongside this we see a massive expansion of health and social initiatives such as

Te Whare Tapa Wha and Whenua Ora (Glover, 2002). As a result, Māori academics recognised the importance of creating their own processes of research, and the need for them to have control of how this was done and used (Powick, 2003). In practice, this then requires research on and for Māori to be undertaken in consultation with Māori. Agreement on the aims and objectives of the research and the questions it seeks to ask are agreed to in advance, ensuring that its contribution is for the betterment of Māori people.

Kaupapa Māori as both a theory and method challenges dominant Pākehā constructions of research, and it accords full recognition of *tikanga* (Māori cultural norms value systems and practices), providing cultural legitimation of both the process and outcomes of research (Bishop, 1996; Smith, 1999). It embodies the idea that research by Māori is for Māori and is not only about taking back control but also about the ownership of knowledge. Walker, Eketone and Gibbs (2006) suggest there are in fact five key principles that underpin Kaupapa Māori; the aim of the research should be about promoting social justice – it requires an epistemological approach that is built upon the 'Māori worldview', it needs to apply important Māori concepts to ensure that key protocols are maintained, for example, *whakawhanaungatanga* (the process of identifying, maintaining, or forming past, present and future relationships), it uses *teo reo* (Māori language) where possible and finally it operates around the principles of *whānau* (family and collective accountability and responsibility).

It is then proposed that Kaupapa Māori research should be done by Māori researchers. Linda Tuhiwai Smith (1999) argues that indigenous research should not only be controlled by indigenous peoples, but also the research should be undertaken by indigenous scholars. When indigenous people become researchers and not merely the researched, the activity is transformed. For example, 'the questions are framed differently; priorities are ranked differently; problems are defined differently; and people participate on different terms' (Linda Tuhiwai Smith, 1999, p. 193). This needs to be not just someone of Māori descent but someone who is knowledgeable about protocols, culture and Māori language. Such researchers are often able to bring a deeper and more comprehensive understanding of Māori because of their positions as insiders (Kiro, 2000). Researching the life worlds of Māori therefore requires the researcher to understand (and respect) the protocols of engagement and be able to follow Māori customs and practice (Glover, 2002).

That said, it is argued that *tauiwi* (non-Māori) can be involved in Kaupapa Māori research. Smith (1999) for example, suggests there are four different strategies non-Māori researchers can take if they want to use a Kaupapa Māori approach. The first is the *tiaki* or mentoring model, in which authoritative Māori people help and guide the research. The second is the *whangai* or adoption model, where researchers are incorporated into the daily life of Māori, and they maintain a life-long relationship that continues beyond the research. The third strategy is a 'power sharing' approach, where researchers actively seek the help of the community to support and develop the research. The final option is the 'empowering outcomes model', which addresses the sorts of questions Māori people want to know and which then ensures beneficial outcomes for them.

These requirements are challenging, especially when undertaking research with young Māori people. In trying to maintain a practice that is committed to a Kaupapa Māori methodology, accessing the 'authentic voice' of young Māori is not straightforward. Not only are their existing ethical challenges of getting consent but also for indigenous populations there are real concerns about how the research is representing Māori and how it will be used. Kidman (2014), for example, when exploring young Māori's relationship with their tribal land, engaged in a detailed process of consultation with local iwi. In a number of hui (tribal meetings), concerns were raised by elders about the use of visual methods, especially of pictures taken by young people of sites of tribal significance such as *urupâ* (burial ground), *marae* (tribal meeting ground) or *wâhi tapu* (an area of special spiritual, cultural or historical significance). They only agreed on the use of photos taken by the young people in special circumstances and required that ownership of these pictures remained in the hands of the local *iwi*.

Kaupapa Māori methodology, can and does, usually draw upon traditional social science approaches to gather data and can follow a similar format to more traditional social science methodologies;

> The methods of data collection in Kaupapa Māori research are not particular to Māori. In other words, getting the process right is the first consideration, and then answering the research question is the next. Answering the question may well draw upon westernized research designs.
>
> (Walker et al., 2006, p. 336)

As a method it may then draw upon experimental and quantitative designs, for example, Theodore et al. (2017) draw upon a Kaupapa Māori methodology in analysing large data sets on what helps Māori graduates complete their degrees. That said, qualitative approaches such as biographical interviews, oral history, storytelling and focus groups do tend to fit more comfortably into a Kaupapa Māori approach (Ruwhiu and Cone, 2010).

Using Kaupapa Māori methodology in youth research

So, what does a research project that is shaped by Kaupapa Māori look like in practice? The following subsections feature two examples; both are projects that aimed to research and understand specific aspects of the lives of young Māori in New Zealand. The first focuses on the lives of young Māori fathers and the second on Māori and Pacific students in a university setting.

Case study one: researching the lives of Māori fathers

Elkington (2017) undertakes research with a small group of young Māori fathers (n8), exploring their everyday lives. Using a Kaupapa Māori approach, it 'centralises Māori aspirations, epistemologies, values and world views as the norm' and aims to 'promote positive Māori outcomes, intervention, and address power imbalances' (p. 5). In keeping with Kaupapa Māori, this approach wanted to challenge negative stereotype images of young Māori fathers and promote positive perspectives that would help find ways of supporting other young Māori fathers.

The approach used traditional social science methods of data collection (semi-structured interviews) and undertook an analysis of the findings by using a narrative approach. In the interview process, Māori tikanga are centralised. At the beginning of the interview, 5–10 minutes are allocated to establish a relationship and common ground (*whakanoa and whakawhanaungatanga*). Food was also provided as is custom, and time was also given to give *tautoko* (support) and *awhi* (embrace), ensuring that any issues the research raised were addressed. In terms of findings, the research highlighted the importance of *whanaungatanga* (their close connection between kinships groups). These were maintained with great care and centred on *āta* (respectfulness), *aroha* (love) and *manaakitanga* (to give back to others). The young men wanted to be good fathers and ensure that their children also understood their responsibilities. They also had a strong sense of their *whakapapa* (genealogy), which had a major impact on their sense of self and practice of child rearing. They also wanted to maintain their *mana* (control) and *mauri* (life force), especially of their *tūpuna* (their ancestors), showing how their approach to parenting was strongly influenced by their own experiences.

A key theme from the research was the importance of finding ways to support the mother of their children. This became a major priority, and ensuring that her aspirations and needs were met was a key driver to the choices the young fathers made. The narratives also showed the importance of the wider *whānau* of aunties, uncles, community leaders and public figures who offered a wide range of support helping them, especially in difficult times, to maintain their responsibilities as fathers.

Case study two: Māori and Pacific voices on student success in higher education

Mayeda, Keil, Dansey Dutton and Ofamo'Oni (2014) used a Kaupapa Māori approach (combined with Pacific methodology) to explore the factors that helped young Māori and Pacific students be successful at university. Much research in this area concentrates on the reasons why Māori and Pacific students drop out of university, providing a negative portrayal of these populations. Less is known about what factors can operate to help them achieve at university. The research stressed research *with* (not 'on') indigenous peoples, 'utilising indigenous literature, providing culturally safe spaces for participants, [and] privileging indigenous voices' (p. 168). When completed, the research made significant contributions by sharing the learning with Māori and Pacific students, writing opinion pieces on international news sites and undertaking of training for academic staff. Similar to the study of Elkington (2017), this study drew upon and used social science methodology to collect data. It recruited over 90 young people with a B− average and constructed 17 focus groups as a way of gathering insights into their experiences of being successful at university. Focus groups were constructed to avoid markers of authority, and facilitators were interspersed around the circle. Respecting *tikanga*, the sessions usually provide food as a way of cultivating social bonds and aroha. Because spirituality is important in both Māori and Pacific cultures, each group was asked if participants wanted to start with a prayer. In most sessions this was agreed. One of the core strategies used by the research team was to have a research team that reflected the diversity of the cohort they were researching, who were also 'culturally competent' and had understanding of protocols and conventions that would help create a safe space that acknowledged and respected participants' culture.

Three main findings were highlighted. First, young people expressed the importance of *whānau* and family networks in helping them be successful. For example, they expressed a wide range of ways that their family helped them, such as providing money and study space at home or/ and releasing them from family duties at times of pressure. Second, young people acknowledged the support they received within the university setting, which helped them generate an identity 'that connected their sense of indigeneity or "Pacific-ness"' (p. 173). This could also be reinforced by having good role models amongst staff that offered them support and encouragement or a curriculum that reflected their culture. Finally, the research, while not explicitly seeking discussions of barriers, created a space for students to talk about racism and what the authors defined as 'everyday colonialism'. This was a major theme, where young people expressed the Eurocentric nature of the university as principally a 'white place' where racism was subtle and not acknowledged. Not only was the curriculum mainly Eurocentric but also much of it worked on a deficit model reinforcing negative stereotypes of Māori and Pacific peoples. In many cases they felt that they were being expected to forsake their identities so that they could 'fit in'. Evidence shows that while this was detrimental, many of the students became motivated to 'prove them wrong'.

What we see in these case studies is that by embedding a Kaupapa Māori methodology into exploring the life-worlds of young Māori, the research process and outcomes can be enhanced in three particular ways. First, it ensures that the approach used is both ethical and respectful to Māori. As discussed previously, much social science research has created either hypotheses that focus on deficit views of Māori culture and practice or interpret findings of the behaviour and actions of Māori through a Western lens. Kaupapa Māori then offers a mechanism that holds researchers to account and ensures that they are both ethical and respectful in their practice. By requiring consultation and active engagement with the Māori community, agreement on the practice and activities of the research have to be constructed to an acceptable Māori ethical framework. It also ensures that Māori *tikanga* are both respected and embedded in the research approach. Second, Kaupapa Māori methodology ensures that the research has relevance and value to Māori. It not only gives control to Māori but also creates a focus, which can make a significant contribution to their self-determinism. For example, much research in this area has not always considered the impact of its research that consistently focuses on 'problems'; a Kaupapa Māori approach ensures a more empowering and positive framework for understanding the lives of Māori. Finally, as we saw in the examples earlier, Kaupapa Māori methodology can help create new understandings that traditional social science research is unable to access. Having Māori as researchers who have understandings of the language and culture alongside the use of *tikanga* can put participants at ease, creating an environment and space that allows alternative explanations and understandings to emerge.

Finally, it is important to recognise that when conducting Kaupapa Māori research it comes with significant challenges, a foremost one being that research is not always about advancing knowledge. Social research can also be about reaffirming existing knowledge. Additionally, the idea that legitimate attempts must be made to transform the research into action that supports indigenous agendas can be a challenge. For example, with respect to Case Study Two, findings from the research were used to guide an advocacy campaign titled, 'I, Too, Am Auckland', in which Māori and Pacific university students expressed verbally the types of everyday racism they experienced on university campus and how they felt university management should intervene. Participants' contributions were posted as a video series on YouTube (Tesiram et al., 2015), which garnered significant mainstream media attention. While the media attention spawned extensive social awareness across New Zealand, it also led to online backlash perpetrated against some video participants. This violated another critical feature of Kaupapa Māori research, which entails protecting participants from research-related harm. To this end, the mix of advocating publicly for indigenous rights and shielding participants from discrimination made full implementation of Kaupapa Māori research principles difficult.

Can Northern theory make a contribution? The case of Pierre Bourdieu

So far, our discussion has concentrated on research methodology, and as we have seen social science can and does have a role to play alongside Kaupapa Māori, but what about social theory? What contribution can Northern theory make to our analysis? We believe that there is much to be gained by creating a collaborative space where ideas from the Northern Hemisphere are drawn upon to help in explaining the experiences of Māori young people. One theorist that we think offers such an opportunity is Pierre Bourdieu. There is scepticism about such collaboration between Northern theory and Kaupapa Māori, seeing it as part of the continuation of colonialism (Pihama and Southey, 2015), but there are others who recognise that there may be much to be gained by integrating different theoretical approaches (Smith, 1999; Smith, 1996; Eketone, 2012; Mahuika, 2015). Similar to Kaupapa Māori, the ideas of Pierre Bourdieu belong to the school of critical theory and can offer important tools that can help illuminate the way that colonialism and capitalism are operating to shape the struggles Māori have for recognition and control. While Connell (2007) is sceptical about Bourdieu's approach in explaining the impact of colonialism, we believe Connell's reading undervalues and mis-recognises the contribution that Bourdieu's work has made to our understanding of colonialism. Go (2013), for example, defends Bourdieu by reminding us that his early ideas emerged from his time and work in Algiers, which was a French colony. Bourdieu's 'theory of colonialism' is a form of racial domination where 'the function of racism is none other than to provide a rationalization of the existing state of affairs so as to make it appear to be a lawfully instituted order' (Bourdieu, 1961, p. 120 cited in Go, 2013, p. 55). This domination is further enforced by both physical and symbolic violence through practices such as land and labour policies which aim to disintegrate the economic and cultural lives of the colonised.

Bourdieu's theorising on 'domination', 'symbolic violence', 'doxia' and 'struggles' are therefore ideal tools to help explore the relationships between Māori and the state. Not only this, but they can also create opportunities for understanding relationships with capitalism, putting a lens on how divisions are created both within and between Māori. Within this, Bourdieu's theory of capitals also introduces into the analysis new ways of understanding the continued marginalisation of Māori from economic opportunities. While Kaupapa Māori theory has a strong focus on the colonising process and the state, this duality sometimes gives less acknowledgement to the broader processes embedded in global capitalism. For example, it is well recognised that there remain major inequalities in New Zealand between Māori and Pākehā, yet these are traditionally understood as consequences of colonialism. What Bourdieu is able to do is show how such relationships have also to be understood in terms of class (France et al., 2017). This would also open up the possibility to theorise economic divisions such as those of the new Māori middle class (Poata-Smith, 2013)

Bourdieu's concept of class also brings to our attention how habitus and different capital(s) can and do contribute to shaping young people's class trajectories. Habitus remains a product of our upbringing and genealogy, not dissimilar to the Māori concept of *whakapapa*. Habitus is interested in identifying the values, beliefs, cultural tastes, consumption patterns and lifestyles that make up who we are. The everyday lives of young people are greatly shaped by habitus, as it is a:

> system of durable and transposable dispositions through which we perceive, judge and act in the world . . . acquired through lasting exposure to particular social conditions and conditionings via the internalizing of external constraints and possibilities.
>
> (Wacquant, 2006, p. 267)

In this context, habitus is our embodied selves that emerge as we grow and move towards adulthood – and an opportunity exists by using this concept to illuminate what habitus looks like for Māori young people. Habitus becomes important at times when we make decisions or try to make sense of our place in the world, as it frames the way we respond to situations and contexts (France and Roberts, 2017). In terms of capital, Bourdieu identifies three main types: economic, cultural and social (Bourdieu, 1984). Economic capital is the income, wealth and assets that young people either possess or own. For the young, this can be more about their parent's income and wealth.

Recent research, for example, has showed that throughout the great financial crisis, parents and grandparents have been increasing their 'gifting' by paying for rent, university fees and travel (France, 2016). Of course, those from wealthy families are able to have access to a large sum of economic capital. How this works for Māori young people, especially those from the 'new middle class', remains under researched. In terms of cultural capital, Bourdieu argues that it is embodied, being a part of a person's history and objectified through the ownership of cultural artefacts that have significant status and recognised value in relationships. The power and influence of such artefacts and practice are usually positioned by being given recognition and status by key institutions or social actors (Swartz, 1997). A wide range of cultural artefacts and cultural activities are of central importance to the Māori life world, and how these forms of cultural capital operate both inside and outside of the culture is an important question when exploring the lives of the young.

Finally, social capital relates to a form of mutual recognition that objectivises social difference while establishing strong ties and networks (Bottrell, 2009). Again, social relationships and networks are a central feature of the Māori life world (for example, *whanaungatanga* and *whānau*), and how these operate in the lives of young people is core to how they live their lives. It is in the struggle within particular 'fields' that these forms of capital can and are influential in ensuring that some groups have access to resources and opportunities. How such capitals work within and outside of Māori culture is a critical question when exploring the lives of the young.

These Bourdieusian concepts create opportunities to explore how a young person's history, relationship with *whānau*, *iwi* and their wider community is impacting on their social identity. It also creates opportunities to examine how young people manage themselves in 'two worlds'. For example, Bourdieu argued that in Algerian individuals had a 'split habitus', living 'between two worlds' and forced to navigate between their traditional way of life and the culture and values of the colonisers (Bourdieu, 1961, p.144). This, combined with Bourdieu's tools such as domination, doxia and symbolic violence, help shine a light on the way the state and capitalism operate to maintain the 'status quo' over the relation that Māori youth have to the process of colonisation in New Zealand.

Conclusion

Constructing research methods and using theories that are able to capture the experience of indigenous populations needs to be culturally sensitive in their making. We have argued here that in Aotearoa, New Zealand, by creating an approach that centralises Kaupapa Māori theory and principles, we believe a more ethical approach to gathering knowledge is achieved. While social science methods and theory are important, we have to recognise it also has a history as being a partner in the colonising process. As a result, its use must be developed in ways that contribute positively to Māori knowledge and development while ensuring that it operates within the boundaries and requirements of Kaupapa Māori. When researching in colonised countries such as New Zealand, the challenges to those who are trained in approaches from the Northern Hemisphere is to move beyond the 'default positions' that locate indigenous worldviews as marginal and Northern science as 'all knowing'. As we have shown, by embedding principles of Kaupapa Māori in our practice, we are able to capture the diverse experiences of young people in New Zealand.

Note

1 https://theecologist.org/2019/jan/31/climate-school-strikes-go-global

References

Belich, J. (1996) *Making Peoples: A History of the New Zealanders* (Auckland: Allen Lane).
Bell, A. (2017) 'Imagining Aotearoa New Zealand: Politics of National Imagining', in A. Bell, V. Elizabeth, T. McIntosh and M. Wynyard (eds.), *A Land of Milk and Honey* (Auckland: Auckland University Press).
Bishop, R. (1996) *Collaborative Research Stories: Whakawhanaungatanga* (Palmerston North: The Dunmore Press).
Bottrell, D. (2009) 'Dealing With Disadvantage', *Youth and Society*, 40(4), 476–501.
Bourdieu, P. (1961) *The Algerians* (Boston: Beacon Press).
Bourdieu, P. (1984) *Distinction: A Social Critique of the Judgment of Taste* (Cambridge, MA: Harvard University Press).
Connell, R. (2007) *Southern Theory* (Crows Nest, Australia: Allen and Unwin).
Durie, M. (1998) *Te mana, te kawanatanga: The Politics of Māori Self-Determination* (Auckland: Oxford University Press).
Eketone, A. (2012) 'Maori Parenting, From Deficit to Strength', *Aotearoa New Zealand Social Work*, 24(3/4), 75.
Elkington, A. (2017) 'The Everyday Lives of Young Māori Fathers: An Explorative Study', *Journal of Indigenous Wellbeing*, 2(1), 3–17.
France, A. and Roberts, S. (2017) *Youth and Social Class: Enduring Inequality in the UK, Australia and New Zealand* (London: Palgrave).
Glover, M. (2002) *A Literature Review and Commentary on the Use of a Kaupapa Maori Approach Within a Doctoral Study of Maori Smoking Cessation* (Auckland: University of Auckland).
Go, J. (2013) 'Decolonizing Bourdieu: Colonial and Post-Colonial Theory in Pierre Bourdieu's Early Work', *Sociological Theory*, 31(1), 49–74.
Hoskins, T.K. and McKinley, E. (2015) 'New Zealand: Māori Education in Aotearoa', in M. Crossley, G. Hancock and T. Sprague (eds.), *Education in Australia, New Zealand and the Pacific* (London: Bloomsbury Publishing), 159–175.

Kidman, J. (2014) 'Representing Māori Youth Voices in Community Education Research', *New Zealand Journal of Educational Studies*, 49(2), 205–218.

King, M. (2003) *The Penguin History of New Zealand* (Auckland, New Zealand: Penguin Books).

Kiro, C. (2000) 'Maori Research and the Social Services', *Social Work Review*, 12, 26–32.

Kuper, A. (1988) *The Invention of the Primitive Society* (London: Routledge).

Macfarlane, A., Glynn, T., Cavanagh, T. and Bateman, S. (2007) 'Creating Culturally-Safe Schools for Māori Students', *The Australian Journal of Indigenous Education*, 36, 65–76.

Mahuika, N. (2015) 'New Zealand History Is Maori History: Tikanga as the Ethical Foundation of Historical Scholarship in Aotearoa New Zealand', *New Zealand Journal of History*, 49(1), 5–30.

Mayeda, D., Keil, M., Dansey Dutton, H. and Ofamo'Oni, I.-Futa-Helu. (2014) '"You've Gotta Set a Precedent": Māori and Pacific Voices on Student Success in Higher Education', *AlterNative*, 10(2), 165–179.

McKinley, E. and Hoskins, T.K. (2011) 'Māori Education and Achievement', in T. McIntosh and M. Mulholland (eds.), *Māori and Social Issues* (Wellington: Huia Publishers), 84–111.

Mutu, M. (2012) 'Musket Wars, Migrations, New Tribal Alignments', in D. Keenan (ed.), *Huia Histories of Māori: Ngā Tāhuhu Kōrero* (Wellington: Huia Publishers).

Orange, C. (2011) *The Treaty of Waitangi*, 2nd ed. (Wellington: Bridget Williams Books).

Pihama, L. and Southey, K. (2015). *Kaupapa Rangahau: A Reader. A Collection of Readings from the Kaupapa Māori Research Workshops Series.* (Hamilton, New Zealand: Te Kotahi Research Institute).

Pihama, L. (2001) *Tīhei mauri ora: Honouring Our Voices: Mana wahine as a Kaupapa Māori: Theoretical Framework* (Unpublished Doctoral Thesis, University of Auckland, New Zealand).

Pihama, L., Cram, F. and Walker, S. (2002) 'Creating Methodological Space: A Literature Review of Kaupapa Maori Research', *Canadian Journal of Native Education*, 26, 30–43.

Poata-Smith, E.T.A. (2013) 'Inequality and Māori', in M. Rashbrooke (eds.), *Inequality: A New Zealand Crisis* (Wellington: Bridget Williams Books), 148–158.

Powick, K. (2003) *Maori Research Ethics* (Hamilton: Wilf Malcolm Institute of Educational Research, University of Waikato).

Rigney, L. (1999) 'Internalization of an Indigenous Anti-Colonialist Cultural Critique of Research Methodologies: A Guide to Indigenist Research Methodology and Its Principles', *Wicazo Sa Review Fall*, 14(12), 109–111.

Ruwhiu, D. and Cone, M. (2010) 'Advancing a Pragmatist Epistemology in Organisational Research', *Qualitative Research in Organizations and Management*, 5(2), 108–126.

Smith, G. (1992) *Tane-nui-a-rangi's Legacy. Propping Up the Sky: Kaupapa Māori as Resistance and Intervention* (Auckland: Research Unit for Māori Education, University of Auckland).

Smith, L.T. (1996) *Nga aho o te kakahu matauranga: The Multiple Layers of Struggle by Māori in Education* (Unpublished Doctoral Dissertation, University of Auckland, New Zealand).

Smith, L.T. (1999) *Decolonising Methodologies* (Otago: University of Otago).

Spyrou, S. (2011) 'The Limits of Children's Voices: From Authenticity to Critical, Reflexive Representation', *Childhood*, 18(2), 151–165.

Swartz, D. (1997) *Culture and Power: The Sociology of Pierre Bourdieu* (Chicago: University of Chicago Press).

Tesiram, M., Vijaykumar, R., William, L., Tevaga, C., McLean, S. and Mayeda, D. (2015) 'I, Too, Am Auckland: Experiences'. Available at: www.youtube.com/watch?v=4iKLJTbN7uc&t (Accessed 14 January 2019).

Theodore, R., Gollop, M., Tustin, K., Taylor, N., Kiro, C., Taumoepeau, M. and Poulton, R. (2017) 'Māori University Success: What Helps and Hinders Qualification Completion', *AlterNative: An International Journal of Indigenous Peoples*, 13(2), 122–130.

Wacquant, L. (2006) 'Pierre Bourdieu', in R. Stones (ed.), *Key Contemporary Thinkers* (London: Palgrave Macmillan).

Waitangi Tribunal. (2014) *He Whakaputanga me Te Tiriti (Report on Stage 1 of the Te Paparahi o Te Raki Inquiry, WAI 1040)* (Wellington, New Zealand: Waitangi Tribunal).

Walker, R. (2004) *Ka Whawhai Tonu Matou: Struggle Without an End* (Auckland: Penguin Books).

Walker, S., Eketone, A. and Gibbs, A. (2006) 'An Exploration of Kaupapa Maori Research, Its Principles, Processes and Applications', *International Journal of Social Research Methodology*, 9(4), 331–344.

Chapter 3

Doing research in organisations

Implications of the different
definitions of youth

Joel Robert McGregor and David Farrugia

Introduction

This chapter interrogates the theoretical definitions of young people in contemporary youth research through an exploration of the institutional and relational practices through which young people 'at-risk' of reoffending are imagined in the case management programs designed to govern their movement out of the juvenile justice system. The aim of the chapter is to interrogate existing concepts of youth in this field which focus on risk and expert authority and which therefore define youth as a fixed object of disciplinary knowledge. Moving beyond this approach, this chapter situates youth as a fluid, relationally constructed and constantly negotiated phenomenon that is not defined in advance of the organisational practices that are used to govern young people's lives. The chapter argues that rather than a preexisting object or life stage, youth is enacted as a complex set of organisationally situated and relational practices that implicate and produce the subjectivities of the case managers that govern them as well as rendering young people themselves governable. These practices – and the ongoing definition and redefinition of youth identities that they involve – are important focal points for youth research. Researching these practices can form the basis for new research approaches that capture the ongoing production of youth within local institutional contexts as well as the effects of these productions on young people themselves.

The intellectual frameworks currently used to conceptualise youth in the juvenile justice system are aimed at fixing the concept of youth in place through the notion of risk. They either essentialise the 'young risky subject', or they critique the way that youth is positioned as an object of governance through the technology of risk. One approach – which dominates the institutional discourses and management techniques of the criminal justice system – is the notion of the 'at-risk' youth. This approach demonstrates an individual subject of risk and responsibility who poses a threat to the moral order of the 'mainstream' and that is defined through technologies of risk assessment. The second – originating in critical social theory – understands youth as a population that is produced and disciplined through the discourse of risk. In other words, while the notion of being an at-risk youth is taken for granted in institutional discourses, critical analysis shows how this subject position is produced through the institutional techniques that mobilise these discourses. What both of these approaches have in common however, is a desire to position youth as objects of expert knowledges, either to facilitate governance or critique. In general, therefore, the ways in which youth are conceptualised in this area have failed to move beyond the 'institutionalised intellectual domain of "youth studies"' (Kelly, 2000, p. 302) to the actual practices that define youth in particular research sites.

In order to move beyond these static notions of youth and risk, this chapter draws on data collected as part of the first author's PhD research, which explores the relational practices of case managers working with young people who have been in custody and are 'at-risk' of (re-)offending. While investigating the desistance practices used in particular organisations, it became clear that participants' classifications of their young clients were fluid and relationally negotiated in ways that go beyond the discursive construction of risk. Instead, youth were defined through relational practices, including the negotiation of intimacy and the construction of family-like relationships between case managers and clients. With these complex and conflicting definitions in mind, the chapter suggests that as an object of study, youth must be approached as a fluid and malleable product of institutional practices rather than as a subject fixed in advance by expert knowledge. The chapter concludes with implications of this shift for conceptualising youth in contemporary youth research.

Case management, risk and youth

The case management of people in justice frameworks is part of a broader ensemble of institutional processes that currently acts to shape and produce what counts as a risk subject (Hannah-Moffat, 2005). Young people who are leaving detention centres are subject to a range of interventions which are designed to mitigate factors leading to (re-)offence. Case management is the institutional technique through which young people are connected to the systems of governmental authorities that shape their post-release experiences. When young people have been identified as being a 'risk', they are allocated a case manager who is tasked with organising interventions into the young person's life that are designed to reduce their risk of returning to custody. These interventions are organised around assessments of the various 'risk factors' that may increase the likelihood of a young person (re-)offending, and notions of risk underpin the governmental interventions through which a young person's subjectivity is converted into a 'case' to be 'managed'.

The case management of young people in justice frameworks contributes to broader trends in the way that both crime and youth are imagined and institutionally governed. These trends are connected with the influence of neoliberal interventions into the social world. For the purposes of this chapter, neoliberalism is approached as a mode of governing that takes place through the production of rational, self-responsible subjects. The emergence of neoliberal modes of government contribute to what the criminologist David Garland (2011, p. 53) has described as a 'crisis of penal modernism' taking place in the 1980s, in which the institutional aims of the penal system shifted from notions of rehabilitation and discipline towards a focus on risk management. The influence of notions of 'risk' in juvenile justice reflects the broader role that risk plays in the neoliberal imagining of the social world (O'Malley, 2004), in which the concept underpins modes of governance that operate through rendering populations calculable and therefore governable through the implementation of technical solutions. In the contemporary juvenile justice system, the concept of risk is deployed in order to render calculable the likelihood of an individual young person reengaging in criminalised behaviour. Coupled with the political rationality of neoliberalism, this has shifted prevention and early intervention programs hosted by nongovernment organisations into critical positions in the governance of crime and in young people's experience of leaving prison.

Neoliberal techniques for governing crime also include the creation of new networks of agencies, practices and discourses which serve to identify the risk factors which influence an individual's likelihood to commit a crime or reoffend. In the process, an enormous field of research has emerged dedicated to identifying the risk factors which predispose young people to participating in crime. This field is too large to cite here, and it includes disciplines such as epidemiology, public health, developmental psychology and psychiatry, as well as positivist criminology (France, 2008). Methodologically, the field is committed to the quantitative measurement of individual level risk factors in their association with various kinds of criminalised activities such as participating in violence, various forms of crime, notions of 'delinquency' and the like. The risk factors are identified through criminogenic-needs assessment instruments such as the Youth Level of Service/Case Management Inventory (YLS/CMI), measured and then correlated to various outcomes connected with desisting from come. The emergence of risk factor analysis has resulted in the institutionalisation of the 'at-risk youth' as the key target for research on young people and crime. The hegemonic position of risk factor analysis also shapes the service sector, which consists of a range of services designed to address particular risk factors and therefore ameliorate the risks of an at-risk youth participating in criminalised behaviour (such as mental health services, employment services and substance abuse services). There is therefore a critical relationship between the organisation of governmental interventions and the technical knowledge brought to bear to fix the at-risk youth in place as an object of governance.

Case management is the practice that brings these services together in the government of a particular young person. A human service practice which has been widely applied across the criminal justice system (Turner, 2012), case management is a key example of the kinds of institutional practices that are deployed in order to govern these imagined risky subjects. In the practice of case management, young people are hosted by a primary organisation who organises an intervention plan based upon their needs, scored through risk-factor assessments. At-risk young people are identified through a 'risk score' which determines the level of intervention they will receive. 'Criminogenic needs' are defined as the factors which are most likely to lead to criminal behaviour. Offenders with a medium to high criminogenic risk score will be targeted for intervention, while the individual scored at a low risk or with non-criminogenic needs will be disregarded as needing intervention (Robinson, 2002). Criminogenic risk factors include mental health problems, substance abuse, homelessness, exposure to abuse, being in out-of-home care as a child, foetal alcohol spectrum disorder or Aboriginality. It is currently accepted within rehabilitation practice that to stop reoffence, the criminogenic needs must be effectively targeted. In the case management model, this would mean that the case plan of a young person would be determined through the identification of these needs, and a case manager would engage with a service who would put interventions in place to address those needs that have been identified. The most common of the specialised services are mental health and job seeking. Through the identification of criminogenic needs, the at-risk young subject is imagined, their risks calculated and their lives governed through the various interventions available that correspond to the risk factors identified in their assessment.

Risk-factor analysis remains the dominant way of understanding young people. It is institutionalised in both juvenile justice and other forms of neoliberal governmentality in fields such as health, employment and homelessness. However, despite its enormous institutional influence, risk factor analysis has been critiqued for the way that it imagines youth and issues such as crime. While the concept of risk is common to a wide array of institutional interventions into the social world (O'Malley, 2004), the application of risk factor analysis to young people in juvenile justice reflects the intertwining of the discourse of risk with developmental psychology and the longstanding association of youth as a time of increased risk to both the self and others (Wyn and White, 1997). Critiques of risk factor analysis have observed that the notion of risk constructs an individualised risky subject that is abstracted from the social world, including the social inequalities that shape young people's lives (France, 2008). In correctional discourses, young people are positioned as an age category which is marked as a period of heightened risk, and a specific institutional apparatus exists that is based on these developmental and risk-based approaches to youth. Moreover, the positivistic methodology of risk factor analysis reifies what may be seen as moral judgements about proper conduct. Measuring a young person's risk of criminal behaviour through a criminogenic-needs assessment assumes an ideal type of young person, based upon 'moral assessments of values, lifestyles and experiences' (Hannah-Moffat, 2005, p. 37). Hannah-Moffat (2005, p. 37) explains, 'the scientific claims of objective assessment mask the inherently moralistic/normative elements of this penal exercise'.

One key theoretical resource for critiques of risk-factor analysis is the concept of governmentality drawn from Foucault (2007). For Foucault, expert knowledges such as risk-factor analysis operate to produce and govern populations in line with the governmental requirements of institutions such as the state. With this body of work in mind, risk-factor analysis may be understood as a normative exercise in the categorisation and government of 'problem' populations, and in the sociology of youth risk-factor analysis has been critiqued in terms of the way that it positions young people within broader power relations and governmental regimes. From the perspective of governmentality, risk is not a taken-for-granted attribute of young people that must be measured but a means by which populations of young people may be brought into being and governed through institutional techniques. Risk in this sense is a form of surveillance and discipline in which power relationships operate through the production of subjectivities and populations. The aim of the government of youth through risk is the production of responsiblised young people who manage the social world as entrepreneurial individuals (Kelly, 2006). Responsibilisation takes place through the institutionalisation of risk discourses within governmental authorities such as juvenile justice systems. Through institutional practices based on the discourse of risk, the 'at-risk youth' is produced and governed in ways that reproduce the power relations of institutionalised expertise and the broader social relations imagined by neoliberal governmentality (Kelly, 2000, 2001, 2006). In this respect, institutional interventions into young people are significant in that they mobilise preexisting discourses in the production of risky subjects. Case management therefore is best understood as the application of risk-factor analysis to individuals through the mobilisation of services that themselves institutionalise the language of risk.

Across this research field, these frameworks conceptualise youth as *fixed in place*, either as risky subjects or as objects of disciplinary power. In the process, young people emerge as static objects of knowledge, defined in advance either through the technology of risk assessment or through the bodies of knowledge and systems of expertise that are brought to bear on contemporary populations. These frameworks shape the preconceptions that youth researchers bring to conceiving of their object of study and lay out the terrain of possible analysis and critique that researchers may participate in. For the risk assessor, the task is to define and measure risks and their association with predetermined outcomes such as desisting from crime. For the governmentality analyst, the task is to identify and critique how young people become objects of neoliberal governance. In both instances, it becomes possible to define and conceptualise youth with reference to systems of technical expertise. In this respect, while these forms of analysis have different theoretical assumptions and political implications, the outcome is an approach to youth that is defined in advance of the lived experiences and practices through which young people are imagined in juvenile justice and case management practices.

In the empirical project that forms the basis for the rest of this chapter, these frameworks were found to be inadequate to understanding how young people are imagined and case-managed in post-release programs. By exploring how the case management of youth takes place in these settings, the remainder of this chapter offers a new reflection on how the empirical object of youth studies is negotiated and produced and reflects on the implications of this for the design and conduct of youth research. In the remainder of this chapter we argue that these intellectual constructions do not account for the multiple, fluid and contested understandings of 'youth' in organisations and cannot be taken for granted as premises for the design and conduct of research. Instead, the research that we draw upon within this chapter highlights how case managers construct clients in ways that reflect a range of factors that are unrecognised and unrecognisable in contemporary constructions of youth. In so doing, we situate research on the production of youth in organisations as a means by which to continue to problematise the empirical focus of contemporary youth research.

The study

The empirical material for this study comes for the doctoral project of the first author, which explores the practitioner's role in youth desistance programs. It examines the relational processes of youth participation in support programs, program functions and desistance from crime. Programs were located in Newcastle, the Central Coast and Sydney, Australia. Qualitative interviews were conducted with 21 practitioners who worked directly with people participating in the desistance process. Interviews were semi-structured with a range of preestablished questions and prompts to guide the interview. The study design aims to capture practices of governmentality in action. However, the outcomes of the project reveal the complex negotiation of intimacy and biographical disclosure that constructs youth in different ways despite this intensely governmentalised arena.

Practitioner knowledge and the conceptualisation of 'youth'

The risk-factor and governmentality approaches to young people are united in their assumption that case management takes place through the application of expert knowledges and technical devices (such as risk assessments) to young people in juvenile justice. However, in what follows, this chapter will suggest that case management takes place not merely through the top-down application of expert knowledge but through complex relational practices that escape the assumptions of risk-assessment (understood either as a neutral technical device, or a mode of governmentality). While there are, of course, power relationships at play in the shaping of case manager and client subjectivities, the way that these are enacted was described by case managers themselves in terms remote from the assumptions of risk-factor governmentality.

Rather than the application of technical knowledge, participants in this project described their capacity for good case management in terms of their biographical experiences. Their desire to work with young people and their capacity to be good case managers emerged from their own experiences of adversity or trauma. It facilitated what they considered to be feelings of empathy and understanding towards their clients. The participants' biographical experiences also shaped their approach to the day-to-day relational practices of case management. Rather than merely addressing various risk factors, case managers described their work as modelled on familial and friend-like relationships and foregrounded the management of friendship, intimacy and a desire for connection as critical to the way that case management takes place. These relationships raise important questions about the way that youth is understood as an empirical object.

Case management and biographical experiences of adversity

Case managers are responsible for conducting risk assessments. In this sense, it is in their case management work that expert definitions of youth are materialised in practice. If young people are positioned as objects of risk management, then this would be anticipated in the forms of expertise and practice deployed in their case management. However, narratives from participants in this project reveal a more complex discursive and relational terrain. Case managers did not necessarily implement the technical language of risk when describing their case management practices. Indeed, the basis for the expertise they deployed in managing their clients came not from these forms of governmentalised knowledge but from personal biographical experiences in which their own capacity to overcome adversity provided the capacity and motivation to facilitate similar experiences for others. Participants often described themselves as coming from positions of marginalisation or as having experienced trauma or abuse in their own lives.

These experiences – and the experience of having overcome them – led to participants feeling that they had a unique capacity to relate to those in similar circumstances and therefore to be good case managers. Participants felt that their personal experiences of trauma or abuse allowed them to communicate, advise and mentor clients and therefore to be good case managers. Tim described his background as 'dysfunctional':

> I was involved in petty crime as a youth. My mother had mental health issues. I didn't meet my father until I was 19 years old. I was adopted amongst all of that and then went back to my mother. . . . I have probably had about three and a half years of homelessness as well.

However, he had subsequently become a successful businessman, and case management was work that he had embarked upon subsequent to becoming established in business and financially secure. Having overcome this marginalisation, Tim regarded his own biography as a concrete manifestation of what he hoped clients could achieve. When Tim was asked about the factors influencing his clients' abilities to avoid returning to custody, he foregrounded a capacity for 'decision-based living' formed through long-term relationships with secure others (such as himself):

> It's got to be internal. . . . There's an old saying, I can lead a horse to water, but I can't make it drink. I've put it down to decision-based living compared

to choice-based living . . . many of these young kids have learnt to survive on their own without . . . a lot of positive input from older people. All they have probably heard, most of the time, is how they are doing things wrong and how they are a blight on the landscape. So, having somebody that they have not had a long relationship with come along and tell them what the boundaries are and how they should do it and how they should structure is not something that people are necessarily going to be able to pick up straight away. . . . People that live by making choices, usually are not taking responsibility for their actions and things they have been involved with. Those that do decision-based living take action through decisions in their life, they take responsibility for things that they have been involved in and the things that they have been given responsibility for.

For Tim, his ability to overcome adversity was a matter of personal responsibility, which he now sees as the critical capacity that he is facilitating in his clients. In the process, Tim enacts a key assumption of neoliberal governmentality, which is the attempt to create personally responsible subjects who can individually navigate inequality and marginalisation. However, the assumptions from Tim do not come from formal risk assessments of young people (such as the YLS/CMI) or from the expert knowledge that is available to him in his work. Instead, these assumptions come from Tim's own experience of marginalisation and his deployment of neoliberal discourses of individual personal responsibility in his narration of himself.

Like Tim, Eve also foregrounded her own biographical experiences in the making of herself as a case manager. However, rather than the personal responsibility of herself and her clients, Eve suggested that her experiences of marginalisation and familial trauma allowed her to connect with clients in a more empathic manner. When she was asked about her motivations for working with juvenile offenders, she said: 'my own personal upbringing, and like I guess, the way that stuff that has played out in my family has probably been a big factor'. When she was further prompted about her upbringing, she detailed her mother's multiple husbands and partners, homelessness, experiences with her mother's drug abuse and domestic violence and her brother's criminal history. However, Eve was able to overcome disadvantages to enrol in a nursing degree in university before she started working with offenders. Eve suggested that her personal history was a 'subconscious thing', she said:

I guess it helps me understand though. Like I the similarities, maybe I can relate to some of the stuff they are going through

Here, Eve suggests that the relatively narrow social distance between her own experiences and those of her clients allowed her to understand and relate to them in ways that facilitated her case management work. This relationship between personal experiences of marginalisation and increased empathy for clients was also described by Debbie, who described her upbringing as 'disadvantaged'. She grew up, primarily, in a single parent household after her mother left an abusive relationship with her father. When asked how her previous experiences play into her own work, Debbie invoked a discourse of 'risk' but then connected this with her capacity for connecting with clients:

> I was a young person at risk. I have a few mental health problems. I was diagnosed with depression, attempted suicide a few times and had an eating disorder. So, knowing where I have come from and where I am now helps me to know that when these young people are at their worst or where at their worst . . . and helping them through that, it kind of just brings it back.

If the expertise that case managers draw upon in legitimising their professional authority does not come from their application of risk discourses, then this destabilises youth as an object of research within existing approaches. In the actual practice of case management, governmental authority comes not from expert discourses but from biographical experiences that provide a sense of competence and the desire to facilitate success. We are not arguing that normative assumptions connected to neoliberalism were not articulated here, as indeed they are in these narratives and those that follow. However, these practices were seen to facilitate a capacity for empathy, understanding and personal connection that case managers considered to be fundamental to their work, and it is here that the meaning of youth is constructed and negotiated. It is in these relational contexts that the work of case management takes place, and so we turn to these practices in the next section of this chapter.

Case management as a relational practice

Case management was not described by participants in terms of the application of technical expertise but as a relational practice that involves the mutual negotiation of identity on the part of both case managers and their clients. From the perspective of both the risk-factor and governmentality approach to juvenile justice practices, the work of case management takes place according to discourses which define young people as subjects of management and that outline the kinds of practices that workers must employ in order to connect clients with services. In this sense, it is not relevant who the particular case manager is, or how they are regarded by their clients, so long as there is 'rapport' between case manager and client (Summers, 2012). However, when asked about their work, case managers were clear that the key task of good case management was the creation and management of a personal relationship and a sense of empathic connection with clients. While this personal relationship was described as key to clients' desistance pathways, the kind of personal relationship mobilised and managed by case managers in their dealings with clients took place through the enactment of identities that were not necessarily reducible to the subject positions defined in notions of case management best practice. The relational practices of case managers moved beyond the bounds of the prescribed case manager-client relationship to form identities that resembled familial or other kinds of intimate bonds, although enacted in the context of the work of case management.

Eve (also quoted earlier) emphasised the need for a 'supportive system' for her clients where they had a network of help to assist them through periods of change. The job of a case manager was to be a part of this support system, which was embedded in the broader social relationships of clients, but which may also come to stand in for other supportive relationships. In this context, Eve suggested that her case management practices often resembled familial bonds, and that her position in relation to her clients was that of a parental or other familial figure:

> Sometimes, it's weird, you end up becoming a surrogate mum or dad or like, you know, yeah a big sister or whatever.

Case managers frequently referred to themselves as like parents, and family-like relationships between the case manager and client were common in participants' accounts of their work. Establishing a relationship that resembled familial or other relationships outside of the juvenile justice context was considered critical to successful case management, since it included experiences of empathy and an authentic personal connection that was necessary for clients' engagement with the case management program. In this context, Maranda suggested that working with young people is about 'being chilled and getting [the] relationship going'. Maranda stressed the importance for the closeness of the relationship with her clients so that they could confide with her. The sharing of information was a critical tool to achieve this:

> They want to know the music you like, they want to know what you did on the weekend. Without doing too much self-disclosure, because that's a big thing in the industry that you have to be conscious of, but just getting that rapport on a more real level.

For Maranda, the relationship she builds with her clients is an important part of normalising case management interventions. The relationship required some level of disclosure about her personal life and interests that encouraged clients to trust her. However, the relationship also required the careful negotiation of the level of intimacy that was permitted in these relationships. In the following excerpt, Maranda was referring to a male client who was in a 'cycle' of substance abuse where he used with his girlfriend and friends. She said she had to emphasise to the client the need for positive relationships in order to break this cycle. In this instance the client took his friendly relationship to a level of intimacy which oversteps the boundaries which she puts in place:

> He said to me once: 'I can't get out of the cycle'. He's like: 'if you and me went out' and I thought 'oh god'. Be he's like 'obviously I would meet a new group of friends and, like, it would open up a whole new life for me'.

In this instance, the client moved beyond the surrogate sister or friend relationship to discuss the way that a girlfriend such as Maranda would be a positive relationship in his desistance pathway. For this client, his case manager represents an imagined future in which he gains access to new social connections and is thereby able to leave the 'cycle' that he feels himself trapped within. The intimacy of the relationship between Maranda and her client is critical to this client's approach to his case management and did not go beyond this discussion of hypothetical social connections that this client would accumulate should he be in an intimate relationship with his case manager. However, while this intimacy is necessary to the case management relationship, it requires case managers to carefully negotiate the boundaries of familial and other kinds of intimacy in order to facilitate an ongoing sense of personal connection, while not transgressing the institutional boundaries defining the relationship between case manager and client.

Nevertheless, some case managers did feel constricted by the institutional boundaries placed around their relationships with their clients. Gloria started working with young people once her children had started school, and her understanding of her clients came from her role as a parent. She said that she related to her clients as she would her children or friends of her children, and compared the experiences of clients to those of her own children:

> There were a lot of young people in the community that didn't quite have the opportunities that my own children had, and I thought I could give back.

From this position as a parent-like figure, Gloria went on to say that everyone had 'challenges and choices', and everyone 'makes mistakes, everyone makes bad choices, but some choices are worse than others'. Gloria said that she is 'just able to be a role model'. However, the parent-like position that Gloria established in her relationships with clients sometimes conflicted with institutional definitions of the case management relationship and limited the level of relationality that Gloria was able to exercise with her clients. She said that, on occasions, she would like to say to her clients:

> I have a free afternoon. I don't have any appointments so let's go take a movie or something . . . why can't I just jump in the car and drive this person and make this life a little bit easier for them.

Wanting to help make her client's lives 'a little bit easier for them' felt commonplace for Gloria, as this is what she would do with her own children, and it frustrated her that she couldn't do this with her clients. These practices, such as going to a movie with a client or driving them to an appointment, did not contribute to the formal desistance plans. However, Gloria felt that they were essential for case managers to build the kind of relationship with clients that would facilitate their ongoing engagement with the service.

Rather than the application of technical knowledge onto a subject of risk, the relational practices of case management involve the navigation of intimacy, authenticity and trust that resemble familial and other kinds of intimate relationships. These examples show that case management is a complex relational practice in which personal connections and the relational negotiation of identity is key to the success of the case management relationship. The negotiation of empathy and the production of familial-like relationships that this entails is not anticipated by the emphasis on risk and intervention foregrounded by both the risk-management and governmentality perspectives, both of which understand case management as driven by technical knowledge deployed on the part of a governmental subject and unable to properly apprehend these relational and institutional dynamics.

However, these are of course not familial bonds, and the negotiation of relationality and intimacy that these case managers describe is a part of the power relationships that shape the relationship between case manager and client. This is a highly asymmetrical relationship, in which case managers both connect clients to services and have the authority to apply disciplinary sanctions to those clients who do not adequately conform to the requirements placed upon them by their case managers. In this respect, these relational practices enact the disciplinary practice of case management in the context of the neoliberal governance of crime and shows how the negotiation of intimacy and trust contributes to the institutional practices deployed to define and govern youth in juvenile justice.

New theoretical sensibilities/doing research in organisations

Bringing theoretical critique to bear on the concept of the 'at-risk youth' has been important for interrogating young people's position within the power relations of neoliberal governmentality. Young people leaving juvenile justice are intensely governed subjects, the targets of a range of discourses and interventions into their lives. The nature of youth in juvenile justice is heavily circumscribed – positioned in terms of risk and defined in terms that make youth amenable to expert intervention. However, neither the subject of risk defined by risk-factor analysis nor the disciplined object of neoliberal governmentality can be easily discerned in these narratives from case managers. Instead, what emerges in these narratives is a relationally constructed and constantly negotiated object – youth as a product of familial ties and negotiated intimacy and as a reflection of the biographical experiences of case managers themselves. Rather than merely subjects of risk, young people emerge here in ways that resemble children, siblings and intimate partners, as well as the case manager's memories of themselves in earlier parts of their biography. In this sense, the object of study implied by existing approaches to youth research in juvenile justice appears absent from the very institutional practices that should implement these concepts in concrete governmental practices. Instead, these narratives enact a fluid and heterogeneous concept of youth that requires new approaches to researching young people.

This argument implies a new object for youth research. Conceptualising youth means theorising something that is under negotiation in a variety of social and institutional settings. Rather than fixed in place by disciplinary technologies, youth is constantly in motion, constructed and reconstructed differently within relational practices that are unpredictable and that require investigation. The key task, therefore, is not merely to analyse a fixed object, even if to critique the way in which it is fixed. Rather, the task is to understand the forms of expertise and relational authority through which youth comes to be defined as a socially intelligible object for researchers and institutions. These relational practices are localised in particular settings and negotiated in ways that create new questions about the basis for governmental expertise and the multifaceted ways in which young people are known and treated within organisations. The nature of youth is not in this sense predictable in advance but is intrinsically malleable in ways that reflect the subjectivities and organisational imperatives at work in the various sites in which youth is constructed. Youth research is relevant within all of these sites and approaches an intrinsically ambiguous object which nevertheless occupies a critical role in important and socially impactful institutions, such as the criminal justice system and the broader terrain of neoliberal welfare institutions.

References

Foucault, M. (2007) *Security, Territory, Population* (London: Palgrave).

France, A. (2008) 'Risk Factor Analysis and the Youth Question', *Journal of Youth Studies*, 11(1), 1–15.

Garland, D. (2011) *The Culture of Control: Crime and Social Order in Contemporary Society*, Kindle ed. (New York: Oxford University Press).

Hannah-Moffat, K. (2005) 'Criminogenic Needs and the Transformative Risk Subject', *Punishment and Society*, 7(1), 29–51.

Kelly, P. (2000) 'Youth as an Artefact of Expertise: Problematizing the Practice of Youth Studies in an Age of Uncertainty', *Journal of Youth Studies*, 3(3), 301–315.

Kelly, P. (2001) 'Youth at Risk: Processes of Individualisation and Responsibilisation in the Risk Society', *Discourse: Studies in the Cultural Politics of Education*, 22(1), 23–33.

Kelly, P. (2006) 'The Entrepreneurial Self and "Youth At-Risk": Exploring the Horizons of Identity in the Twenty-First Century', *Journal of Youth Studies*, 9(1), 17–32.

O'Malley, P. (2004) *Risk, Uncertainty and Government* (London: The Glass House Press).

Robinson, G. (2002) 'Exploring Risk Management in Probation Practice: Contemporary Developments in England and Wales', *Punishment and Society*, 4(1), 5–25.

Summers, N. (2012) *Fundamentals of Case Management Practice*, 4th ed. (Belmont, CA: Brooks/Cole).

Turner, S. (2012) 'Case Management in Corrections: Evidence, Issues and Challenges', in F. McNeill, P. Raynor and C. Trotter (eds.), *Offender Supervision: New Directions in Theory, Research and Practice* (New York: Willan Publishing), 344–366.

Wyn, J. and White, R. (1997) *Rethinking Youth* (Crows Nest, Australia: Allen and Unwin).

Chapter 4

They look before they leap

Conceptualising young people as digitally
competent risk takers and its implications
for ethical internet research

Matt Hart

Introduction

In this chapter I explore some of the complexities involved in researching young
people's intimate and social online practices. This work is informed by the challenges and dilemmas I have encountered in my time speaking with young people
as an internet researcher over the previous seven years. In so doing, I highlight
the sometimes frustrating and paradoxical nature of online research involving
young people. As scholars of youth, we are often tasked with overcoming con-
trived bureaucratic or institutional hurdles which impact our creativity and autonomy (Calvey, 2008). Yet, in spite of our efforts to conduct ourselves ethically,
our young research participants are often adept at creating unexpected situations
which we must reflect on in order to elucidate best practice.

My work broadens the argument that many approaches taken by human research
ethics committees (HRECS), university research ethics boards (URECS) or institutional review boards (IRBs) are either outdated or ignorant of the nuances of internet
spaces or cultures (O'Connor, Madge, Shaw and Wellens, 2008; Convery and Cox,
2012). This outdatedness is manifestly present in the fixation on risk elements, such
as being able to verify and ensure participants give informed consent (Bruckman,
2002; Hudson and Bruckman, 2004). Such a fixation owes, in part, to entrenched
conceptualisations of young people as either 'at-risk' or 'vulnerable' (McLeod,
2012) or their inhabiting a position of transitional change (Furlong, 2013; see also
Furlong and Cartmel, 1997). However, these key definitions are problematised
by the conceptual contradictions and ambiguities that occur when these terms are
used in an increasingly interdisciplinary manner; particularly when notions of
vulnerability are contrasted against ideas of 'resilience' (Hanewald, 2011). On one
side of the argument are scholars advocating for the protection of young people from harm (see, for example, Livingstone et al., 2011). On the other are those
seeking to promote a 'risk-positive' discourse, one that argues that only by being
exposed to risks can young people adapt to and learn from life's problems and
therein maintain a sense of wellbeing and resilience (see, for example, Bengtsson
and Ravn, 2018; Case, 2006; Cense, 2019; Hart and Third, 2013; Naezer, 2018).

Research involving young people under the age of 18 is further 'complicated' (Lenhart, 2013) when it examines their sexuality and online sexual practices due to contradictions within legislation. For example, in the UK and Australia the age of sexual consent is deemed to be 16 and over (Richards, 2018), but at the same time – under certain jurisdictions – any 'sexually suggestive' image of an adolescent may also be considered child pornography (Albury, 2015, p. 1738). In such a context, visual research involving nude selfies and young people is, therefore limited (cf. Naezer, 2018) because HRECs and IRBs deem such research as too risky to approve. Consequently, most internet researchers interested in understanding young people's online sexual experiences elect to conduct research primarily with 'young adults' aged 18 and over (see, for example, Tiidenberg and Gómez Cruz, 2015; Powell and Henry, 2014). Such research is guided by broad definitions of 'youth' or 'young people' that align with the World Health Organisation (WHO), which conceptualises youth in terms of being a period between 15 and 24 years of age (WHO, 2014).

Certainly, an anxiety over the pedantry of HRECs was instilled in me as a postgraduate student, when I originally designed my research project on young people's nude selfie practices on the social media site Tumblr. Despite suggesting that adolescents – those under the age of 18 – were likely to be sharing nude images of themselves on Tumblr – and that we should understand why – I was advised by my colleagues at the time that I would encounter 'less hassle in terms of getting ethics clearance' if I just 'study young people aged between 18 and twenty-five (25) in line with the WHO definition'. As an inexperienced PhD student, I internalised this advice, but in hindsight, I realise now that this was indicative of a broader mindset within academia, one in which we as researchers are so constrained by a bureaucratic system, designed not only to minimise risk for our participants but also the institutions whom employ us. However, in excluding people who are deemed too young 'for their own sake', we lose the salient, rich stories and experiences of those on the cusp of adulthood, a critical juncture in their development (Schulenberg, Sameroff and Cicchetti, 2004). This is something I will return to later in the chapter.

Despite brushing aside this immediate ethical complexity, the research project discussed here still contained several other complex, sensitive dilemmas or challenges. Given the physical constraints of a book chapter, I shall limit this discussion to three here. The first involved the difficulty of recruiting young people in a diffuse, online environment. The second emerged out of the tension between my ethics committee's need for me to ensure my participants were over the age of 18. The last concerned the problematic nature of the ownership of research data and a participant's right to privacy (or to eschew it). The chapter concludes, having reflected on the complexities of my research, with a discussion on how the concept of 'edgework' (Lyng, 1990; 2004) can help frame young people's digital competency for negotiating risk and thus challenge established conceptualisations of young people online as 'vulnerable'.

Architecture and assumptions: difficulty in online recruitment

My research initially involved an ethnographic immersion into the visual social media platform Tumblr. Launched in 2007, Tumblr enables its users to post text, video and audio and fashion highly customisable profile pages (far beyond the limited potential of Facebook or Twitter profiles). In so doing, Tumblr users can create reflexive, sociopolitical spaces in which to participate in fandoms (Kanai, 2015) or belong in safe, like-minded spaces (Hart 2015, 2018a) and engage in personal or political action (Fink and Miller, 2014). Tumblr can be broadly defined as a social networking site (SNS), in that it contains unique, user-made profiles, which themselves contain friends lists, comprised of other users with which the profile has a connection; these features can produce streams of user-generated content in which interaction can occur (Ellison and Boyd, 2013, p. 158). In this way, Tumblr is largely consistent with other social network/networking sites (SNSs) like Twitter. For example: Tumblr users can 'like', 'reblog' (share) and hashtag (sort) content.

However, profiles on Tumblr are not necessarily public or even semi-public – they can be entirely private. Unlike Facebook, 'friendship' on Tumblr can be asymmetrical, similar to Twitter, with a following/followed model that does not presume reciprocity. Further, this friendship may be obfuscated entirely, such that Tumblr users rarely publicise or make visible their connections with or to other Tumblr profiles. It is tempting to think of Tumblr as a 'networked public' (Boyd, 2010), in that it shares some of the same affordances of the replicability and searchability of Facebook or Twitter. However, Tumblr has the added affordance of *pseudonymity*. Unlike Facebook, Tumblr users are under no obligation to use their 'real' names or have a limit on the amount of Tumblr profiles (and by extension, identities) they can articulate.

I draw attention here to the 'architecture' of Tumblr, as one of the first mistakes I made was underestimating how my lack of knowledge in comparison to my participants *of the platform* contributed to issues in recruitment, and indeed my use of Tumblr offers a rather interesting research experience in terms of its access to participants. I wanted to 'see' the nude selfie community, but Tumblr is in essence a diffuse mass of individual profiles. Adding further complexity, Tumblr profiles lack the permeance found on Facebook – Tumblr users create and delete their profiles on an ad hoc basis – sometimes treating their accounts with abandon, at other times strategically treating them like 'burner phones' and discarding them when necessary (Hart, 2017). Because Tumblr profiles are fluid and ephemeral, it seemed pointless to post a recruitment flyer to my blog and hope that people would notice it. Who would know where to find me? It was more appropriate for me to search for them. I did this not by searching for *the* nude selfie sharing community (as if it were a physical thing I could find) but by searching the hashtags #nude and #selfie and approaching individual users directly. This involved sending users a private message with a brief outline of my research project and an invitation to participate via an interview (the process then followed standard ethics committee procedures via sending each user a participant information sheet, consent form and so on).

While this approach solved my initial recruitment problem of 'how' to sample, a few problems arose, problems that really relate to outdated ethics procedures. Anyone who has ever received a random phone call or spam email understands the annoyance of a cold-call approach, especially when further hindered by the cold/direct/formal language used within ethics information forms, somewhat like terms and conditions jargon, as required by the ethics committee who approve a research project. Initial responders were not shy in accusing me of being a market researcher and that no, they would not be interested in participating. Further to the ethics requirements it also became apparent that there was something wrong about my initial greeting message. My attempt at informality perhaps was not sitting well with the young people I was approaching. This issue became very clear when one young woman accused me of being a 'pic thief' wanting to 'cop some free nudes'.

As a white, middle-class, heterosexual man from an Australian university, I had initially (and foolishly) failed to be cognisant of how it might look to a young person to be approached out of the blue by a man online claiming to be a researcher; really only I knew my intentions were genuine and noble (from a professional and empirical perspective). Realising my naïveté, I modified my introduction message to include not only the links to my research project but to make them aware of my academic footprint – my university profile page, my academia.edu profile page and so on. I draw attention to this outcome in an attempt to advise any internet researcher wishing to approach potential participants in a similar manner on the value of their academic footprint. Being able to provide my credentials, to seem 'authentic' as it were, made an inordinate difference in recruitment. Once I was able to prove *my* authenticity they were more trusting of me, and my response rate improved.

Anxiety over veracity: the pressure for informed consent in online research

After overcoming the recruitment difficulty, I gathered a sample of 25 young Tumblr users within the space of a month. However, in line with the ethical requirements, before interviews could begin, I was required to verify their identities, but more specifically, determine that they were over the age of 18. The way the HREC deemed I should do this was to request that each participant send a scanned copy of their personal identification documents such as their birth certificates, driver's licenses or passports.

The scepticism of my HREC with regard to the veracity of my participants' ages and abilities to provide informed consent was directly linked to the internet's propensity for anonymity, which has its roots in the formative discourse around identity which emerged out of the global uptake of the internet in the late 1980s and early 1990s. On 5 July 1993, the now infamous Peter Steiner cartoon was published in *The New Yorker* bearing the caption: 'On the Internet, nobody knows you're a dog', which came to represent the zeitgeist around the internet and disembodied self-representation. We could, according to pioneer internet theorists, be whoever we wanted to be 'behind the screen' in the new 'virtual frontier' (see, for example, Turkle, 1995; Rheingold, 2000). We were supposedly able for the first time to reinvent ourselves in 'cyberspace', free from the shackles of racial, sexual or other forms of embodied oppression. The cartoon, according to Castro-Leon and Harmon, 'endures as an icon of internet culture' and issues around anonymity (2016, p. 27). These early concerns around 'authenticity' and 'trust' pervade academia and shape much of what researchers are able to 'do' online (De Laat, 2008).

An outcome, I argue, is that under particular circumstances, the requirement for absolute proof of identity restricts research in the online environment. Given how protective young people are of their private space, and supported by their knowledge of social media platforms, their embracing of the ability to articulate identities in pseudo/anonymous spaces (Hart, 2017; Binik, Mah and Kiesler, 2010), and the ease of access to photo-manipulation software which enables users to create and share fake documents, demonstrates that there is a certain intrinsic safety in how young people operate online. In such a situation, I argue that it is difficult for an internet researcher – particularly one whose research methods are entirely based around interacting online – to ever truly hope to verify (with any real certainty) an individual's identity. Identification documents can be forged or Photoshopped. Obviously, I am not making the case that we should abandon the need for verification from our participants. Indeed, given the nature of my research, both I and my supporting university were keen to avoid any inadvertent collection of child pornography or exploitation material.

However, after learning how much of their personal information they would need to provide in order to satisfy my ethics committee in order to establish they were who they claimed to be and that they were capable of consenting to the research, a number of the participants withdrew from the study. Their discomfort was understandable; while I had established myself as a real researcher, I could empathise in the trepidation of being required to give a relative stranger on the internet a copy of their records. One workaround I propose if other researchers find themselves in a similar position is to consider the use of Snapchat. By creating an academic snapchat profile, participants could send their information for a short time only – enough for the researcher and colleague to verify names and ages – and then the data would disappear. If either the researcher or colleague was to screenshot anything they received, the participant would be notified, and the breach of privacy would likely destroy any trust and potential research partnership, resulting in the loss of the participant. By embracing ephemerality, a relationship of trust can be built while satisfying ethical requirements regarding veracity and consent.

I offer the workaround as even with the best laid plans, sometimes research participants can throw a proverbial spanner in the works. One of my initial research participants had gone through the standard process as permitted by my HREC: he was sampled, provided a participant information sheet and consent form and had shown me the required documents earlier to confirm his identity prior to commencing our interview. At the conclusion of one of our connections, however, the young man who had claimed to be 18 admitted to providing false information (a fake ID). He confessed to being 17 'but turning 18 in a month'. He was so interested in the project because it 'would give people like (him) a voice' that he felt the need to lie so he could participate. Despite his desire to have his story told, and my moral conviction torn between the ethics of giving a young person a voice or silencing it, the only option was as permitted by my HREC to ensure that I deleted his data and remove him from the study.

Current legal frameworks around young people and nude selfies are complex, stemming in part from the conflation between nude selfies and 'sexts' (Albury, 2015) but also in contradictory legislation that deems young people under the age of 18 legally unable to give consent, even if they are over the legal age to consent to sexual intercourse. Put in simpler terms, any image of a young person 'in a sexual context' (where what constitutes 'sexual' appears to be highly subjective), is deemed to constitute child pornography 'even if it is a selfie' (Albury and Crawford, 2012, p. 469). It is for this legal reason that HRECs and IRBs are extremely strict with internet researchers involved in studying young people's nude selfies and participant veracity.

However, this complex conflation and discourse is 'out of step with the perceptions of young people . . . who view themselves as having full sexual agency' (Ibid., p. 464). One way we could acknowledge young people's agency is to draw on the notion of *Gillick Competence*. In the UK, the right of a child under the age of 16 to consent to medical treatment was decided by the House of Lords in 1986 under *Gillick v West Norfolk and Wisbech AHA*. Here, a mother of girls under the age of 16 objected to their doctors prescribing contraceptive medication without her consent. The House of Lords ruled that a child under the age of 16 had 'legal competence' to consent to the medical examination and treatment 'if they had sufficient maturity and intelligence to understand the nature and implications of that treatment' (Griffith, 2016, p. 244). In this context then, assessing whether a young person is able to demonstrate Gillick competence rests upon their maturity to make decisions for themselves and to understand and be able to consent to research – and that a parent's authority is not absolute (O'Reilly, Dogra and Daneil, 2013). Clearly the details need to be considered, yet the context is already here. Again, I bring forward these options in a direct attempt to demonstrate plausible workarounds that are within reach.

Ownership of data: the dilemma of the best of intentions

The last complexity I discuss in this chapter is the tension encountered between the well-intended ethics principals which guided my research project and the wishes for autonomy and respect expressed by the participants. Prior to commencing the interviews, these participants had the option to formally dis/agree to my incorporating some of their uploaded nude selfies from their Tumblr profiles into my analysis. My rationale for requiring consent for this outcome related to triangulation of data, particularly for further analysis in any future publications. While consenting to this data collection was entirely voluntary, much time is needed to ensure identification of participant information is kept secure. While I was fortunate that all participants were willing to provide consent, I highlight here that it is difficult to establish and guarantee nondisclosure of identity and no adverse link to researched knowledge and processes. The following is an outcome that came from my attempt to address this nondisclosure of identity.

I draw the reader's attention here to the work of Tiidenberg (2014), who draws on Markham's (2012) concept of 'ethical fabrication' in her work on adults and nude selfies on Tumblr. Tiidenberg provides the option to alter her participants' images by running them through an application that subjected them to a series of filters that included hiding watermarks drastically changing the colours and placing 'modesty blocks' over genitalia. Tiidenberg (2015) took guidance from the Association of Internet Researchers (AOIR) 2012 ethics guidelines and fellow AOIR ethics committee members in her decision to protect her participants' identities and is arguably what most would regard as 'best practice' in this research context. When my participants became aware that this practice was built into my work, things became complicated. When my participants read the participant information sheet and consent form and became aware that I would need to anonymise their images, by either cropping, pixelating or blurring out any identifying features such as face, tattoos and so on, making clear that I would change the composition of any participants' selfies by flipping (mirroring) the image to further prevent anyone from using a web service to reverse-search the image and trace it back to my participants' blog, many were very annoyed.

Confidentiality is often touted as critical when researching with children and young people, given their prescribed status by researchers and care workers as 'vulnerable' (Kendrick, Steckley and Lerpiniere, 2008), and as such, anonymity should be a guarantee (Masson, 2002; Hill, 2005). However, unlike Tiidenberg's (2014) participants, many of the young people I approached were reticent to continue with my study upon learning that I would fundamentally change the look of their nude selfies in order to include them in my study:

PARTICIPANT: Before we start will you show me what pictures from my blog you'll choose to include, if any, right?

ME: Of course!

PARTICIPANT: You won't have to censor my face btw

ME: I appreciate that, but it's a requirement of the ethics board who permitted me to conduct the study to remove any elements that might identify you.

PARTICIPANT: Um wait a sec my pictures will get credited right? Like you'll mention my blog or name won't you?

ME: I can't, I'm sorry. Your blog/name are also censored as part of the de-identifying
process that is intended to protect you.
PARTICIPANT: Well those are my pictures. . . . I mean if you use them and don't
even credit me it's like you're basically plagiarising my art. Sorry, but I'm out.

The reaction given by the participant was a common reaction shared amongst
many of my would-be participants, most of whom withdrew from the study altogether after our conversation inevitably covered this sticking point.

Their desire to be identified in the research is consistent with existing ethics
literature which notes that children and young people often want to be named in
scholarly research, usually because they want the right to exert their own identity
and are proud and excited to have their voices heard (Heath, Brooks, Cleaver and
Ireland, 2009; see also Kendrick et al., 2008; Edmond, 2005; Alderson and Morrow, 2011). However, the young participants in my study who insisted upon being
identified are somewhat unique, in that many considered themselves sex workers
or 'cam girls' (Senft, 2008). In this sense, their desire for autonomy and identification stems from a need for recognition of ownership over their images, rather
than out of pride of involvement alone. From the perspective of a researcher trying to minimise potential harm, it seems axiomatic that censoring and protecting
the identities of my participants would be a figurative 'no-brainer'. However, by
altering the image in any form, I would, as the participant points out, be plagiarising *their* work. Indeed, some of the young women I spoke with went on to explain
how they made a living off their nude selfies on Tumblr. One participant described
it as being 'no different to any other type of artist producing work on commission'
by a benefactor or patron.

Unfortunately, I was heavily constrained by the ethics requirements of my university and had no choice but to let the individuals withdraw from the study. This
outcome created two interesting tensions for me as the researcher: the first being
that I found myself asking the rhetorical question: *at what point does data stop
belonging to the participant and start belonging to the researcher?* The second
tension was the realisation that a participant might be leveraging my research for
their own personal gain.

Without thinking, I had initially fallen into the epistemological mistake of
thinking that the data *I* had collected, and that which was going to be subject to
my analysis, was mine, *and* I was being ethical at the same time. Plagiarism was
the furthest from my intentions; indeed, the whole point of anonymising my participants was to protect their privacy. I bring this discussion to the forefront, as it
is equally important for HRECS and IRBs to become cognisant that in removing
our participants' autonomy, by threat of removal of the study, we may inadvertently cause other harm. As is often the case in participatory research, participants
involved in generating material or artefacts that form part of the analysis feel a
strong sense of ownership of the data that is coproduced with the researcher. Such
feelings are particularly true in methods such as 'photovoice' (Vaughan, 2016),

wherein participants have had an active role in generating the data and may take offence to the idea of a researcher imposing their will upon the meaning or the potential 'harm' of an image.

The second tension, regarding incentives, is also interesting. Scholars have long contested the ethical implications of providing incentives for participation (Pittman and Sheehan, 2017). Some argue that providing financial benefits for participants as compensation for their time and effort is itself a risk of harm-causing – such as giving money to studies involving addicts (McKeganey, 2001). Conversely, others insist that incentives prove valuable, as young people respond well to short-term motivators (Grant, 2014). Interestingly, this discussion is frequently framed in terms of what opportunities or harms (financial or otherwise) the researcher can impart or offer to their participants – not how the participant can leverage opportunities themselves (Hopkins, 2010).

Ultimately, I did not think my participants sought to use my study as a platform for self-branding, though even if that was the case, I do not see it as being exploitative on the participants' part. Rather, the possibility seemed to me to be a demonstration of their savviness and acumen! As researchers we place considerable significance on the benefits that young people, as a whole, gain by participating in our research (McCarry, 2012). However, this benefit is often framed in feminist terms such as giving our participants 'voice' or a chance to be heard. What I learned and have discussed here, from my participants, is that what we as researchers consider to be of benefit may indeed work against our ideals. I therefore argue that our current outlook may well undermine the autonomy of young people and be disrespectful of their competency for risk management.

Crowding edges online: young people's digital competency

Throughout this chapter I have described three complexities that entangled my research process: how platform architecture and insider/outsider status can impact on the ability to successfully recruit and how both the need for participant veracity and ethical fabrication – our very own ethics principals – can harm young people. I completely admit that during my research I had internalised a traditional ethical perspective, albeit one that tried in earnest to adopt a feminist paradigm of care. Yet I now see that in so doing, I perpetuated a perspective which limited the autonomy of the young people I sought to empower. Through conducting the research, in working with and speaking with these young people it became clear not only how cognisant of online risks they were but how competent they were in minimising or successfully negotiating associated risks.

My history of research work outlines in detail just how knowledgeable young people are of social media and how well versed the skills they have developed over time in order to safely negotiate the risks of sharing their nudes online are (Hart, 2017). For example, they deploy 'burner' profiles or use strategic hash tagging and participatory practices which limit their public visibility and therefore reduce chances of being discovered (Hart, 2018b). Such skills and knowledge are quintessential trademarks to what Stephen Lyng (1990, 2004) refers to as 'edgework'. Edgework is about voluntarily engaging in risky behaviour because it is thrilling, affirming, authentic and seductive. To engage in edgework is to 'tread boundaries' (Shay, 2017) between life and death, consciousness and unconsciousness, sanity and insanity or order and chaos. The challenge of edgework is to 'tread' those boundaries as close to the 'edges' as possible without 'falling over' and losing one's life, sense of self or general wellbeing. The way in which edgeworkers maintain their sense of control over the dangers is to deploy their learned knowledge, honed skills and intrinsic personal characteristics – what Lyng (1990) refers to as 'having the right stuff' or a basic survival instinct (p. 859). I argue that the young people I worked with in my research fit this profile. While aware that historically, edgework was criticised for its focus on the 'hyper masculine' world of adventure or extreme sports, emergency work and war (Newmahr, 2011), in recent years it has been used by scholars to help understand white collar rogue-trading (Wexler, 2010), 'pro-anorexia subcultures' (Gailey, 2009), sadomasochism (Newmahr, 2011) and videogaming (Shay, 2017).

In wanting to conceptualise young people who take risks online via their nude selfies – as intimate edgeworkers – as digitally competent, I hope to reduce the problematic notion of 'digital nativity'. As in previous research, I am careful to argue that not *all* young people possess the skills, knowledge or *competence* to safely tread the boundaries inherent in such risky behaviour. However, rather than continue to persist with the dichotomy of young people as at-risk or vulnerable, or of being 'in transition' (Furlong and Cartmel, 1997), I propose that we all look at digital competence when designing a study, when interpreting data and when establishing our ethical boundaries. Such a notion carries the torch from Albury and Crawford (2012), who call for a need to respond to the 'realities of young people's experiences, and the role played by technologies' (p. 471), as in opening up new room for discussion on how, for *some* young people, voluntary engagement with risk can offer an outcome that is a more wholesome and emotionally rewarding experience for both researchers and those being researched. How we bring HRECs and IRBs up to speed with such contemporary thinking, how ethics best practice can adapt while maintaining order and minimising new harms that emerge in the digital age is the focus we need to adopt. The challenge is evolving and of great interest to all involved in research.

References

Albury, K. (2015) 'Selfies, Sexts, and Sneaky Hats: Young People's Understandings of Gendered Practices of Self-Representation', *International Journal of Communication*, 9, 1734–1745.

Albury, K. and Crawford, K. (2012) 'Sexting, Consent and Young People's Ethics: Beyond Megan's Story', *Continuum*, 26(3), 463–473.

Alderson, P. and Morrow, V. (2011) *The Ethics of Research With Children and Young People: A Practical Handbook* (London: Sage).

AOIR. (2012) 'Ethical Decision-Making and Internet Research: Recommendations From the AoIR Ethics Working Committee (Version 2.0)'. Available at: https://aoir.org/reports/ethics2.pdf.

Bengtsson, T.T. and Ravn, S. (2018) *Youth, Risk, Routine: A New Perspective on Risk-Taking in Young Lives* (London: Routledge).

Binik, Y.M., Mah, K. and Kiesler, S. (2010) 'Ethical Issues in Conducting Sex Research on the Internet', *The Journal of Sex Research*, 36(1), 82–90.

Boyd, D. (2010) 'Social Network Sites as Networked Publics: Affordances, Dynamics, and Implications', in Z. Papacharissi (ed.), *Networked Self: Identity, Community, and Culture* (London: Routledge), 39–58.

Bruckman, A. (2002) 'Ethical Guidelines for Researching Online', *College of Computing: Georgia Institute of Technology*. Available at: www-static.cc.gatech.edu/~asb/ethics/ (Accessed 17 July 2019).

Calvey, D. (2008) 'The Art and Politics of Covert Research: Doing "Situated Ethics" in the Field', *Sociology*, 42(5), 905–918.

Case, S. (2006) 'Young People "At Risk" of What? Challenging Risk-Focused Early Intervention as Crime Prevention', *Youth Justice*, 6(3), 171–179.

Castro-Leon, E. and Harmon, R. (2016) *Cloud as a Service: Understanding the Service Innovation Ecosystem* (New York: Apress).

Cense, M. (2019) 'Navigating a Bumpy Road. Developing Sexuality Education that Supports Young People's Sexual Agency', *Sex Education*, 19(3), 263–276.

Convery, I. and Cox, D. (2012) 'A Review of Research Ethics in Internet-Based Research', *Practitioner Research in Higher Education*, 6(1), 50–57.

De Laat, P.B. (2008) 'Online Diaries: Reflections on Trust, Privacy, and Exhibitionism', *Ethics and Information Technology*, 10(10), 57.

Edmond, R. (2005) 'An Outsider's View of the Inside', in D. Crimmens and I. Lyme Regis Milligan (eds.), *Facing Forward: Residential Child Care in the 21st Century* (Dorset: Russell House Publishing).

Ellison, N. and Boyd, D. (2013) 'Sociality Through Social Network Sites', in W.H. Dutton (ed.), *The Oxford Handbook of Internet Studies* (Oxford: Oxford University Press).

Fink, M. and Miller, Q. (2014) 'Trans Media Moments: Tumblr, 2011–2013', *Television & New Media*, 15(7), 611–626.

Furlong, A. (2013) *Youth Studies: An Introduction* (London: Routledge).

Furlong, A. and Cartmel, F. (1997) *Young People and Social Change: Individualisation and Risk in Late Modernity* (London: Open University Press).

Gailey, J. (2009) 'Starving Is the Most Fun a Girl Can Have', *Critical Criminology*, 17(2), 93–108.

Grant, R.W. (2014) *Strings Attached: Untangling the Ethics of Incentives* (Princeton: Princeton University Press).

Griffith, R. (2016) 'What Is Gillick Competence?', *Human Vaccines & Immunotherapeutics*, 12(1), 244–247.

Hanewald, R. (2011) 'Reviewing the Literature on "At-Risk" and Resilient Children and Young People', *Australian Journal of Teacher Education*, 36(2), 16–29.

Hart, M. (2015) 'Youth Intimacy on Tumblr: A Pilot Study', *YOUNG*, 23(3), 193–208.

Hart, M. (2017) 'Being Naked on the Internet: Young People's Nude Selfies as Intimate Edgework', *Journal of Youth Studies*, 20(3), 301–315.

Hart, M. (2018a) '#Topless Tuesdays and #Wet Wednesdays: Digitally-Mediated Neo-Tribalism and NSFW Selfies on Tumblr', in A. Hardy, A. Bennett and B. Robards (eds.), *Neo-Tribes: Consumption, Leisure and Tourism* (Cham: Palgrave), 207–209.

Hart, M. (2018b) '"It's Nice To See You're Not The Only One With Kinks": Presenting Intimate Privates in Intimate Publics on Tumblr', in A.S. Dobson, B. Robards and N. Carah (eds.), *Digital Intimate Publics and Social Media* (Cham: Palgrave), 177–191.

Hart, M. and Third, A. (2013) 'Why Tumblr Fosters Deep and Enduring Forms of Intimacy Online'. Available at: http://onlineopinion.com.au/view.asp?article=15666 (Accessed 24 June 2019).

Heath, S., Brooks, R., Cleaver, E. and Ireland, E. (2009) *Researching Young People's Lives* (London: Sage).

Hill, M. (2005) 'Ethical Considerations in Researching Children's Experience', in S. Greene and D. Hogan (eds.), *Researching Children's Experience: Approaches and Methods* (London: Sage).

Hopkins, P.E. (2010) *Young People, Place and Identity* (London: Routledge).

Hudson, J.M. and Bruckman, A. (2004) '"Go Away": Participant Objections to Being Studied and the Ethics of Chatroom Research', *The Information Society*, 20(2), 127–139.

Kanai, A. (2015) 'WhatShouldWeCallMe? Self-Branding, Individuality and Belonging in Youthful Femininities on Tumblr', *M/C Journal*, 18(1). Available at: http://journal.media-culture.org.au/index.php/mcjournal/article/view/936 (Accessed 1 March 2018).

Kendrick, A., Steckley, L. and Lerpiniere, J. (2008) 'Ethical Issues, Research and Vulnerability: Gaining the Views of Children and Young People in Residential Care', *Children's Geographies*, 6(1), 79–93.

Lenhart, A. (2013) 'The Challenges of Conducting Surveys of Youth', *Pew Research Centre*. Available at: www.pewresearch.org/fact-tank/2013/06/21/the-challenges-of-conducting-surveys-on-youths/ (Accessed 11 July 2019).

Livingstone, S., Haddon, L., Görzig, A. and Ólafsson, K. (2011) 'EU Kids Online II: Final Report 2011' (London: London School of Economics & Political Science). Available at: http://eprints.lse.ac.uk/39351 (Accessed 15 July 2019).

Lyng, S. (1990) 'Edgework: A Social Psychological Analysis of Voluntary Risk Taking', *American Journal of Sociology*, 95(4), 851–886.

Lyng, S. (2004) *Edgework: The Sociology of Risk-Taking* (London: Routledge).

Markham, A. (2012) 'Fabrication as Ethical Practice', *Information, Communication & Society*, 15(3), 334–353.

Masson, J. (2002) 'Researching Children's Perspectives: Legal Issues', in A. Lewis, G. Lindsay and G. Buckingham (eds.), *Researching Children's Perspectives* (London: Open University Press), 34–45.

McCarry, M. (2012) 'Who Benefits? A Critical Reflection on Children and Young People's Participation in Sensitive Research', *International Journal of Social Research Methodology*, 15(1), 55–68.

McKeganey, N. (2001) 'To Pay or Not to Pay: Respondents' Motivation for Participation in Research', *Addiction*, 96, 1237–1238.

McLeod, J. (2012) 'Vulnerability and the Neo-Liberal Youth Citizen: A View From Australia', *Comparative Education*, 48(1), 11–26.

Naezer, M. (2018) 'From Risky Behaviour to Sexy Adventures: Reconceptualising Young People's Online Sexual Activities', *Culture, Health & Sexuality*, 20(6), 715–729.

Newmahr, S. (2011) *Playing on the Edge: Sadomasochism, Risk and Intimacy* (Bloomington: Indiana University Press).

O'Connor, H., Madge, C., Shaw, R. and Wellens, J. (2008) 'Internet-Based Interviewing', in N. Fielding, R.M. Lee and G. Blank (eds.), *The SAGE Handbook of Online Research Methods*, 2nd ed. (London: Sage), 416–434.

O'Reilly, M., Dogra, N. and Daneil, P. (2013) *Research With Children: Theory and Practice* (London: Sage).

Pittman, M. and Sheehan, K. (2017) 'Ethics of Using Online Commercial Crowdsourcing Sites for Academic Research', in M. Zimmer and K. Kinder-Kurlanda (eds.), *Internet Research Ethics for the Social Age: New Challenges, Cases and Contexts* (New York: Peter Lang), 177–186.

Powell, A. and Henry, N. (2014) 'Blurred Lines? Responding to "Sexting" and Gender-Based Violence Among Young People', *Children Australia*, 39(2), 119–124.

Quinton, S. and Reynolds, N. (2018) 'The Changing Roles of Researchers and Participants in Digital and Social Media Research: Ethics Challenges and Forward Directions', in K. Woodfield (ed.), *The Ethics of Online Research* (Bingley: Emerald Publishing Limited), 53–78.

Rheingold, H. (2000) *The Virtual Community: Homesteading on the Electronic Frontier* (Cambridge, MA: MIT Press).

Richards, M. (2018) 'Why the Age of Sexual Consent Continues to Be a Worldwide Challenge', *The Conversation*. Available at: http://theconversation.com/why-the-age-of-sexual-consent-continues-to-be-a-worldwide-challenge-94334 (Accessed 8 July 2019).

Schulenberg, J.E., Sameroff, A.J. and Cicchetti, D. (2004) 'The Transition to Adulthood as a Critical Juncture in the Course of Psychopathology and Mental Health', *Development and Psychopathology*, 16(4), 799–806.

Senft, T. (2008) *Cam Girls: Celebrity and Community in the Age of Social Networks* (New York: Peter Lang).

Shay, H. (2017) 'Virtual Edgework: Negotiating Risk in Role-Playing Gaming', *Journal of Contemporary Ethnography*, 46(2), 203–229.

Tiidenberg, K. (2014) 'Bringing Sexy Back: Reclaiming the Body Aesthetic via Self-Shooting', *Cyberpsychology: Journal of Psychological Research on Cyberspace*, 8(1). Available at: https://cyberpsychology.eu/article/view/4295/3342 (Accessed 9 February 2018).

Tiidenberg, K. (2015) 'Great Faith in Surfaces – Visual Narrative Analysis of Selfies', in A.A. Allaste and K. Tiidenberg (eds.), *In Search of . . . New Methodological Approaches to Youth Research* (Newcastle Upon Tyne: Cambridge Scholars), 233–257.

Tiidenberg, K. and Gómez Cruz, E. (2015) 'Selfies, Image and the Re-Making of the Body', *Body & Society*, 21(4), 77–102.

Turkle, S. (1995) *Life on the Screen: Identity in the Age of the Internet* (London: Simon and Schuster).

Vaughan, C. (2016) 'Different Lenses: Navigating Ethics in Cross-Cultural Research Using Photovoice', in D. Warr, M. Guillemin, S. Cox and J. Waycott (eds.), *Ethics and Visual Research Methods: Theory, Methodology, and Practice* (Basingstoke: Palgrave Macmillan), 19–30.

Wexler, M. (2010) 'Financial Edgework and the Persistence of Rogue Traders', *Business and Society Review*, 115(1), 1–25.

World Health Organisation. (2014) 'Recognising Adolescence'. Available at: http://apps.who.int/adolescent/second-decade/section2/page1/recognizing-adolescence.html (Accessed 18 July 2019).

Theme II

Digital research

Chapter 5

Critical reflections

Merits of using youth-centric technology in keeping young people safe across Europe

Darren Sharpe, Spyros Spyrou and Shain Akhtar

Introduction

This chapter draws on the lessons and experiences from an EU-funded project carried out by an interdisciplinary research team, youth work practitioners and international body of young people. The chapter illustrates how participatory research done well can lead to the coproduction of digitals tools for safeguarding young people in the 'real world', while also empowering vulnerable groups of young people in becoming active and engaged citizens. This project was designed primarily in response to the inconsistency and gaps in youth-led resources currently available to support the safeguarding of children and young people throughout the European Union and online. The project built on primary research to codevelop a cross-culturally transferable e-learning tool to promote early routes to help for young people on the move across Europe. The focus of this chapter is on the complexities and benefits – theoretically, and in practice – in coproducing digital tools with young people who experienced shared histories of state care, forced migration, dentation and displacement.

The project achieved its aim in raising the profile of a group of young people who experience adversity as European citizens capable of knowing, understanding and responding to their own risks. We also achieved our aim in the codevelopment of a game-infused e-learning tool to empower young people from across Europe to learn more about the different child protection systems in existence and provide youth work professionals with a novel tool for tackling a challenging societal issue.

Understanding the precarity of unaccompanied migrant children

The contemporary world is experiencing an unprecedented movement of people across countries and continents, and we are learning to deal with all the challenges and complexities this migration brings, particularly in the case of unaccompanied migrant children (Hopkins and Hill, 2010). The recent flows of refugees from the

Middle East to Europe have accentuated the need to attend to these movements with the necessary sensitivity and urgency, especially in relation to those populations who appear to be more vulnerable, such as unaccompanied, smuggled or trafficked children (Feijen, 2008).

Although not the only social group that requires special attention, young people who are on the move are clearly in need of safeguarding. As discussed by Klepp (2010), there is no uniform child protection system in place within the EU to keep children and young people safe from harm. This shortcoming gains significance when considered in light of existing evidence that favours early help. On the one hand, there is longstanding and widespread international agreement that readily available early help for children and families can stop problems from escalating and prevent maltreatment before it occurs (MacMillan, 2010; Laming, 2003, 2009). There is significant evidence that harm from maltreatment is common, but often hidden, and that most children and young people in need cannot easily access services (Harker et al., 2013; Walsh and Brandon, 2012).

We draw on the lessons and experiences from a collaborative project carried out by a diverse group of academics, researchers, practitioners and young people. It illustrates how participatory projects, based on the active engagement of young people, can facilitate a creative and productive process for developing tools for safeguarding young people, while also empowering them to tackle their safeguarding needs both online and offline as active and engaged citizens. Although the primary goal of the project was the development of a Gamified e-learning tool to promote health and early access to safeguarding services for young people on the move in Europe, the focus of this chapter is on the participatory process of codeveloping a youth-centric digital tool.

Although the outcome or product of the project (the production of a Gamified e-learning tool) remained a clearly defined goal for all participants from the very beginning of the project, it was also clear that the process through which this would result was equally important. Treating participation as a process rather than merely an outcome recentres attention on the actual relations, negotiations and practices that unfold during the participatory process, which ultimately matter as much for young people's development as the quality of the outcome of the participatory process. The project faced the challenge of ensuring a productive and fulfilling collaborative experience for young people coming from diverse ethnic, cultural and linguistic groups working across national contexts, an issue that we explore in much more detail in the chapter. The overall framework of the project enabled groups of young people to provide insight into their own concerns and cultural contexts, through a supportive mechanism that sought to achieve voice, impact and improvement within social policy and social work environments.

From this blended intergenerational and multicultural context, this chapter first provides a brief introduction to the project, and its objectives are outlined. This is followed by a discussion of the participatory process of youth engagement in researching, analysing, conceptualising and developing the e-learning tool. There is a focus on both the strengths and challenges of working collaboratively with diverse groups of young people across national contexts to achieve a common goal and an examination of the various needs that stem from the participatory process through a culturally sensitive lens. This is followed by a discussion of young people's reactions to the game, and how their feedback, combined with the 'bottom-up' approach adopted by the team, helped make adjustments to the game and how this offers a dynamic model for game development through participatory engagement. The chapter concludes with reflections on the significance of this kind of research-informed, participatory, youth-engagement process for addressing the safeguarding needs of young people on the move.

Keep me safe in Europe: a participatory youth project

This participatory project, titled Keep Me Safe in Europe, offered here as a case study of youth engagement in applied research, was funded by Erasmus + and ran for a period of 24 months (2014–2016). The project built on the learning and experiences of the partner organisations gained through previous relevant funded national and transnational youth projects that centred on young people's experiences of violence and abuse in Europe. As part of the project, groups of young people from three different countries (the UK, Greece and Cyprus) worked together in a collaborative manner in order to develop, with the help of a number of experts (including academics and researchers from the fields of anthropology, sociology, psychology and social work, practitioners involved with youth support services and game design and development experts) a gamified e-learning tool.

In this project, an EU citizenship model was adopted based on the participation of young people that recognises the importance of youth voice and nonformal learning. The emergence of childhood and youth studies since the late 1980s, together with the establishment of the United Nations Convention on the Rights of the Child (UNCRC) in 1989, has brought about an unprecedented interest in child and youth participation in research. While participation may come in a variety of forms, from the mere soliciting of young people's views on a research topic to youth-led research projects where young people play a leading role in all stages of the research process, it is well-established that participation offers clear advantages to young people, the production of new knowledge and society at large (Fraser, Lewis, Ding, Kellett and Robinson, 2004; Kirby, 1999). Yet still, the youth participation movement cannot stand still and should strive to reflect the times in which we live. For instance, research and policy addressing the needs of digitalised youth falls behind general youth participatory practices. Led by the previous Children's Commissioner for England, there is now growing momentum internationally to bring the UNCRC up to date by recognising and addressing children's digital rights (see Livingstone, Lansdown and Third, 2017).

In this project, not only are young people's rights as citizens acknowledged, respected and safeguarded through their participation in research, but their perspectives are made visible and integrated into the research knowledge produced as part of a democratic process (see especially Percy-Smith and Thomas, 2010). Likewise, young people's participation often leads to more valid research findings that are attuned to the realities of young people's lives, while youth-led research is often more likely to address power inequalities in research, given that it is young people themselves who are carrying out the research (Schafer and Yarwood, 2008). The young people who participated in the project explored their own solutions to neglect and abuse risks inherent within their daily lives, in their local communities, on the internet and in their social media environments.

Methodological aspects of the project

The project was sponsored and approved by the European Commission, ethical approval was gained from the Faculty of Health, Social Care and Education Research Ethics Panel at Anglia Ruskin University, European University Cyprus and SEERC Research Ethics Panels, and also Walsall County Safeguarding Board. We registered Anglia Ruskin's research ethics approval with our respective ethics bodies. Both the research and practice were iterative processes where we learnt as we went along. In practice, we produced young-people-friendly paperwork and codesigned learning sessions based on the principles of learning by doing. We also learnt how to reflect together and find solutions in monthly telecom meetings involving primarily the adult researchers. We discussed, debated and discovered new ways to involve the young cocreators in the codesign process in safe and meaningful ways.

The project fostered the service-learning approach, which is a method of teaching, learning and reflecting frequently used in youth work. As a teaching method, it falls under the philosophy of experiential education. More specifically, it integrates meaningful community service with instruction and reflection to enrich the learning experience, teach civic responsibility, encourage lifelong civic engagement and strengthen communities for the common good. It also promotes active learning, which is a process whereby the young people cocreate the learning environment. The coinquirers in our project engaged in activities such as role playing, reality playing, small groups and other introspective challenging activities that promote critical thinking. The cooperative learning experience was entertaining, with high returns in terms of recall for young people. In the following we describe the four stages we followed in our participatory approach.

Phase One prioritised the recruitment, training and support of the young coinquirers. All the sites ran at least one learning session per month with a group of young coinquirers (aged 15–24). The coinquirers from the three countries were brought together at the project's first transnational meeting in Greece, where the young coinquirers gained exposure to a range of participatory methods from experienced youth coaches. The meeting offered opportunities for the young coinquirers to refine and practise the participatory methods they would later use to gather local knowledge. The young coinquirers left the meeting with an increased understanding of the European context of abuse and neglect experienced by young people and enhanced skills in the planning, running and recording of activity-based workshops aimed at children and young people. The young coinquirers also had the opportunity to test out their initial thoughts and ideas on this substantive topic area and received immediate feedback in a supportive environment from peers and adult practitioners/academics. In parallel, adult members of the team had the opportunity to network and share amongst themselves the latest safeguarding information/resources they had uncovered in their desk-top research and cross referenced the key issues to be included in the e-tool. They also agreed on milestones for sharing work with the goal of harmonising the fieldwork in the development of the e-learning tool and guide. All of the groups had started to gather and share information on neglect and abuse by the end of Phase One. The young researchers then returned home in small groups and led local workshops with groups of vulnerable young people to develop storylines and scenarios, based upon real situations and perceptions of accessing early routes to find support for neglect and abuse with which to populate the game. The storylines were brought together into the game to allow users from across Europe to learn more about the different safeguarding systems in existence across the EU and culturally specific issues in recognising, telling and seeking help with neglect and abuse.

One of the main challenges of Phase One was to help young people from different cultural backgrounds, who speak different languages, to sit together in groups and cooperate to produce the first storylines. The use of two languages – Greek and English – was a considerable barrier for the young coinquirers. The stories shared presented some difficulties in terms of understanding the issues and recognising unpredictable behaviours. This was particularly prevalent when the UK group presented stories on child sexual exploitation, bullying, domestic abuse and neglect to the Greek group, who had young people that had been displaced due to turmoil from countries from which they had arrived. This presented some anomalies in terms of responses from the groups, with the UK group wanting to be proactive and identify solutions, versus the Greek group not feeling the same – in essence, dealing with bullying and neglect. What was evident during the development of this work was that young people in the UK had greater exposure to the topic areas within schools, colleges and wider participation groups, from a theoretical base, while the young people from Greece had little understanding of the subject area due to the lack of exposure and varied background of the participants present. Also, there was a question of what was deemed as acceptable in terms of behaviours from the Greek and UK young people, particularly around cultural sensitivities, in relation to use of language. This challenge was overcome by pairing fluent bilingual youths with monolingual members of the same team, thus promoting a culture of collaboration and monitoring and supervising the working teams through their respective leaders. The cultural differences challenged coinquirers but in turn enriched the coproduction process, creating greater opportunity to identify risk and protective factors to build into the scenarios modelled in the game. Boyle and Harris (2009) highlight the challenges to coproduction but argue that the key to reforming public services is to encourage users to design and deliver services in equal partnership with professionals.

Mutual respect and acceptance are not a given state of mind amongst people of different cultural backgrounds. The young coinquirers were to some extent constrained by their local biographies but were supported in developing cultural competence to understand, communicate with and effectively interact with other young people and adults across the multicultural team. Respect and acceptance were promoted by sharing personal experiences and providing fun bonding activities for the young coinquirers. Five mixed working groups were formed, and each group had representatives of the three countries. The previous two actions facilitated the necessary transnational cohesiveness for the game. It should be taken into consideration that many of the young researchers have themselves experienced abuse and neglect, and they have used their own personal experiences to inform the stories that were produced by each group. This was a liberating experience for many of them, but still a lot of effort was made to ensure that they did not reveal more than they felt comfortable with, and that they could withdraw from the group at any time. This concern was also built into the gamified game, where the player has the option to press a 'panic button' and leave the scene of the game should they feel overwhelmed by the story content.

The ethical complexities of a participatory project where a number of the young participants might themselves have had direct experiences of violence or neglect should not be underestimated. The adult facilitators in the project had to ensure that the young participants would be protected throughout the process from unintentional disclosures or the possibility of emotional trauma resulting from the recall of painful experiences. For example, we gave guidance on not reading project material late at night, provided local safe spaces to discuss ideas before sharing them with the larger group and worked hard collaboratively with their carers, parents and organisations to ensure that a wrap-around support system was there for each young person. The benefits of drawing on participants' personal experiences had to be constantly checked against the possible negative consequences of doing so for their emotional wellbeing. This was in relation to young people sharing their own stories and the impact it had on them emotionally during group discussions and allowing for young people to feel safe enough to share them with the wider group, with support from staff present as and when required. At the formation stage of the UK group, young people were asked to develop and agree a set of rules that would cover the sharing a sensitive information with others. The rules were something the group adhered to and recognised as an important feature in relation to the development of this work.

It is also worth mentioning that the young people came from diverse cultural settings, which had different understandings and practices about safeguarding. Thus, a substantial amount of time was spent during the first session to ensure that all young coinquirers reached a consensus on basic concepts and terms used throughout the project. The cultural differences could merely be acknowledged and be considered as a factor in the design of the game. For instance, terms such as 'participation' or 'coproduction' carried different cultural and linguistic meanings across the group and had to be negotiated early on to allow for a fruitful and commonly shared trajectory for the project. Also, the graphic description of the characters and places young people would naturally go to seek help varied across the participating countries, and therefore common sense comprises needed to be made. For instance, characters shared different ethnicities, gender and evolving storylines. The places young people can go to seek help was simplified to home, school and friends, a terrain which all the collaborators and users inhabit. We recognised however, that the quest for cultural competence is a dimension of the game that needs further study in order to achieve a fully localised game for each respective country of the transnational team. An example of localisation in games is that a game that is set in the Second World War would have all swastika flags removed for the German version, as Nazi symbolism is banned in Germany. The subject of safeguarding also presented some difficulties in relation to young people's understanding, with the cultural backgrounds of the group also having an impact on exploring the subjects, that is, for some young people survival (being safe) was ultimately the key principle, with other issues being secondary.

The importance of respecting and accepting diversity in all its forms was also discussed. The past experience of the senior researchers was vital in designing activities that promoted interpersonal relationships in a friendly and accepting environment. Leisure activities were also built into the programme to help young researchers socialise outside the more official project environment. Given their diverse backgrounds, establishing common ground amongst the young participants was an ongoing process that required not only the encouragement of respect for difference but also finding common or shared experiences and interests that allowed for cross-national collaboration.

Phase Two consisted of an interactive, fun and playful transnational meeting in Cyprus. The 'Make, Play and Do' meeting brought together the users, developers, designers and partners to play, wireframe and storyboard in order to visualise what they needed and wanted from the e-learning tool. The coproduction of the game began at the meeting and continued on their return home. Feedback was continually shared to drive the game design. In order for the young researchers to effectively steer the direction and development of the game through the local workshops, teams acquired the need for structure, which reflects the game development process. All the teams consulted and tested features of the game with a mix of social workers, custody officers, general practitioners and other professional groups, as well as youth participation groups to ensure that storylines had validity, and also accurately reflected statutory policies and procedures.

The development of the game was not without its challenges, primarily due to the detail of the content. It was necessary to reduce the content in order to get the main points across, without losing the essence of the story. Young people had different ideas on solutions, which generated some debate amongst the groups. The UK being diverse and young people coming from different abilities and backgrounds, there was constant pressure on staff to take stock of the outcomes of the groups, ensuring that the group had a common understanding and that their views influenced the development of the work stream. The challenges of coproducing knowledge should not be underestimated. A careful balance needed to be stuck in listening, synthesising and ejecting information and keeping everyone on board with how ideas and solutions were adapted and perhaps reworded to fit the needs of a European audience. The emerging ideas for the e-learning tool were brought to the attention of relevant child-safeguarding boards and/or the ministries responsible for children and young people's welfare in each country to gain professional input and endorsement. Between the two phases, an alpha of the game was developed.[1] In game development, a project goes through this process:

- Alpha: first playable version, story outlined, core featured implemented
- Beta: functionally complete, most features implemented, ready for the main bulk of testing
- Gold Master/Release: feature complete, all issues and development complete, ready for release

An abstract story model was built by researching the patterns presented in the set of stories created in the first phase, and the first stories to be 'played' were implemented in the game. The player had to choose the main character from several options with different life background stories, all with some episodes connected with neglect and abuse. The gameplay consists of exploring a town space and interacting with characters (family, friends and social workers) and institutions (social services, schools) in the context of a running story that makes the player react to problematic situations.

In Phase Three, a beta version of the game was created and rolled out to be trialled and tested with the inclusion of a 'how-to' guide. Each team encouraged groups of children and young people in their locality to trial the game and feedback their recommendations for improvement. Walsall Council led on the adaptation of the assessment guide originally developed in a separate project to accurately capture children's and young people's views of the game. In Phase Four, a showcase event was organised in London and Greece to launch the e-learning tool and guide. Key stakeholders were invited and learnt about the background and development of the game and were given plenty of time to test it out and provide feedback. Young researchers were also presented with the Open College Network qualifications they had earned through their active participation in this project.

To summarise, research conducted with young people questions traditional methodological premises by challenging the relationship between the young person and the researcher. This impacts on power relationships, as the target of research (the young person) becomes a collaborator in the research process. Collaborating with young people challenges the researcher's status as the expert in charge of administrating the research process. The researcher's task is to share their expertise with young people and professionals. In joint production of knowledge, both young people and adults contribute to the collection and analysis of research data (Törrönen and Vornanen, 2014). This type of research undermines the construction of a 'monopoly of knowledge' on the traditionally exclusive basis of adult- and researcher-centred approaches. The collection and analysis of research data are the result of collaborative action, rather than the accomplishments of a single researcher or research team. Young people's participation also supports and reinforces the research methodology by ensuring that the target of the study is actively involved in empirical research (Faulkner, 2010).

Unpacking the complexity of digital research and creation of digital context for young people

The young researchers provided the stories for the Gamified e-tool, and this was very useful in conceptualising potentially dangerous circumstances that cannot be easily identified by senior researchers who have different experiences and understandings of safeguarding. For example, there is extensive reference in the game to social media and online dangers that are more pertinent to the specific age group. Such age-relevant stories might not have been included in the game had young people not been involved in all the stages of the project. The young researchers helped to develop the language and expressions used in the game that are most appropriate to their age and culture, making the tool more realistic and culturally sensitive. They provided extensive feedback on the characters (age, gender, appearance, role in the game), the plots and the different options that are presented to them (for example, at the points that players have to make a choice, there may be a separate option asking them if there is something else that they would choose that is not offered as a built-in option by the game) and the layout for the whole game. Pleasingly, there was also a large amount of positive, detailed feedback provided even for cosmetic things, such as the background music, the font of the letters or the time that elapses between stories. This is demonstrative of the genuine interest in the development of the game shown by the young people and is greatly attributable to the ownership given to them.

One of the main concerns of all the people who were involved in designing the specific tool was to ensure that the 'how-to' guide does not serve simply as a manual with instructions for the game. Therefore, a section has been included that refers to the support that should be offered to users at different stages and what we should take into consideration. The support provided to young people who play the game should be the following:

• When they start to play the game, they will be informed that they may view something that disturbs and upsets them or makes them feel uncomfortable. This is not self-evident since most games are designed to help young people relax and not to inform them about something as important as safeguarding
• It should also be taken into consideration that some young people may not recognise that they are exposed to abuse and neglect in their everyday lives. Therefore, it was important to build into the game features that allow them to refrain from the game and take them directly to appropriate resources to deal

with abuse and neglect. It is one of the main reasons why it is advisable to use this game with bigger groups as an educational tool, or with the presence of a social worker or another mental health professional

- Playing the game will show the young people some ways to talk about their own experiences of abuse or neglect or the experiences of people they know (for example, parents, siblings, friends, classmates). It is important to understand that they should help others voice similar experiences or report such cases for them in order to become active ambassadors against abuse and neglect. This is essential in order to combat forms of violence (such as bullying) that are very common, have taken enormous dimensions and are often taking place in front of others who do not know what to do. If we achieve this it will make a difference in the lives of many young people

- Through the game, the players will learn how to ask for help, and the game will include various resources that they can access no matter which part of the country they live in. Lay people tend to believe that this information is readily available to everyone in today's societies, but this is often not the case for children and young people who are exposed to, or experience, abuse and neglect. For this reason, the e-online tool can be accessed from any device and also played offline. This e-online tool can be extremely useful for young people who migrate to Europe. Although at the time we put together the proposal and got the funding, we did not have in mind the flow of refugees and immigrants to Europe, this online tool can cater for the safeguarding needs of these young people who were violently removed from their houses and found themselves in a very different cultural context

It is important to consider that parents or carers can use this e-tool as a way to talk to their children/young people through the game about scenarios of abuse and neglect to which they are exposed. They can resort to the manual and the guidelines for some relevant information, and there may also be links to other relevant sources of information. If parents avoid talking to their children about safeguarding because they are not sure how to approach the topic and what kind of information to provide, this e-tool tool provides a service to help with this. Parents/carers are advised to play the game themselves in order to know better how to guide their children, and to be aware of the situations to which young people will be exposed.

However, since many families/carers may not be aware of the abuse or neglect that their children/young people have experienced, they may also experience shock. They will have to process the overwhelming news fairly quickly and offer appropriate support (which is something this online tool can help them with). This situation is even more demanding in cases where a relative or family friend/ acquaintance is involved in the abuse or neglect. In any case, they may also need to access information on where they could ask for help for themselves, as well as for their children.

Last but not least, we should refer to social workers, teachers, therapists or other mental health professionals who are working with young people. They need to play the game first, so that they can understand its rationale and how it can be used to introduce young people to the concepts of abuse and neglect, to empower them to talk about their own or others' experiences of abuse and neglect and where to look for help. Then, according to their own training, the context and the group of young people that they work with, they can choose how and when to introduce it. They can ask young people to play it as a group talking about the choices that they would make and where they believe these choices could lead them and use the game as an interactive training platform.

In other cases, they may opt for an individualistic approach that will enable them to 'protect' young people and give them the opportunity to reflect on their own experiences. Given that the game is built mainly around three types of abuse, and that there is no direct reference to neglect, they may want to discuss with young people examples of neglect and how they could lead to abuse. The whole philosophy of the game and the 'how-to' guide is to provide a framework of con- tact support to all interested parties in the form of training them to recognise and talk about abuse and neglect, learning how to avoid it and where to ask for help.

Finally, it should be stressed that young people should not be led to believe that things are always as simple and straightforward as presented in the game format. Abuse and neglect may take on different forms that are occasionally supported by cultural or religious practices. Moreover, some young people may try to access the appropriate services and still fail to receive the support that they need. This is a delicate issue that we need to deal with, since we can never devise a game that can take into account all the different endings that a case of abuse or neglect may have in real life. Therefore, we should alert young people to the fact that this e-tool is meant to provide them with guidance on which are the most appropriate actions to take and to help them understand that they always have a choice (even if it is the lesser of two evils).

Conclusion

Keep Me Safe in Europe is unique in its merging a video gameplay experience and feel with learning about neglect and abuse. The game was built from the start with a general multidimensional story model, so that it was possible to 'plug in' new stories that impacted the main characters' lives along different dimensions in positive or negative ways. The game was expanded twice during the project, but its story model remains open for further expansions. This results in a mediated and curated experience that can reach a wide audience, all in the context of a carefully safeguarded digital environment. Keep Me Safe in Europe is also widely acces- sible from browsers and devices and has specific features to facilitate its usage in classes and for facilitating interactive discussions of the themes presented.

Without collaborating with a range of young people, acting as coinquirers throughout the duration of the project, comprised of vulnerable groups to trainee social workers, the project could not have achieved the depth and quality that it has. Exposure to the project fostered cross-cultural dialogue and built resilience in young people's understanding of neglect and abuse from multifaceted positions. Providing good research skills training not only provided the young researchers with knowledge on how to stay safe but also accountability in their decision-making and actions. Learners were awarded OCN Level 2 in Safeguarding, OCN Level 2 in Mentoring and the opportunity to achieve the Youth Pass. Good research-skills training allows young researchers to express themselves naturally, honestly and empirically. How young researchers then translate these skills and attributes into an ethical code of conduct depends upon how they are supported and steered.

This project raises the profile of vulnerable young people as European citizens capable of knowing, understanding and responding to their own risks. The project framework enabled groups of vulnerable young people to provide insights about their own concerns and cultural context through a supportive mechanism that seeks to achieve voice, impact and improvement within social policy and social work environments. In that sense, we feel that the project and the participatory approach we followed provides a much needed, sensitively informed tool for addressing young people's safeguarding needs while on the move in the rapidly changing social scene of Europe.

The web site for the game is here:
   http://kmse.open-lab.com/

The game can be played and downloaded from here:
   http://kmse.open-lab.com/play-the-game/

Acknowledgements

We would like to acknowledge the young researchers whose efforts and hard work contributed to the success of the study. We would also like to thank the contributors to the project and expert advisers on the drafting of this work. They are Froso Kalyva, Nicos Sozos, Pietro Polsinelli and Edward Smith.

The project is funded by Erasmus +, which is an EU programme for education, training, youth and sport. The project builds on a prototype game called Keep Me Safe funded by the Daphne-YOU RESPOND (2010) and informed by the study called Recognition, Telling and Seeking Help with Abuse and Neglect, funded by the Office of the Children's Commissioner in England 2014.

Dr Darren Sharpe was supported in part by the National Institute for Health Research (NIHR) Collaboration for Leadership in Applied Health Research and Care (CLAHRC) North Thames at Bart's Health NHS Trust. The views expressed are those of the author(s) and not necessarily those of the NHS, the NIHR or the Department of Health and Social Care

Note

1 Unity is a games engine that allows for multi-platform (Android, iOS, Playstation, Xbox, PC, Mac) development without additional services or applications. It is easy to

use across all disciplines due to its use of standard GUI techniques and naming conventions, without sacrificing versatility, and it even allows for easy expansion/augmentation by the development team. Unity uses C#, a common programming language across app and game development, allowing for new coders (whether new to the company or new to the project) to easily understand the code base and immediately integrate into the team and work processes.

References

Boyle, D. and Harris, M. (2009) *The Challenge of Co-production* (London: New Economics Foundation).

Faulkner, J. (2010) 'The Innocence Fetish: The Commodification and Sexualisation of Children in the Media and Popular Culture', *Media International Australia*, 135(1), 106–117.

Feijen, L. (2008) 'The Challenges of Ensuring Protection to Unaccompanied and Separated Children in Composite Flows in Europe', *Refugee Survey Quarterly*, 27(4), 63–73.

Fraser, S., Lewis, V., Ding, S., Kellett, M. and Robinson, C. (eds.). (2004) *Doing Research With Children and Young People* (London: Sage).

Harker, L., Jütte, S., Murphy, T., Bentley, H., Miller, P. and Fitch, K. (2013) *How Safe Are Our Children?* (London: NSPCC).

Hopkins, P. and Hill, M. (2010) 'The Needs and Strengths of Unaccompanied Asylum-Seeking Children and Young People in Scotland', *Child and Family Social Work*, 15(4), 399–408.

Kirby, P. (1999) *Involving Young Researchers: How to Enable Young People to Design and Conduct Research* (York: York Publishing Services).

Klepp, S. (2010) 'A Contested Asylum System: The European Union Between Refugee Protection and Border Control in the Mediterranean Sea', *European Journal of Migration and Law*, 12(1), 1–21.

Laming, H. (2003) *The Victoria Climbie Inquiry* (London: The Stationery Office).

Laming, H. (2009) *The Protection of Children in England: A Progress Report*, Vol. 330 (London: The Stationery Office).

Livingstone, S., Lansdown, G. and Third, A. (2017) *The Case for a UNCRC General Comment on Children's Rights and Digital Media: A Report Prepared for the Office of the Children's Commissioner of England* (London: LSE Consulting).

MacMillan, H.L. (2010) 'Commentary: Child Maltreatment and Physical Health: A Call to Action', *Journal of Pediatric Psychology*, 35(5), 533–535.

Percy-Smith, B. and Thomas, N. (eds.). (2010) *A Handbook of Children and Young People's Participation: Perspectives From Theory and Practice* (London and New York: Routledge).

Schafer, N. and Yarwood, R. (2008) 'Involving Young People as Researchers: Uncovering Multiple Power Relations Among Youths', *Children's Geographies*, 6(2), 121–135.

Törrönen, M.L. and Vornanen, R.H. (2014) 'Young People Leaving Care: Participatory Research to Improve Child Welfare Practices and the Rights of Children and Young People', *Australian Social Work*, 67(1), 135–150.

Walsh, K. and Brandon, L. (2012) 'Their Children's First Educators: Parents' Views About Child Sexual Abuse Prevention Education', *Journal of Child and Family Studies*, 21(5), 734–746.

Chapter 6

Digital modes of data collection in mixed-methods longitudinal youth research

Julia Cook and Dan Woodman

Introduction

Contemporary youth research is marked by a constellation of approaches and interests. Within this diversity there are, however, two dominant streams: youth transitions research, often using survey questionnaires or mixed methods, and youth cultures research, likely to draw on ethnographic (often insider) approaches. Digital methods are gaining popularity in youth research (see Robards and Lincoln, 2017; Hart, 2017) but are rarely integrated into large scale mixed-methods studies. In this chapter we discuss a recent use of digital data collection as part of the Life Patterns study, a long-running mixed-methods study of two generations of Australian young adults. Specifically, we discuss how this digital data collection was integrated with the larger program of research, and some of the challenges that this entailed. The Life Patterns study began in 1991 and was originally developed to track transitions to 'adult' statuses, focusing on young adults' experiences of education, employment, relationships and health and wellbeing. For this reason, the data collected for it – both survey and interview-based – generally focused on major milestones and experiences of key institutions. Over the past decade the focus has broadened to include a greater emphasis on making sense of these milestones and turning points in the context of everyday life. To help facilitate this focus on everyday life, in 2017 a digital method of data collection was added to the suite of methods used in the study. This allowed participants to document their activities and experiences over a week, in real time, providing a complex snapshot of their everyday lives.

The digital method of data collection that we discuss in this chapter was the foundation of a smaller study embedded within the broader Life Patterns project, which explored the impact of new employment patterns on young adults' lives beyond work, focusing particularly on their relationships. We began sampling for this study from the existing pool of Life Patterns participants who were aged 28–29 when the study took place in 2017, asking these participants if they were willing to recruit a significant other (such as an intimate partner). The sample of 53 (including 16 significant others) were asked to make multiple posts each day using a mobile phone application (or app) for a week, before taking part in an interview that discussed these posts. In this chapter we discuss some of the challenges that we encountered, as well as, in many cases, the opportunities that these challenges afforded us.

We begin by discussing the research design, focusing especially on the challenges that we encountered while designing a mode of data collection that was appropriate for the existing Life Patterns sample and yet met the aims of our study. We then reflect on the operationalisation of the method, focusing on the practical and interpretive challenges that it provoked, before considering the ways in which it aided us in capturing some of the complexities that characterised our participants' lives. Finally, we address how our study is placed within the ongoing Life Patterns research program, and how the insights that it produced both differed from and complemented those that have emerged from the wider study, adding to the complex picture of young adults' lives that it has built up over time.

Research design

As our study was situated within an existing research program (Life Patterns) one of the key challenges that we contended with was the need to design the project in a way that aligned with our aims while also building upon the substantial preexisting data. This was particularly relevant to our approach to data collection and sampling. The core of the Life Patterns research program is annual surveys with the entire sample (n = 520 in 2017) and biennial interviews with a sub-set of 30–50 participants. The design of the study meant that the types of experiences and changes that were captured through these methods were often focused on major events such as new jobs or milestones within families and intimate relationships. For instance, the participants who have taken part in the qualitative aspect of the project have, when possible, been followed longitudinally, with some interviewed up to seven times. This means that a significant portion of the interviews have often taken on the character of an update, focusing on what has changed and what has remained the same since the last interview. While the qualitative data collection added depth and insight into the everyday lives of participants missing in many longitudinal studies, Life Patterns lacked the type ethnographic insight that characterises some of the best youth research.

Our study sought to contribute to the existing research program by specifically considering the impact of work on young adults' *everyday* lives. This research topic was underpinned by the aim of adding depth and nuance to the existing data to better capture the complexities that characterise young adults' lives. Considering this aim, we sought to integrate a new mode of data collection into the existing research program, drawing inspiration from digital ethnography. Digital ethnographic methods have been used extensively in research on youth cultures, and have been particularly successful in revealing some of the intricacies of personal experience and expression (for recent examples see Abidin, 2017; Hart, 2018). Recognising the rich data collected in these studies of youth culture was a driver of our attempts to bring a type of ethnographic closeness into a large-numbers study of youth transitions and to thus better capture the complexities that characterised our participants' lives.

The form that the digital mode of data collection could take was heavily determined by the Life Patterns participants' use of digital technologies. In the 2013 survey, the participants were asked to comment on what they used social media for, and how important it was in their life via an open response question. Although a range of responses were received, we found that a significant proportion of the participants used social media as a tool for keeping in touch with those who were important to them and preferred to use private messaging over more visible functions (echoing the findings of previous studies, see Boyd, 2008). Data from the same survey also showed that most of the participants engaged with social media frequently, with 40% checking it many times a day, 27%a few times a day, and 18% once or twice a day, leaving only 15%using some form of social media less than once daily.

Although these data were collected four years prior to the design of the present study, they nevertheless provided an indication of the nature of the participants' engagement with social media. The data suggested that while observation of participants' existing social media profiles was unlikely to provide a sufficiently detailed sense of their everyday lives, most of them were engaging with digital platforms regularly, meaning that doing so was probably part of their everyday routines. Based on these insights we determined that it was likely that a large proportion of the participants would be willing and able to engage with a digital space multiple times each day, but it would be necessary to elicit a form of digital engagement from them rather than observing their existing modes of engagement.

Significantly, while we were originally inspired by the successes of digital ethnographic methods, these insights prompted us to diverge from what are often considered to be some of the key conventions of ethnography. Ethnography, along with its digital variant, remains deeply contested, evading definition despite myriad attempts (see Pink et al., 2015). Yet, in much of the literature it appears that ethnographic methods generally diverge from other qualitative methods (such as interviewing) due to their focus on observation (Gobo and Marciniak, 2016). While both the necessity and the feasibility of spending extended periods of time with a specific, often unfamiliar group of people as suggested by early ethnographers has been challenged on several fronts (see, for instance, Madison, 2011), the ethnographic method nevertheless maintains an enduring relationship with the observation of already-occurring social phenomena. By inviting our participants to a specific digital space that they (for the most part) did not already inhabit, and by relying on data that they curated, but which was elicited from them, we stepped towards the margins of ethnography, even as we were able to gain access to their everyday experiences in a new way. Although, as we discuss in the course of this chapter, this meant that we could capitalise on some of the benefits that have resulted from ethnographic studies in youth research, it also provoked several challenges.

While searching for an appropriate digital platform we contended with concerns about privacy and data security. Although we initially considered using a social media website such as Facebook, well-publicised concerns about privacy policies and (mis)use of data (Baruh and Popescu, 2017) ultimately deterred us from pursuing this option. We turned our attention to other platforms available as smartphone applications. The study of the implications and usage of smartphones signifies a rapidly expanding area of research interest (Lasén, 2015). Apps form a central part of this. Curiously, while sociologists have studied apps by participating in their design (Neves, Franz, Munteanu and Baecker, 2017), producing critiques and commentaries on them (Thomas and Lupton, 2016) and studying individuals' use of them via both self-reported content (Hobbs, Owen and Gerber, 2017) and log data (Kaufmann, 2018), little research has made use of apps to solicit data from participants. Indeed, the only studies doing so stem from market research (see Erickson, 2017). For this reason, there was little guidance available as to an appropriate app for our study. Ultimately, we selected an app based on our requirements for data security as well as functionality. Specifically, we chose an app named 'Slack' because it provided us with a password protected digital space that was visible only to the participant and ourselves and because the administrators could guarantee the security of the data that was uploaded to the app. Additionally, it was free to download and use (aside from costs associated with internet connectivity and uploading and downloading data) and allowed the participants to easily post text, images and videos in real time. We considered that some of the potential participants may not own or use smart phones and determined that if this were the case we would request that they use the app online via a computer. However, this situation did not arise during recruitment.

Turning to sampling, as we were working within an existing research program, the pool of participants we could sample from was predetermined. The cohort of Life Patterns participants whom we were interested in were originally recruited from secondary schools in Victoria, New South Wales, Tasmania and the Australian Capital Territory in 2005, when they were aged 16–17. Although the sample originally included approximately 4,000 participants, by the time we conducted our study with them in 2017, when they were aged 28–29, they numbered 520. However, attrition did not occur evenly throughout the sample in the years spanning 2005–2017. By 2017 the sample was comprised of approximately two-thirds women and was skewed towards those who were tertiary educated and working in professional forms of employment. Although this aligns with patterns found in the attrition of other longitudinal studies of youth transitions (see Chesters et al., 2018), it nevertheless meant that some pathways and experiences were over-represented, while others were reflected by few of the participants. In short, just as the preexisting sample shaped the way in which we could engage with the participants digitally, so too did it shape the demographics and experiences that we could target while selecting our sub-sample.

We focused particularly on those who had experiences of insecure work and/or nonstandard hours when recruiting our subsample. We defined nonstandard hours as work which included night or evening shifts, weekend work, public holidays and/or variability in one's working schedule, and we identified these participants using their responses to a survey question asking them if their work fit into any of these categories. Although, as already mentioned, the Life Patterns sample is skewed towards those in professional occupations which are commonly associated with 9–5 Monday-Friday work schedules, we nevertheless found that a majority of participants reported working nonstandard hours. This appeared to be due primarily to (typically unpaid) overtime that they engaged in outside of the formal hours of their employment, a practice that many of these participants identified as necessary to 'keep up' with their workload and the demands of their position.

We also wanted to recruit participants experiencing employment insecurity. Operationalising insecurity turned out to be challenging. We initially intended to use the participants' employment contract type (e.g., permanent, renewable, fixed term, casual, etc.) and numbers of jobs held over the previous five years as a measure. However, while reviewing the participants' open-text responses to a 2016 survey question asking them how their working conditions effected their lives we found that many of those who were employed on casual contracts did not view their work as insecure. In response to this the 2017 survey included a yes/no question asking the participants whether they had experienced job insecurity over the last five years and an open-text question asking them to comment on the impact of job insecurity on their lives. Notably, we found that, just as many of the participants working on casual-or fixed-term contracts did not experience their employment as insecure, many of the participants employed on permanent contracts reported experiencing job insecurity at the time at which they were surveyed. Considering these findings, we used the subjective measure of job insecurity that was included in the 2017 survey to identify the sub-sample that we could recruit from.

As part of our recruitment process we asked the existing Life Patterns participants whom we contacted to invite a significant other who they tried to spend time with in a given week to take part in the study. The aim of this was to gain an understanding not only of what our participants' day-to-day lives and schedules looked like but also of how they intersected with the lives and schedules of those around them. The 53 participants that took part in the study included 37 existing Life Patterns participants and 16 significant others, meaning that just under half of the participants recruited someone into the study. The significant others included 11 spouses or partners, three housemates, one workmate/friend and one sibling. Interestingly, although the participants were simply given the option to recruit anyone that they spent time with in an average week, none of them recruited an individual who they solely identified as a friend, and 14 of the 16 individuals who were recruited into the study lived with the person who recruited them.

While we were cognisant of some of the specific challenges associated with conducting research with individuals who are known to each other – for instance, the possibility that the pairs would be able to identify each other in publications

arising from the study – we also encountered a scenario that we had not anticipated. We found that by the time that we interviewed them two of the 16 individuals who were recruited into the study were experiencing interpersonal conflict
with the individual who had recruited them. As a result, at the beginning of two
interviews that were intended to focus on the work that was performed to ensure
that schedules could align, we found that the interviewees were actively avoiding the individual whom they had previously sought to spend time with. In each
instance, rather than avoiding questions about aligning schedules entirely we
instead probed sensitively in this area, and in so doing revealed a complex picture
of the role of work and time pressures in interpersonal conflicts. Ultimately, this
experience characterised much of what we found during conducting this study:
many of the challenges that we contended with in turn provided opportunities to
uncover complexities about young adults' lives that we may not otherwise have
accessed.

Reflection on the method

Now that we have established the design of the research, we turn to some of the
challenges that we encountered as well as some of the unexpected opportunities
that they afforded us. We begin by discussing some of the interpretive and practical challenges that were associated with our digital mode of data collection before
moving on to considering how this method was able to access data that could
speak to the complexities that characterise young lives.

While our use of an app for data elicitation provided several opportunities to
better understand the complexities that characterise young adults' lives, it also
presented challenges. There is a grammar of social media that, just as all data
is shaped by the social grammar of that form of communication, shapes what is
presented. For instance, we found that many of the photos that the participants
uploaded onto the app were of food, often with a stylised presentation, that they
were either preparing or about to consume. Food and meals were not mentioned
directly in the document given to the participants outlining the aspects of life
that they may like to post about (although they were implicit in activities such
as domestic labour and socialising). The ubiquity of food posts may highlight
the importance of food practices to conviviality and sociality (Neely, Walton and
Stephens, 2014). However, the images tended to be of food alone and appear
prompted by the popularity of the practice of sharing stylised images of food via
social media platforms (Holmberg, Chaplin, Hillman and Berg, 2016). While the
broad social implications of this practice have been addressed (Bouvier, 2018),
little research has considered its place within and utility for understanding individuals' everyday lives.

Much like the interpersonal conflict between some paired participants that had
arisen by the interview stage of the study, the volume of food-based images was
unexpected. However, we again sought to consider how it may be of relevance
to the aims of our study. While the aesthetics of the participants' images and the

specifics of the food that they photographed was not of great utility to the aims of our study – more likely evidence of a contemporary social media aesthetic than an emergent finding about sociality – we nevertheless found that the images that they provided allowed us to elicit insight into their lives. For instance, in many cases we were able to use these images to prompt discussion of whether they ate alone or with others, whether they took breaks from activities such as work to eat, whether they left their desk or workplace to eat and whether they cooked or found themselves too tired to do so, instead ordering take away (as we observed in many cases).

However, while this specific challenge offered unanticipated and ultimately productive insights, this was not the case for all the challenges that we encountered. For instance, at one stage during the study the servers at the Slack app's central headquarters went down for approximately a six-hour period. We were able to work around this issue by contacting our participants and asking them to record any posts that they planned to make elsewhere temporarily and upload them when Slack was online once again. However, while this work-around sought to minimise the impact of this unanticipated disruption on our study, it did not negate its effects. For instance, we found that the participants recorded few posts during this time, and that those which they did record and later upload were generally brief and did not include images. Ultimately, this disruption lay outside of our control and highlighted the largely unavoidable perils of relying on a third party for a technology that is necessary for a project like this.

We also found that our participants' strong degree of familiarity with mobile phone apps was both an opportunity and a challenge. As already mentioned, all the participants whom we contacted and asked to take part in the study owned a smartphone and were familiar with their use, including those who initially showed interest but ultimately elected not to take part. Hence, we did not need to ask participants to post to an alternative forum. However, while the participants' familiarity with smartphones meant that they were able to find and download the Slack app with relative ease, it also meant that many of them did not closely follow the instructions that we provided about the specific ways in which we were asking them to use the app, probably viewing them as unnecessary. Hence, we initially found that many of the participants did not post in the specific 'channel' (forum or online space within the app) that we requested them to, meaning that we had difficulty identifying where they were posting, and in some cases they were not able to view their posts. While these initial experiences necessitated asking the participants to post elsewhere, and in some cases involved phone conversations in which one of us directed them to the correct channel, we eventually found that our instructions were much more likely to be followed when they were included in a condensed form in an email or text rather than in the fact sheet that we had originally provided. This experience ultimately demonstrated to us some of the considerations that must be attended to while asking participants to interact with a familiar platform (mobile phone applications).

However, despite the practical challenges related to the specific method of data collection, this approach nevertheless afforded us substantial opportunities to better understand the complexities that characterise young adults' lives. As already mentioned, the existing modes of data collection within the Life Patterns study (interviews and surveys) generally produced data that provided a broad impression of the participants' lives. Detailed data does emerge from the regular in-depth interviews but has tended to be compartmentalised into different themes pursued in each round of interviewing. While we had previously asked questions of the 'tell me about an average day' type in the interviews, this did not mimic the real-time data about everyday experiences that we could elicit by having the participants regularly checking in and engaging with us via the app. This 'ethnographic' addition, particularly when used as a guide to in-depth interviews, affords comparatively greater insight into the intersections of experiences and demands on their time in an everyday context.

Turning to an example drawn from our data, we found that two participants – Lily and Daniel – each experienced job insecurity. They were each employed on short fixed-term contracts and dedicated a significant portion of their time to seeking future employment. They found themselves in similar situations and would be expected to provide similar responses to survey questions about employment, as well as to interview questions about their general experience of and plans for employment (as they each emphasised the need to continue to accumulate skills, experience and professional networks in their chosen industries). Yet, the data that were elicited via the app presented a contrasting impression of their experiences. Specifically, by gathering a sense of Lily and Daniel's schedules via their daily posts we found that while Lily's schedule was filled with networking events and voluntary work for organisations within her industry, as well as TED talks and books about motivation and self-improvement, Daniel's schedule was comparatively empty, with most of his hours outside work spent either with his housemates or alone pursuing leisure activities such as watching television.

Evidently, while Lily and Daniel's employment situations were similar, and they spoke about their situations and their plans in broadly comparable ways, their everyday experiences differed substantially. For instance, while they each emphasised the need to accumulate skills, experience and professional networks to position themselves for future employment, Lily did so via extensive participation in networking events, voluntary work and engagement with 'self-help' texts and resources outside of work, while Daniel did so by taking up professional development opportunities that were offered within his role at his workplace. Similarly, Lily and Daniel each emphasised the stressful nature of working on a fixed-term contract and reported that it impacted negatively upon their social lives. For Lily this was because a large portion of her time outside of work was dedicated to networking events and voluntary work within her industry, leaving limited time and energy for socialising. In contrast, while Daniel's schedule was comparatively empty, seemingly leaving sufficient time for socialising, due to the short-term nature of his employment and his uncertainty about finding further employment in the same geographical area, he felt that there was little point 'putting down roots' by joining local clubs or sports teams or making a concerted effort to socialise and form friendships at work.

Ultimately, while Lily and Daniel each experienced insecure work and expressed similar general sentiments about its impact on their lives as well as how it could be managed in their future planning, by engaging with their day-to-day experiences we were able to gain detailed insight into the specific ways in which it impacted upon their lives. Significantly, we found that lives that can look the same from a cross-sectional and even longitudinal perspective using discrete data points, or even using qualitative interview data, can look different as they unfold in real time in their ethnographic richness, even when accessed via an attenuate form of ethnographic data.

Integrating digital methods into longitudinal research

While the use of the app as a tool to collect data from our participants produced several fruitful insights in isolation – shedding light on the complexities of young lives in much the way that we have shown – it was also utilised for a second purpose. Specifically, after completing data collection via the app we used the participants' posts as an elicitation tool during an interview that took place in the weeks that followed. We used the posts as part of an ice-breaker activity at the beginning of the interviews, selecting three to four posts and either asking participants questions about them or asking them to elaborate upon them. These posts were generally selected because they presented some degree of ambiguity, or they touched upon an area of interest to the project such as the participant's experience of balancing work with other aspects of their life.

Discussion of the participants' posts generally provided a very successfully entry-point into the interview. We were able to discuss aspects of their everyday lives, as well as their plans and ambitions. For instance, some of them posted about a house they wanted to buy or a job that they were applying for, and familiarity of this type helped to build rapport. Additionally, the use of data from the app in an ice-breaker activity set the tone of the interviews. Beginning the interview by discussing specific experiences or anecdotes generally appeared to lead the participants to continue to provide a similar level of detail. This was also aided by the fact that they were aware that the interviewer already had a general understanding of their circumstances, as well as by reference back to posts from the app, which where relevant throughout the interviews. As a result, the interview data that we collected was based more on stories and discussions of specific experiences than it was on more general explanations. The example that follows provides a snapshot of how an interview conducted using the app data as an elicitation tool compares to an interview conducted with the same participant in a previous round. While the issue of quality or validity in qualitative interviewing has received a number of oft-cited treatments (Kvale, 2007; Flick, 2007; Seale, 2004) and is dependent on the epistemological and methodological underpinnings of the research in question (Roulston, 2010), recommendations have generally converged on the claim that rich, detailed and specific data offers a greater resource than generalised discussion, for instance, on justifications rather than explanations and experiences.

2008 interview with Laura

[After establishing that the participant lived in a residential college associated with her tertiary institution]

INTERVIEWER: Ok. Have you ever lived in Melbourne in a, in a shared accommodation or outside the residential house?

PARTICIPANT: Umm no I have only ever lived in this student village at Deakin.

INTERVIEWER: Oh.

PARTICIPANT: I have never lived anywhere else in Melbourne.

INTERVIEWER: And why is that? Why did you decide to live in the residential village?

PARTICIPANT: Umm well when I first got into my course at Deakin umm my sister already lived there so she could vouch for me that it was a good place to live. Umm and it is a very secure environment because there is a whole management team there who make sure everything is running smoothly and everyone is safe and comfortable umm in that living environment. Umm so I had that recommendation and once I got there I just really liked it and didn't want to leave so there I stayed.

2017 interview with Laura

INTERVIEWER: The way in which your hours are concentrated a bit later in the days – it seems to have moved your whole day up a bit.

PARTICIPANT: Moved forward, yeah.

INTERVIEWER: You also touched on the fact that it can be difficult to get together with friends who have a standard work week. Is there any other kind of impact on your life?

PARTICIPANT: Um, when I get home from work, I, yeah, it kind of changes a bit of my home routine, because you know, I'll wanna put on washing or, you know, kind of cook dinner at ten o'clock or whatever. And then I'll think, oh maybe I won't do that because I don't want to make too much noise in the house. Of . . . everyone else who doesn't do that. Um, but sometimes I think, 'No. I'm sorry guys. I've got to do it, I've got to do it tonight'. (laughs)

INTERVIEWER: I'm interested, because you work slightly different hours to the rest of the people in the house, do you think that that helps you to get some time when everyone's not sitting around, some time alone in the house?

PARTICIPANT: That's true. Yeah. That's a good point. Yeah, that's kind of my time to access, you know? The kitchen, the laundry.

In addition to illustrating the level of nuance that was reflected in the interviews when the data collected from the app was used as an elicitation tool, the example also hints at how the interviews and the app allowed us to capture data which would not only supplement but *compliment* and iteratively shape the more generalised data that was collected via the annual surveys. The digital mode of data collection that we developed did not simply sit alongside the existing longitudinal Life Patterns project. Rather, the findings from this study contributed to the iterative approach that has guided the design of the Life Patterns research program since its inception (for further discussion see Woodman and Tyler, 2007; Tyler, Cuervo and Wyn, 2011).

Conclusion

Over the course of this chapter we have discussed some of the challenges that were encountered while developing and operationalising a digital mode of data collection in the context of an existing longitudinal study. As this chapter was written after data collection was concluded, it may appear that the study was designed from the outset to produce data that could feed back into the wider Life Patterns research program. This was, however, not the case. The digital mode of data collection was initially intended solely as a means of gaining insight into the participants' day-to-day schedules and routines, essentially acting as a qualitative time-use diary. However, once we began the empirical portion of the study we quickly found that the data that we collected from the participants' posts had other utilities. In many cases they included substantial reflections on their lives, and contained a multimodality and degree of specificity and depth that was not present in the survey and interview data informing the wider study. Additionally, the use of posts taken from the app as an elicitation tool in the interviews was originally intended as a means of bridging between the two stages of data collection.

While it was intended that the ice-breaker activity that made use of the participants' posts would elicit detailed and specific data, it was not anticipated that this use of the data would set the tone of the interviews more generally. Needless to say, while we anticipated that the interviews that we conducted would contribute to the wider longitudinal project in the same way as those conducted in past rounds, we did not foresee the level of detail that they contained and were therefore pleasantly surprised by their eventual contribution to the wider study. Our experience ultimately evidences some of what stands to be gained by being flexible while collecting data with young adults and by allowing oneself to be guided by their participants, especially in research that seeks to capture a nuanced account of the complexities that characterise their lives.

Funding acknowledgements

The study discussed here, including the digital data collection, was supported by an Australian Research Council (ARC) DECRA fellowship for Dan Woodman – DE160100333. The broader Life Patterns study has been funded by several research grants from the ARC and other sources, most recently the ARC grant – DP160101611.

References

Abidin, C. (2017) '#familygoals: Family Influencers, Calibrated Amateurism, and Justifying Young Digital Labour', *Social Media + Society*, 3(2), 1–15.

Baruh, L. and Popescu, M. (2017) 'Big Data Analytics and the Limits of Privacy Self-Management', *New Media & Society*, 19(4), 579–596.

Bouvier, E. (2018) 'Breaking Bread Online: Social Media, Photography, and the Virtual Experience of Food', in N. Namaste and M. Nadales (eds.), *Who Decides? Competing Narratives in Constructing Tastes, Consumption and Choice* (Brill: Leiden), 157–172.

Boyd, D. (2008) 'Why Youth (Heart) Social Network Sites: The Role of Networked Publics in Teenaged Social Life', in D. Buckingham (ed.), *Youth, Identity, and Digital Media* (Cambridge, MA: MIT Press), 119–142.

Chesters, J., Smith, J., Cuervo, H., Laughland-Booy, J., Wyn, J., Skrbiš, Z. and Woodman, D. (2018) 'Young Adulthood in Uncertain Times: The Association Between Sense of Personal Control and Employment, Education, Personal Relationships and Health', *Journal of Sociology*, 55(2), 389–408. doi:10.1177/1440783318800767

Erickson, G.S. (2017) *New Methods of Market Research and Analysis* (Northampton, MA: Edward Elgar Publisher).

Flick, U. (2007) *Managing Quality in Qualitative Research* (London: Sage).

Gobo, G. and Marciniak, L. (2016) 'What Is Ethnography?', in D. Silverman (ed.), *Qualitative Research*, 4th ed. (London: Sage), 103–118.

Hart, M. (2017) 'Being Naked on the Internet: Young People's Selfies as Intimate Edgework', *Journal of Youth Studies*, 20(3), 301–315.

Hart, M. (2018) '#Topless Tuesdays and #Wet Wednesdays: Digitally-Mediated Neo-Tribalism and NSFW Selfies on Tumblr', in A. Hardy, A. Bennett and B. Robards (eds.), *Neo-Tribes: Consumption, Leisure and Tourism* (London: Palgrave Macmillan), 207–219.

Hobbs, M., Owen, S. and Gerber, L. (2017) 'Liquid Love? Dating Apps, Sex, Relationships and the Digital Transformation of Intimacy', *Journal of Sociology*, 53(2), 271–284.

Holmberg, C., Chaplin, J.E., Hillman, T. and Berg, C. (2016) 'Adolescents' Presentation of Food in Social Media: An Exploratory Study', *Appetite*, 99(1), 121–129.

Kaufmann, K. (2018) 'The Smartphone as a Snapshot of Its Use: Mobile Media Elicitation in Qualitative Interviews', *Mobile Media & Communication*, 6(2), 233–246.

Kvale, S. (2007) *Doing Interviews* (London: Sage).

Lasén, A. (2015) 'Rhythms and Flow: Timing and Spacing the Digitally Mediated Everyday', in J. Wyn and H. Cahill (eds.), *Handbook of Children and Youth Studies* (Singapore: Springer), 749–760.

Madison, S. (2011) *Critical Ethnography: Method, Ethics and Performance* (Thousand Oaks, CA: Sage).

Neely, E., Walton, M. and Stephens, C. (2014) 'Young People's Food Practices and Social Relationships: A Thematic Synthesis', *Appetite*, 82(1), 50–60.

Neves, B.B., Franz, R.L., Munteanu, C. and Baecker, R. (2017) 'Adoption and Feasibility of a Communication App to Enhance Social Connectedness Amongst Frail Institutionalized Oldest Old: An Embedded Case Study', *Information, Communication & Society*, 21(11), 1681–1699. doi:10.1080/1369118X.2017.1348534

Pink, S., Horst, H., Postill, J., Hjorth, L., Lewis, T. and Tacchi, J. (2015) *Digital Ethnography: Principles and Practice* (London: Sage).

Robards, B. and Lincoln, S. (2017) 'Uncovering Longitudinal Life Narratives: Scrolling Back on Facebook', *Qualitative Research*, 17(6), 715–730.

Roulston, K. (2010) 'Considering Quality in Qualitative Interviewing', *Qualitative Research*, 10(2), 199–228.

Seale, C. (2004) 'Quality in Qualitative Research', in C. Seale, G. Gobo, J.F. Gubrium and D. Silverman (eds.), *Qualitative Research Practice* (London: Sage), 407–419.

Thomas, G.M. and Lupton, D. (2016) 'Threats and Thrills: Pregnancy Apps, Risk and Consumption', *Health, Risk & Society*, 17(7–8), 495–509.

Tyler, D., Cuervo, H. and Wyn, J. (2011) 'Researching Youth Transitions', in S. Beadle, R. Holdsworth and J. Wyn (eds.), *For We Are Young . . . Young People in a Time of Uncertainty* (Melbourne: Melbourne University Press), 88–104.

Woodman, D. and Tyler, D. (2007) 'Participatory Approaches to Longitudinal Research With Young People', Youth Studies Australia, 26(2), 20–26.

Chapter 7

Revealing intimacy through digital media

Young people, digital culture and new research perspectives

Cosimo Marco Scarcelli and Arianna Mainardi

Introduction

The internet represents an important part of teens' everyday life (Boyd, 2014; Livingstone et al., 2011), and the mediatisation of life affects social relations (Couldry and Hepp, 2013), intimate life and sexuality (Döring, 2009; Mowlabocus, 2010). The amount of research being conducted on intimacy and digital media has increased in recent years but has maintained a focus on effects, presented as polarised between positive and (overwhelmingly) negative aspects (Döring, 2009; Chronaki, 2014). Sexual culture and its connection with media and technology is treated as problematic (Livingstone and Bober, 2005), and the discourses are full of moral panic (Buckingham and Jensen, 2012). Because of both cultural taboos and ethical and methodological difficulties, young people's engagements with intimate issues remains a relatively unexplored area. Young people's experiences in relation to intimacy are frequently 'sensationalized, silenced, caricatured, pathologized and routinely undermined' (Renold, Ringrose and Egan, 2015, p. 1).

In our opinion, to conduct fruitful research into intimacy, young people and digital media, it is necessary to take three initial steps: abandon a deterministic approach to technology, to youth and to sexuality in order to wear a more complex lens that is better able to read the society; consider young people that use media as active users; move beyond the reductive question of whether sex in media is 'good' or 'bad', avoiding a deterministic approach and focusing instead on media practices that are shaped by a drive to make sense of media cultures (Couldry, 2004, 2012) and sexual culture (Attwood and Smith, 2014).

We regard intimacy as a relational concept that can be redefined in research practice, and seek to problematise what it means to share intimacy during research. In this chapter, we want to translate the approach that we have explained into instruments which can be used to work on intimacy, young people and digital media in a more reflexive way, a way that places the participants themselves at the centre of research and recognises their agency in a society where mediatisation and media culture cannot be ignored.

In pursuit of this aim, we have isolated two principal topics that we consider to be paramount in the field: the online-offline continuum and the issue of agency;

and the question of who decides to participate in our research. This chapter grew out of considerations that arose from our first research projects (our PhD theses) in the field of young people, digital media and intimacy (Mainardi worked on girls' everyday use of digital media and Scarcelli worked on teens, intimacy and digital media.)

Online + offline = experience

The relationship between online and offline has long been seen as dichotomous. The literature around the argument treats online and offline as opposed concepts that divide experience, on the one hand the concept of the authentic life (offline) and, on the other hand, the production of a second, online self (Keen, 2007; Lanier, 2010; Turkle, 1995, 2011). In the earliest studies of the digital realm (Heim, 1993; Thu Nguyen and Alexander, 1996), virtual space was conceived of as an improvement on real space. These scholars described online spaces as without materiality and disembodied, where there is a hyper-realisation of reality (Doel and Clarke, 1999), a zone rich in freedom and isolated from external reality, where it is possible to suspend the physical self. Other authors described the virtual world as a fake, a bad copy of reality (McLaughlin, Osborne and Smith, 1995). In other words, the group of scholars that Bingham, Valentine and Holloway (1999) defined as debunkers, regarded offline and online as separated and different worlds. Following this analysis, many of the works in the first period of study of the internet and its effect on identity focused on identity multitasking, gender-swapping or virtual beautification – topics connected to the idea that there was an equation between body and identity that the internet was able to deconstruct.

Thanks to the arrival of the social web and of the new analysis concerning digital culture and digital media (see, for example, Bakardjeva, 2005; Baym, 2000; Jenkins, 2006), the attitude that separated body and digital media has been invalidated. These new approaches demonstrate that what in the past has been defined as 'virtual' life, decontextualised and disembodied, presents different characteristics. The use of the resources that the internet provides creates spaces for expression of the self and provides the users with instruments that enable them to give sense to everyday life and to the forms of social action. Physical and digital spaces, body and representation, intertwine in a continuum that goes beyond the dualism of real/virtual or online/offline (van Doorn, 2011).

What we explain here also concerns intimacy, gender and sexuality. The internet, even if it does not permit a physical copresence, transmits information, drives, affects, desires, ideas and definitions that can be used in physical and discursive practices. Physical and digital spaces are part of a continuum (Boyd, 2007; Livingstone and Helsper, 2010) in which the distinction between real and virtual, online and offline loses its rigid meaning. Users pass easily between one dimension and the other, mixing different forms of communication, both mediated and face to face (Orgad, 2007; Slater, 2002). This framework implicates three main thematic considerations:

1   Online interactions, especially for the 'always on' generation are co-implicated in a unique horizon of meaning, a unitary experience in which online is an essential part of offline
2   Online spaces are bounded by offline norms connected to gender, age, social capital, etc.
3   Online spaces have their own rules and peculiarities and there exist ideas on behavioural normality and what may or may not be done in online spaces

Dealing with the online-offline continuum

In order to avoid counterpoising online and offline (Leander and McKim, 2003) when we study intimacy and digital media, and translating this approach into research practices, we must not dissolve the bond between online and offline, and so we must employ methods that can move easily between these spaces without constructing artificial boundaries. This means articulating the continuum between online and offline in everyday life and recognising the complexity of intimacy and its variations inside and outside of digital platforms. In this sense, we need to construct a new research path composed of two mainstays: the linguistic deconstruction of borders and the use of social media as narrative supports.

We must avoid perpetuating the idea that there is a rigid partition between online and offline and instead favour a more dynamic approach that is able to look at experience while still recognising specific online characteristics. A linguistic deconstruction of borders consists in the interviewer's dialectic ability to discursively reconnect online and offline experiences. Online and offline may be useful terms for specifying where, for example, an actor performs her\his identity in a specific moment, but they must not become a border that describes those experiences as groups of separated entities. For this reason, it is important to redefine the expressions that the interviewer uses during the interviews, avoiding the use of words connected to online and offline when it is not necessary: why create a barrier when it is important to leave the interviewee free to move between her\his experiences? This is particularly true when we are working on intimacy: when the disclosure process both in digital spaces and in discourse is not so direct, there is a trust path between the parties that can only be slowly constructed.

Digital media as narrative supports

The second mainstay of our research path is represented by the use of digital media as a 'narrative support'. In order to move fluidly between online and offline during the interviews we decided to bring the digital into the narration (the interviews). The starting point is that digital and mobile media become meaningful when they contain traces of intimate moments in young peoples' lives. Youths regard their smartphones as the keepers of their emotions, contained within intimate photos, messages and videos. In everyday life we can commonly 'see' the seams between online and offline when someone shows another something on her\his smartphone to support her\his narration. So why not encourage them to use these supports when they relate their experience to the interviewer?

In qualitative research on youth and digital media, combining traditional methods with characteristics of digital media, using pages and profiles for analysis, or as prompts for interviews and focus groups, is not a new technique. Robards and Lincoln (2017) introduced a novel approach with their 'scroll back method' that focused on Facebook and consisted of a call to 'attend more closely to the temporal dimensions of sustained use, uncovering the archival nature of these Timelines, and investigating changes in disclosure practices over time' (pg. 6). But the use of digital media as a 'narrative support' adds something different and original because it does not originate with the researcher, but with interviewees who autonomously decide to make use of it; we do not ask interviewees to show us content on their smartphones\tablets\laptops because we are conscious that these digital media could represent very intimate objects for these young people.

The first step to using digital media as a 'narrative support' in interviews with young people is the preparation of the setting, which can break down some of the normative (if unarticulated) barriers surrounding the idea that (according to many adults) social media are connected to 'not serious' activities (social networks, videogames, and so on). An interview is frequently perceived by the interviewees as a serious activity where, consequently, smartphones and other digital technology are banned. Before starting the interview, we usually explain to the interviewees that they are free to use their smartphone during the interview. Smartphones could be used to better explain something they are telling us about, or if they prefer, to show us examples – through the phone – of photos, videos, internet links, etc., that might help to demonstrate what they are talking about. This simple step permits us to move towards the possibility of using these media as a 'narrative support' and lets the interviewee understand that we regard digital media as a part of their culture.

Some interviewees felt comfortable showing us photos and videos to support their narration and asked us, 'can I show you', revealing, with this phrase, a certain reserve about using the smartphone (or other portable technology) during the interview. For example, during a study on young people and sexting, one interviewee, speaking about the possession of pornographic material on his smartphone, decided to take out his phone and show the interviewer what he was talking about. In that moment the interviewee opened up a new intimate space between himself and the interviewer – a space where he is totally trusting his interlocutor and feels that he is not being judged by the interviewer. It was a cathartic moment where we felt the interviewer had been completely put into play for the entire interview and had to move carefully. The smartphone is considered as an intimate space by young people (Vincent and Fortunati, 2014), so sharing its contents with the interviewer was a sign of trust that the interviewer had to take into account. If the feeling of safety is breached an interview can fall apart, and to navigate this we decided to not be intrusive. For example, we never touch the smartphone to navigate the photo gallery or to see the video better, as this could constitute an invasion of personal space.

When we work on intimacy, we must feel ready to enter deeply into touch with interviewees, but some visual content might provoke a stronger reaction in the interviewer than a verbal description. When employing the use of digital media as narrative supports in the realm of intimacy, we therefore must be ready to be especially open to understanding interviewee motivation, rather than judging them, leaving our own preconceptions fully aside. This episode permitted us to enter into the interviewee's world, unpacking with him the meaning he gave to the video he shared with his friend and why it was funny to them. In other words, he permitted us to better understand what issues like pleasure, amusement and shame meant to him; it was a great chance for us to go in depth into the creation of meaning, peer culture and media culture related to those practices.

In general, as Robards and Lincoln (2017) described when speaking about the 'scrolling back method', permitting the interviewees to use digital media as a 'narrative support' means working together with the participants to make sense of everyday digital performance (Robards and Lincoln speak of a 'digital trace'). It opens new spaces for the negotiation of our comprehension of young people's meaning in relation to intimacy and its expression. This was also the case in our previous research on young people and digital intimacy (Scarcelli, 2015a, 2015b): speaking about gender roles and self-presentation, a large proportion of the interviewees stated that lots of girls on Facebook showed their bodies naked or semi-naked. The use of a laptop as a narrative support permitted us to understand what the teens meant when they said naked (referring frequently to girls who were wearing bikinis, for example) and that when they spoke about a great number of girls who showed their nudity online they were all referring to the same two or three profiles and that in reality they were reproducing the discourse of adults on the risks of the internet, with particular relation to sexual predators and a strong persistency of the double standard.

Digital media as 'narrative support' permits an analysis that allows both the interviewer and the interviewee to understand intimacy and identity as processes and to look closely at the shaping of intimacy and identity performances. In other words, digital technology as 'narrative support' is another form of disclosure by the research participants that, when speaking about intimacy, creates intimacy with the researcher, giving them access to their own intimacy and maintaining control of the situation by deciding how to expose that intimacy and where to avoid the researcher's gaze. An example of this last case was a young girl, who during an interview about the representation of the body in the social media, when scrolling through her smartphone's photo album, said to the interviewer: 'no, this photo is not for you [laugh], I can explain to you what it is, but I cannot show it to you . . . it shows too much [laugh]'. She was defining her intimacy during the interview, explaining that she was disclosing with the interviewer but that there were some barriers that she preferred to maintain.

Using digital media as 'narrative support' could also put the researcher in a challenging situation because this method could catapult the interviewer into the intimate life of the interviewee. This means, as we have stated, that we have to be prepared to deal with the different content that the interviewees might show us, concentrating more on the construction of meaning and appropriation practices that the interviewee could help us to understand, than on the content that he\ she is showing to us. In other words, this kind of method could help us to better illuminate the process of attribution of meaning and so become a support for the researcher's comprehension rather than a 'crowbar' to gain access to the interviewee's intimacy. Because it is a method that focuses on the construction and co-analysis of the interviewees' paths of meaning, we decided never to report a description of the content that the interviewees showed us during our research in our papers/reports in order to protect the interviewees' intimacy and respect the personal spaces that they kindly opened up to us. In our opinion, when we are working with intimacy (especially that of young people) we must enter gently into the personal spaces that they permit us to enter and leave them just as gently.

Young people, agency and online research

The idea of using agency as a lens for observation is increasingly employed to reflect upon the condition of youth in contemporary society. It is adopted by researchers from different theoretical positions and therefore produces different and complex interpretations (Coffey and Farrugia, 2014). Some authors have focused on the lack of studies that recognise young people as active actors and citizens in our society (Buckingham, 2008), while some others have highlighted the risks in overemphasising the choices available to young people without taking into account the structural conditions that shape their agentic chances (e.g., Gill, 2007; Harris and Dobson, 2015). Discussing digital culture, a current strand of research has explored new challenges and opportunities opened up by the use of digital media amongst young people – where participatory culture and the increasing diffusion of mobile technologies are seen as new tools to showcase young people's voices and bring their subjectivities into public spaces. Against this background, other scholars have discussed how important it is to consider the structural constraints that challenge young people's agency, even in the online world – avoiding the risk of considering the internet as a space free from power relations (De Ridder, 2017; Mainardi, 2018). If the issue of agency is a vexed question in research with young people (Heath, Brooks, Cleaver and Ireland, 2009), new challenges appear in digital media research in relation to intimacy: how do youth actively negotiate what is public and what is private online in order to build their subjectivities? What is the relationship between researcher and subjects in digital research?

Public, private and privacy

To answer this first question, as researchers we think we should begin by considering that, despite having a large 'public' component, social media are an important space of expression and autonomy for many of the young who actively use with online resources to create intimate spaces in which to develop their gender identities and sexual relationships (De Ridder, 2017). The first step of any research that aims to respect the agency of young people must take into account the nuanced notion of 'public' in the realm of social networks. Indeed, the youths we have encountered consciously produce a personal and situated understanding of what is private and what is public on social networking sites, recognising, for instance, that once online they have to manage and address different and diverse audiences (Boyd, 2010). The implication for research is that it must be flexible and open to reflexivity, a clear indication that methods must be developed to create a research path which can satisfy youths' need for disclosure, while remembering that the key to comprehension is in the hands of those same young people.

Indeed, once online, young people develop different strategies in order to control their online relational and intimate spaces. We should consider that the new regime of visibility, fostered by the everyday use of social media, makes the boundaries between public and private more porous, so the issue of privacy becomes more relevant, for both interviewer and interviewee. We consider the issue of privacy online to be strictly linked to the capacity of the subject control his/her own data and so consider it to be a fundamental brick in the wall of youth intimacy. As shown in the research we conducted (Mainardi, 2018; Scarcelli, 2015a), youth awareness of the management of privacy settings should not to be taken for granted. Indeed, it was common for the young people interviewed to not always be able to define the privacy standards proposed by the SNS, but they were decidedly aware of the content they wanted to share compared to the audience they wanted to reach – friends or adults. In fact, not infrequently elaborate social stenographic techniques (Boyd and Marwick, 2011) were put in place to 'protect' their posts from the gaze of adults and to build freer spaces of intimacy with their female friends for the discussion of issues considered intimate, such as sexual and gender experimentation.

During the research, a female interviewee agreed to meet us for a second interview. The case involved a girl aged 16 and female researcher. The second encounter was organised through Facebook Messenger; indeed during the first interview the girl actively added our contact to her Facebook account via her smartphone. The second meeting gave us a chance to discuss in depth a selfie that the girl had decided not to share on her Facebook account because she considered it too intimate in the way it showed part of her body. Enthusiastically, she offered to meet us again: 'Yes, I would love to (meet for another interview). I didn't get bored, on the contrary, I talked about myself like I don't talk often'. We discussed how and when to meet via the Facebook chat platform. The second discussion allowed us to interrogate the possibilities and constraints of gendered representation on Facebook, and how what is considered intimate or public online is strictly related to the regime of visibility that affects different subjects differently. This example helped us to understand that the researcher risks not considering the profound diversity of discursive and social practices in which youth are immersed when online (see Boyd (2010), for instance, with regard to gender and age). And moreover it showed us that intimacy is redefined in research practices which produce forms of complicity when the research relationship (online and offline) is based on the girl's/interviewee's needs and decisions.

Therefore, 'public' content (what a researcher can see online) does not necessarily have a unique meaning which anyone can access, and whether or not content is accessible to the researcher, it has to be inserted into a complex web of relational practices that we must listen to and respect – combining interviews and digital platforms to achieve the goal of building a research path based on listening. This is the true indication of method because it makes us aware that not only should we ask subjects for their own narratives (as in the case with the interview detailed here) but that in order to achieve this goal we have to expand our own research toolbox into the online realm. Indeed, in the next section we discuss how digital media can be a good ally in a research practice that aims to respect young peoples' voices by exploring the potential of SNS to give youth a more active role in the research relationship.

The relationship between researcher and subjects in digital research

When considering new challenges posed by digital and online data, we claim, researchers need to redefine the research relationship itself, beginning by recognising young people as a constitutive part of the process of knowledge production on the topics of research in an online setting – the research process developed online should be understood as a relationship and not as an opportunity to collect data. In our experience we were also confronted with the choice of using of social networks as devices within the research relationship. At the end of each interview we therefore asked the interviewees if we could send them a 'friend request' on Facebook in order to stay in touch and possibly deepen our understanding of some topics that had emerged during our conversations. The moment of accepting friendship on Facebook is a crucial one because it represents the first step in entering the online world of the interviewee and is a true act of faith on their part.

Confronted with the decision of which kind of Facebook profile to use for the research – personal or ad hoc – we opted for creating a 'research profile' instead of using the personal profile of the researcher. This said, the researcher was clearly identifiable, their face was shown in the profile picture and their age and a reference to the university for which the research was conducted were included on the page. In this way, young people were immediately informed of the page's 'professional' character, and they consciously decided whether or not to allow us to enter as researchers into their online space. This is a crucial added value compared to interviews that do not lead to friendships on Facebook and therefore leave the researcher outside the shared online space. To be fair, this choice was also made in order to maintain boundaries between the intimate world of the researchers and that of the interviewees. Reflecting on this decision, two points come to mind. On the one hand, we believe it is right to put the interviewees in a position that clearly shows the presence of the researcher in their

Facebook audience, if they want to allow him/her to be part of their Facebook world. On the other hand, we think that it is necessary to further reflect on this matter. Some of the results from our research show that where mutual complicity is built – for instance when the researcher decided to share personal experiences and some part of his/her world beyond research during the interview, such as his/her experience with social media – there is a potential for greater collaboration in terms of knowledge sharing between researcher and subject, and this can be further explored in an online context.

As mentioned earlier, social media is a space of negotiation for young people, a fluid and dynamic space that responds to the needs of relationships and intimacy; results show that this is also true of the research relationships that occurs on social media. Indeed, in many cases the interviewees accepted the researcher's friendship request with enthusiasm 'Yes of course I'll add you here directly (via smartphone)', in some cases the request was not accepted, in other cases the friendship was removed a few months after the interview and some profiles were even closed during the research. In doing this, the young people were actively negotiating the space they wanted to share with the researcher. The research relationship that is built through social media can, therefore, have a more ephemeral component than meeting face to face, as well as empower young people to choose how far they wish to develop the research relationship.

The most relevant outcome we observed in our online interaction with the interviewees lay in the possibility of expanding the spatial and temporal dimension of the face-to-face interview. Indeed, in our experience, Facebook can, for instance, be a place to observe young people's activities, but it can also be a material digital space through which to nurture the research relationship, one which allows us to discuss research topics removed from the time and space dynamics of the interview – often determined by the researcher. Consequently, having a research profile on a social network – on Facebook for instance, as we did – could provide a new communication tool between interviewer and interviewee, one that goes beyond the interview.

Participants in the research were encouraged to take an active role and, through digital technologies, to produce and circulate their narratives. That methodological approach sought to leave room for the agency of the subjects in an online context. By using digital technologies, therefore, young people could gain power in the research process, thus challenging the roles embedded in the interview. For instance, through private chat, some young people actively contacted the researcher when they wanted more explanation about the research. During our research some youths even decided to use Facebook Messenger to send us articles related to the topics of research, to show us self-made content or to further discuss issues raised in the interview. On the one hand, this enriched our analysis with material shared directly by subjects who we are not usually able to reach through interview. On the other hand, it made us aware of the potential use of SNS in the research toolkit to give young people an instrument with which they can be more active in the research relationship.

To briefly sum up, by adopting a social network like Facebook in the research methodology, we give the interviewee the ability to manage the research relationship in terms that he/she can accept, reject or cancel at any point. Second, we open up spaces for interaction and sharing – e.g., when young people decide to share articles – that transcend the interview scenario (and that are jointly managed by the researcher and the interviewee). Finally, entering the online space becomes a crucial tool for creating a respectful and clear research relationship – not only to observe subjects but also to nourish the relationship within and beyond the interview, giving girls and boys the chance to pursue their own actions.

Conclusions

In this chapter we hope to have demonstrated the need to adopt a methodological approach that puts the subject at the centre of research, in order to listen to her/his voice and understand her/his specific cultural appropriation of digital media and the meaning she/he associates with intimacy in this context and in order to avoid the risk of neglecting young people's voices. We have also seen how online and offline spaces are not two opposite and detached elements but represent aspects of everyday life that are constantly intertwined in the life of young people as well as in the practice of research. Defining the continuum between online and offline living spaces, and not reproducing dichotomies, is clearly important for those who want to understand the life experiences of young people with respect to gender and sexuality in contemporary society. It is also a methodological indication which, as we have shown, translates into the possibility of using digital media not only as a new space for observing youth practices but also as a research tool.

Digital media provide narrative supports that integrate and enrich the moment of the interview. Social network resources – like Facebook Messenger – can be used to redefine the space and time constraints of the research relationship. What we have learned from our research is that both of these scenarios have been taken up by the youth themselves. We claim that beginning with a respectful and clear research relationship between researchers and subjects makes it possible to redefine research practices by reshaping the boundaries that we usually consider established: e.g., researcher/participant, online/offline – fostering a relationship in which both researchers and subjects build 'trust paths' to create comfort in sharing intimate digital narratives.

In so doing it is possible to gain access to the new spaces of intimacy opened up by the use of digital media and at the same time respecting young people's experiences and points of view. Furthermore, we can recognise digital media as resources in the research process, able to challenge the normative relation between the viewer (the researcher) and the observed (the subject involved), opening up new spaces for participant agency. Moreover, young people are often treated as if they lack knowledge and authority of their experiences and behaviour, especially regarding their sexuality (Chronaki, 2014) – recognising youth agency in digital research means bringing their competences and expertise to the fore as a meaningful element of the knowledge we build around digital society as a whole.

References

Attwood, F. and Smith, C. (2014) 'Porn Studies: An Introduction', *Porn Studies*, 1(1–2), 1–6.

Bakardjeva, M. (2005) *Internet Society* (London: Sage).

Baym, N. (2000) *Tune In, Log On: Soaps, Fandom, and Online Community* (Thousand Oaks: Sage).

Bingham, N., Valentine, G. and Holloway, S.L. (1999) 'Where Do You Want to Go Tomorrow? Connecting Children and the Internet', *Society and Space*, 17(6), 655–672.

Boyd, D. (2007) 'Why Youth (Heart) Social Network Sites: The Role of Networked Publics in Teenage Social Life', in D. Buckingham (ed.), *Youth, Identity and Digital Media* (Cambridge: MIT Press), 119–142.

Boyd, D. (2010) 'Privacy and Publicity in the Context of Big Data', *WWW. Raleigh, North Carolina*, April 29. Available at: www.danah.org/papers/talks/2010/WWW2010.html.

Boyd, D. (2014) *It's Complicated* (New Heaven: Yale University Press).

Boyd, D. and Marwick, A.E. (2011a) 'Social Stenography: Privacy in Networked Publics', *Paper Presented at International Communication Association, Boston, MA*. Available at: www.danah.org/papers/2011/Steganography-ICAVersion.pdf.

Buckingham, D. (2008) *Youth, Identity, and Digital Media* (Cambridge, MA: MIT Press).

Buckingham, D. and Jensen, H.S. (2012) 'Beyond "Media Panics"', *Journal of Children and Media*, 6(4), 413–429.

Chronaki, D. (2014) 'Young Adults' Stories With Sexual Conduct During Childhood and Teenage Life: An Alternative Approach to an Ever-Going Debate', *International Journal of Media & Cultural Politics*, 10, 101–107.

Coffey, J. and Farrugia, D. (2014) 'Unpacking the Black Box: The Problem of Agency in the Sociology of Youth', *Journal of Youth Studies*, 17(4), 461–474.

Couldry, N. (2004) 'Theorising Media as Practice', *Social Semiotics*, 14(2), 115–132.

Couldry, N. (2012) *Media, Society, World* (Cambridge: Polity Press).

Couldry, N. and Hepp, A. (2013) 'Conceptualizing Mediatization: Contexts, Traditions, Arguments', *Communication Theory*, 23(3), 191–202.

De Ridder, S. (2017) 'Social Media and Young People's Sexualities: Values, Norms, and Battlegrounds', *Social Media+ Society*, 3(4), 1–11.

Doel, M.A. and Clarke, D.B. (1999) 'Virtual Worlds. Simulation, Suppletion, S(ed)uction, and Simulacra', in M. Crang, P. Crang and J. May (eds.), *Virtual Geographies: Bodies, Space, and Relations* (London: Routledge), 261–283.

Döring, N.M. (2009) 'The Internet's Impact on Sexuality: A Critical Review of 15 Years of Research', *Computers in Human Behavior*, 25(5), 1089–1101.

Gill, R. (2007) 'Critical Respect: The Difficulties and Dilemmas of Agency and "Choice" for Feminism', *European Journal of Women's Studies*, 14(1), 69–80.

Harris, A. and Dobson, A.S. (2015) 'Theorizing Agency in Post-Girlpower Times', *Continuum: Journal of Media & Cultural Studies*, 29(2), 1–12.

Heath, S., Brooks, R., Cleaver, E. and Ireland, E. (2009) *Researching Young People's Lives* (London: Sage).

Heim, M. (1993) *The Metaphysics of Virtual Reality* (New Heaven: Oxford University Press).

Jenkins, H. (2006) *Convergence Culture* (New York: New York University Press).

Keen, A. (2007) *The Cult of the Amateur: How Blogs, MySpace, YouTube, and the Rest of Today's User-generated Media Are Destroying Our Economy, Our Culture, and Our Values* (New York: Doubleday).

Lanier, J. (2010) *You Are Not A Gadget: A Manifesto* (New York: Alfred A. Knopf).
Leander, K.M. and McKim, K.K. (2003) 'Tracing the Everyday "Sitings" of Adolescents on the Internet: A Strategic Adaptation of Ethnography Across Online and Offline Spaces', *Education, Communication & Information*, 3(2), 211–240.
Livingstone, S. and Bober, M. (2005) *UK Children Go Online: Final Report of Key Project Findings* (London: LSE).
Livingstone, S., Haddon, L., Görzig, A., et al. (2011) *EU Kids Online II: Final Report 2011* (London: LSE).
Livingstone, S. and Helsper, E. (2010) 'Balancing Opportunities and Risks in Teenagers' Use of the Internet: The Role of Online Skills and Internet Self-Efficacy', *New Media & Society*, 12(2), 309–329.
Mainardi, A. (2018) '"The Pictures I Really Dislike Are Those Where the Girls Are Naked!". Postfeminist Norms of Female Sexual Embodiment in Contemporary Italian Digital Culture', *Modern Italy*, 23(2), 187–200.
McLaughlin, M.L., Osborne, K.K. and Smith, C.B. (1995) 'Standards of Conduct on Usenet', in S.G. Jones (ed.), *CyberSociety: Computer-Mediated Communication and Community* (Thousand Oaks: Sage), 90–111.
Mowlabocus, S. (2010) 'Porn 2.0: Technology, Social Practice and the New Online Porn Industry', in F. Attwood (ed.), *Porn.com: Making Sense of Online Pornography* (New York: Peter Lang), 69–87.
Orgad, S. (2007) 'The Internet as a Moral Space: The Legacy of Roger Silverstone', *New Media & Society*, 9(1), 33–41.
Renold, E., Ringrose, J. and Egan, R.D. (eds.). (2015) *Children, Sexuality and Sexualization* (London: Palgrave Macmillan).
Robards, B. and Lincoln, S. (2017) 'Uncovering Longitudinal Life Narratives: Scrolling Back on Facebook', *Qualitative Research*, 17(6), 1–16.
Scarcelli, C.M. (2015a) '"It Is Disgusting, But . . .": Adolescent Girls' Relationship to Internet Pornography as Gender Performance', *Porn Studies*, 2(2–3), 237–249.
Scarcelli, C.M. (2015b) *Intimità Digitali* (Milano: FrancoAngeli).
Slater, D. (2002) 'Social Relationships and Identity Online and Offline', in L.A. Lievrouw and S. Livingstone (eds.), *Handbook of New Media: Social Shaping and Consequences of ICTs* (London: Sage), 533–546.
Thu Nguyen, D. and Alexander, J. (1996) 'The Coming of Cyberspace Time and the End of Polity', in B. Schields (ed.), *Cultures of the Internet* (London: Sage), 9–13.
Turkle, S. (1995) *Life On Screen: Identity in the Age of the Internet* (New York: Touchstone).
Turkle, S. (2011) *Alone Together* (New York: Basic Books).
van Doorn, N. (2011) 'Digital Spaces, Material Traces: How Matter Comes to Matter in Online Performances of Gender, Sexuality and Embodiment', *Media, Culture & Society*, 33(4), 531–547.
Vincent, J. and Fortunati, L. (2014) *The Emotional Identity of Mobile Media* (London: Routledge).

Theme III

Ethical dilemmas

Chapter 8

Researching young people's experiences

An African-centred perspective of consent and ethics

Loretta Anthony-Okeke

Introduction

The thrust of this chapter is to stimulate discussion and reflection on the potential of African-centred consent process in educational research, particularly for African researchers trained in Anglo-Western methodologies and researchers of young Africans. The goal of this chapter is not to discountenance or disparage commonly applied Anglo-Western ethical frameworks. Rather, it intends to provoke consideration, discussion and reflection on an alternative method of ethics in relation to seeking young African people's participation in research in a way that facilitates their development and empowerment to make informed decisions about research participation.

Young people's consent has been sought and used extensively for many years in educational research. In educational research and related fields of inquiry, the processes and procedures for seeking consent with children and young people has been a matter of concern. There are tensions between developing a sound knowledge base for practice that have implications for children and young people and the need to have a duty of care towards them (Alderson and Morrow, 2011; Bourke and Loveridge, 2014; Harcourt and Conroy, 2011; Morrow, 2008; Thomson, 2008). African-centred ethics emerges from an Afrocentric paradigm, Afrocentricity, which centres the African knowledge and value system about lived experience (Asante, 1988). Ethical review boards in Anglo-Western universities operate their own ethical guidelines, and these principles are determined by the historical and cultural norms guiding the societies within which these institutions are located. However, little thought is given to its suitability in navigating ethical issues and consent in researching experiences outside of this context. Asante (1987) finds that there are shortcomings to Western concepts and methods of truth and knowledge. He asserts that knowledge and ways of knowing cannot be separated from specific cultural experiences. Owusu-Ansah and Mji (2013) suggest there is need to 'enrich existing Western knowledge and methodologies' with African ways of knowing (2013, p. 1). African knowledge systems inform a worldview of relational realities and ways of knowing – the importance of individual and collective harmony to knowledge; the significance of peer-oriented and participatory learning for knowledge acquisition; a knowledge system that is based on oral traditions of lived experiences and activities mediated through cultural artefacts of indigenous ceremonies and rituals such as storytelling.

Researchers from former colonised societies, such as African communities, have highlighted the dilemmas in applying Western models of thought and methodologies to researching African experiences (Alkebulan, 2007; Asante, 2016; Mazama, 2003). Some have offered extensive criticism of dominant Euro-Western research and knowledge paradigms that privilege the researcher as producer of knowledge while erasing the voice of the 'other' (Chilisa and Koloi, 2007). Other scholars have contributed usefully to the discourse by proposing appropriate research practices informed and driven by an African-centred ethics framework for researching historically oppressed groups (Mkabela, 2005). This is particularly important for Anglo-Western educated researchers of African student experience. According to Chilisa (2009),

> Ethical frameworks from a Euro-Western perspective invariably centre on the relationship between the researcher and the researched . . . [and normalises] knowledge systems that affirm and privilege Euro-Western knowledge systems and deficit literature, theories and thinking about former colonised societies.
>
> (2009, pp. 422–423)

This issue is problematic for the following reasons:

* Definitions of competency and consent vary from one cultural context to another; there are invariably tensions in the application of ethical standards from one cultural context to another
* There is little understanding about the role of the individual in research in relational terms, i.e., to the communal/group/collective role of significant others (such as community, parents/carers, teachers, peers, etc.) in determining consent
* Conceptions of competency can inform ways in which conventional or unconventional principles of consent and ethics can be adopted to address ideas of communality and collectively inherent in diverse value systems
* Applying Euro-Western centric definitions and assessment of competence to post-colonial African cultural contexts affirms and privileges 'deficit literature, theories, and thinking about former colonised societies' (Chilisa, 2009, p. 423) and its members, be they at home or in diaspora
* Paradigmatic changes in research since the early 20th century neither reflect nor adequately address the need for promoting a cyclical and iterative process of collaboration and dialogic interaction between the researcher and the researched concerning issues of consent and ethics
* There is much difficulty in identifying historically and culturally relevant principles of decision-making in young people as they relate to establishing consent in research, and the processes and procedures for requesting young people's consent and respecting their refusal to participate in youth research

For any ethical framework to be effective, it must incorporate the cultural elements and nuances that influence the worldview of the researcher/researched in terms of how they *know* and *see* consent in the research process; which, I argue, merits further consideration beyond whether or not the consent is informed.

African knowledge and ways of knowing are inextricably linked to African history, cultural contexts and worldviews. Consequently, there is a need for a reimagining of current consent processes in educational research involving young people in order to address these issues. An African-centred ethics framework seeks to address these by recognising, centring and activating (1) an African-centred perspective of consent and rights; (2) young Africans' competence as research participants; (3) consent agreements as social practice rooted in African ways of knowing and values and (4) the African researcher's response to and responsibility in the consent process. The following questions thus become central: how can an African-centred framework be applied in navigating consent issues in researching the perspectives of young Africans in diaspora? Can Anglo-Western educated African scholars apply both African and Anglo-Western knowledge systems to researching young people from former British colonies?

These complexities (addressed in detail here) include resisting the need to apply the dominant Anglo-Western constructs of consent and ethics to methods of assessing young people's competence, particularly when these are not compatible with the researcher's agential role as transformative 'healer' (Chilisa, 2009); which as discussed in the following section, I understand to mean a role that involves a purposive intent to question/address ethical concerns through transformative praxis. They also involve negotiating a balance between the valued norms of the communities in which the researched are born and bred, and the ethical guidelines of the institution from where the research is carried out (Chilisa and Koloi, 2007). They require dealing with the recognition, acknowledgment and legitimisation of the young people's decision-making in issues of consenting to participate in the research. Integral to the consent process is grounding ethical principles in the researcher's historical and cultural perspective, even when this may seem at odds with normalised and marginalising hegemonies of scholarly endeavour (Chilisa, 2009).

Consequently, while some of the same considerations may apply irrespective of the who is conducting the research, Anglo-Western educated researchers, such as myself, researching with young Africans who themselves have Anglo-Western-based education, are addressing these concerns from a perspective grounded in both African and Anglo-Western knowledge systems. With that in mind, there is an even greater need for such researchers to avoid diluting that which grounds the validity and trustworthiness of research but to hold themselves to even higher ethical standards.

A note on the Afrocentric paradigm

The Afrocentric paradigm is a philosophical and theoretical worldview based on the subjective and agential role of Africans in deepening understandings of their lived experience. This worldview is derived from Afrocentricity (Asante, 1987,

1990, 2003), an African-centred (intellectual) perspective of reality and knowledge and value systems framework. Afrocentricity is grounded in African identity which surfaces, centres, locates and orients the African people (Mkabela, 2005, p. 179) in the research process.

Baugh and Guion (2006) noted that while the Afrocentric method is widely used in researching with African people, an African perspective is applicable to examining similar issues common to a broader range of indigenous or marginalised groups in a number of former colonised societies. According to Chilisa (2009), an Afrocentric methodology privileges African conceptions of reality and value systems in such a way that informs and views human existence in relation to others' existence. Afrocentricity as a system is based on ethical principles that are considered compatible with those principles underlying qualitative research in the field of social science (Chilisa, 2009):

- Researcher as transformative 'healer'
- Ethics grounded in deep respect for spirituality, religious beliefs and practices of others
- *Ubuntu* and the centrality of respect for self and 'other', agreement and consensus
- Ethics underscored by relational and dialogic interaction between researchers and the researched

The researcher as transformative healer

The view of the transformative role of the researcher in the research process implies that the researcher embarks on self-reflection and self-questioning well before embarking on a critical aspect of the researcher and researched relationship such as seeking consent. A transformative role can offer the researcher a period of reflection on and questioning of their ethical responsibility in transforming society. Such considerations lead the researcher to a place where they begin to interrogate:

- Power relations with regard to their positionality and how this might inform the researcher/researched relationship
- The researcher's approach to knowledge production and ownership
- The impact of deficit discourses and literature about former colonised and historically marginalised groups on the researched
- Ways postcolonial frameworks can be used to privilege knowledge and value systems of the researched

Ethics grounded in deep respect for spirituality, religious beliefs and practices of others

Ethical protocols built on a deep respect for the religious beliefs, spirituality and practices of participants in a research project that embraces their biographical information offer an enhanced research inquiry (Chilisa, 2009). The

Afrocentric approach to consent as the central act in ethics emphasises and fully expresses the duty of the researcher to the researched to carry out the consent process with the 'care, love for one another, empathy, and compassion' (2009, p. 421), while being grounded in and guided by an understanding of the essence of humanity as informed by the African value system. A communal and collective existence based on a connectedness that begins at birth and transcends death – between the physical and spiritual, the living and nonliving. A life in which everyone is commonly known in and communicated with on relational terms – such as *nne m* (my mother), *nna m* (my father), *nwanne* m (my brother/sister) in Igboland.[1] An understanding of sacred-ness and sacred spaces that can be closed or open depending on who wishes to access them and why. This understanding helps the researcher to begin to view their existence in relation to that of the researched, to empathise with the researched and privilege their experience and in so doing begin to view the researched as competent and capable of consenting to their involvement in research. Thus, dominant meanings of consent are disrupted, and deficit conceptions of requesting and respecting consent become decolonised.

Ubuntu and the centrality of self-determination, agreement and consensus

Ubuntu is a worldview of humanism originating from the Bantu people of Southern Africa. Louw (2006) describes it as an African value system that underscores the interconnectedness of the human and physical world, and the natural and the supernatural, and privileges 'the "I/we" relationship', thus informing the researcher/researched relationship. A relationship that expresses itself in the inextricable binding of one's humanity to another in a nonlinear, circular movement of knowledge allows the researcher to draw on personal history, cultural points of reference and experience. This in turn allows a researcher to ground ethics protocols, so as to promote transformation, development and self-determination in the participant and their community.

The Anglo-Western concept of consent emphasises the I/you individualistic perspective (Louw, 2006). This perspective is likely to reproduce rather than reduce the power imbalances that were a feature of much of the research during colonial times and promote what Shrag (2010) refers to as *ethical imperialism*. There is also a suggestion that in the *Ubuntu* context, ideas about collectivity might be better suited to ethical principles guiding research with individuals from indigenous communities (Morreira, 2012).

I argue that in addition, the *Ubuntu* value system can be used to locate the place from where the consent process, as a central act in ethics, is conducted. Such value system is particularly significant in terms of increasing students' participation in research and collaborative research between researchers in the Global South and the Global North (Chilisa and Koloi, 2007). In accepting the knowledge of the researched of issues of competence and consent, their drive for self-determination through participating in research about their lived experience is promoted.

Ethics underscored by dialogic interaction between researchers and the researched

Being an ethical researcher goes beyond merely acknowledging ethical principles and guidelines, submitting an ethics protocol and passing the ethical review board, and consigning a brief explanation of the consent process to a section of the research project. The I/you individualistic perspective of consent does not adequately address the question of positionality – of who is giving consent, what their consent entails and what the outcome of consent is (Nyamnjoh, 2006). Requesting and respecting the consent of the researched involves a concerted effort on the part of the researcher to initiate dialogue with the researched which addresses these concerns, not merely as a 'tick-box' aspect of the research process but throughout all stages of the research process, and arrives at a consensus in keeping with the I/we relationship. Thus, according to Chilisa (2009), ethical considerations include, on one hand 'consent agreements' (p. 421) invoking consensus, and on the other, 'circles of discussion' (p. 421) informed by the connectedness based on *Ubuntu* principles.

Both dimensions of consent must inform the researcher's decisions and actions in such a way that the individual in the research is privileged, the consent process becomes an important part of a complex research process, the historical and cultural perspective of the researched and the community they belong to is respected within the consent process, significant others in the researcher's life are included in the consent process and in the research, understandings about the interconnectedness of the physical and spiritual world are deepened and the researcher exercises their agency as transformative *healer* to promote the community harmony and balance of the researched. There is growing evidence that former colonised communities are increasingly seeking and engaging with ethical guidelines within their own communities that privilege the cultural perspective of its members. By drawing on cultural points of reference, they are increasingly able to interpret and apply broader ethical principles within their own unique contexts.

African-centred perspective on consent and rights

African-centred perspective of consent and rights is based on the Afrocentric epistemological and methodological foundations of thought and action about the centrality of African ways, interests, values and perspectives related to the consent process in research (Chawane, 2016). Afrocentricity is consistent with the African worldview and culture about consent and rights. Applied to ethical processes in educational research, it is a viewpoint that promotes relational and community-centred ways of seeking and obtaining consent. African-centred consent considers the consent giver as integral to the research process and seeks to engage them in the construct of building knowledge about what consent is, what they are giving consent to and what they are giving consent for. This experience of consent-seeking and -giving also brings to the fore the notion that the research participant – the consent giver – is also being positioned to give their accounts, and accounts on behalf of others, about a specific phenomenon. Consent thus involves the understanding that there can be multiple perspectives of consent. It then becomes the responsibility of the researcher to develop a framework for consent built on a deep respect for these multiple perspectives. One that recognises and acknowledges agreement and consensus as an integral aspect of the consent process. One that legitimises the notion that consent is not fixed or rigid but flexible and open-ended. One that underscores the importance of the consent process being applied as an iterative process of ongoing consultation and agreement with the consent giver about what they are agreeing to. One that goes back and forth to question dominant Anglo-Western discourse around consent practices for young people deemed competent and autonomous to give consent. One that approaches consent from a standpoint that is sensitive and responsive to the needs and interest of the consent giver and to the harmonious existence of the community to which they belong. What follows is an African-centred consent framework, which focuses on positioning the 'researched' as a competent consent giver.

Young people as competent consent givers

African-centred consent informs our construction of young people as active research participants and informs a new epistemological import of consent in researching young people. Applying Anglo-Western methods to assessing young African participants' competence to give informed consent is problematic. Decisions about competence in African-centred consent is taken collectively and on the basis of whether the young person is seen by the community as being capable of owning a description of only themselves, not in addition to others that they may be required to speak for. African ways of knowing about competency can require a reliance on spiritually centred notions of wisdom, which can determine whether consent to participate in the research process promotes collective survival of the community (Ngara, 2007). In African-centred consent-giving, there is no absolute knowledge of competency; the researcher, the researched and the community co-construct competency based on their own experiences and come to an agreement. The notion of young people's competency to consent to participate in research is both complex and infinite; therefore, consent is mediated by the consciousness of all about what competency represents, and this is integrated in the development of the consent interchange. Particularly for young people, this can entail affirmation of self and indigenous subjectivity in the consent process. Furthermore, including young people in dialogue about competency and engaging them in assessing their competency as research participants is a credible way of designing the consent process.

Consent agreements as social practice rooted in African ways of knowing values

Research participation is usually preceded by the individual's written consent. The process of obtaining written consent is a key principle of Western-oriented ethics. However, the African setting is one that is built on rich oral traditions where agreement and consensus is given and taken verbally on the basis of culture, history and ecology. For Anglo-Western-educated African researchers, research ethics require further thought and reflection. To be effective in upholding the principles of research ethics in their host institution and the community in which they are conducting the research, African-centred consent should not be seen as just about Africa or African culture. Rather, it proposes a firm commitment on the part of the researcher to legitimise the young people's knowledge systems about competence to participate in research, based on comprehension of informed consent, in a way that would be an appropriate complement to their specific settings. For the young Africans participating in the research, their perception of consent is informed and shaped by both their African and Anglo-Western worldviews. It is important to acknowledge that this context has the potential to enrich the consent process. In so doing, the young person is located as the key agent in the consent agreement whereby there is respect and mutual exchange of information between the consent giver and seeker (Mkabela, 2005). To this end, African-centred consent encourages a reconceptualisation of the researcher's immersion in the cultural and social practices of the young people as well as the design of a consent protocol using the artefacts and methods native to the young participants in the research. In the African context, a young person is a young person of every adult in the community. Consent-giving is therefore not the monopoly of the consent giver.

The African researcher's response to and responsibility in the consent process

Anglo-Western educated researchers from former British colonies can have 'postcolonial baggage' (Costandius, 2008) arising from years of immersion in an education system in which the language, worldviews and lifestyles of the coloniser are embraced and privileged. They can straddle both African and Anglo-Western worlds and affect the research process, particularly their perception and understanding of the consent process as it relates to ethical guidelines prescribed by their host institutions (Chilisa, 2012; Chilisa and Ntseane, 2010; Chilisa and Preece, 2005; Howe, 2008). For an African researcher within this context, navigating Anglo-Western academic spaces informed by and often reflecting colonial epistemologies can require a surfacing, questioning and eventual reimagining of those research practices, which marginalise critical inspection of 'common' interpretation and practice of consent. Why, for instance, are research methodologies in relation to ethics and consulting with the researched that are rooted in dominant Anglo-Western hegemonic practices articulated as universal for the former colonised? Why is research ethics problematised as a power struggle that the researcher engages in with the researched? The African researcher is invited to recognise and address the 'role of imperialism, colonisation and globalisation in the construction of knowledge' (Chilisa, 2012, p. 8). These concepts function in ways that allow the binary classification of ethical processes into the norm (Anglo-Western knowledge systems) and the 'Other' (African or Indigenous knowledge systems). Thus, central to any decisions the African researcher makes is consideration of whether within the consent process they are acting 'as knowledge imperialists and colonisers . . . under the guise of scholarship, and authority' (Chilisa, 2009, p. 417) in the African student experience.

African-centred consent process and researching young people's academic experiences in Nigeria and England – lessons from the field

Employing African-centred ethics is not simply a means to understand and render more efficient existing ethics status quo, rather, as I describe and discuss shortly, it is about the ethical decisions and actions informed by reflection on how best to transform or question or change it. Further reflection on an African-centred framework in practice, as a means of navigating some of the challenges with seeking young people's consent, can increase understanding about the dilemmas discussed in the previous sections, as will be demonstrated shortly.

In a study conducted with 18 young Nigerian students in Nigeria and England (17 to 18 years old), I proposed an exploration of international students' understandings and experiences of independent learning within a college setting through the medium of student vlogs (video blogging) and interviews. In seeking the consent of the young people to participate in the study, I developed a framework for consent grounded in the African-centred ethical framework in the context of ethical research with young people. The young people and members of the young people's community were given the opportunity to consent by being informed of the research and the consent process through formal and informal African-centred structures of oral explanations, agreement and consensus, dialogue and particularity. Central to this process was encasing consent in an Afrocentric framework that privileged a cyclical nature of the researcher/ researched relationship and identified the young people as unique agential individuals, while acknowledging the elevated levels of consent-seeking which underscore the collective dimension of consent as is obtained in their individual communities. This consent process also involved making sense of the ethical guidelines designed to suit my host institution's particular aims and goals and thinking more about how this might conflict or compliment my own aims and goals as researcher – such as being bound by the institution's prescribed deadlines for data collection, which I found failed to recognise that there are complex layers of consent-seeking and -giving that are required in the African context that may not be navigated within a given period.

Negotiating students' consent with a college form meeting planned by the researcher and the appointed gatekeepers, the form tutors, to introduce the researcher and the research project was itself an implication of power, but it could not be avoided. I would not have had access to the students otherwise. Phrasing introductions as 'I am a former teacher and head teacher and now studying a PhD in England', and 'I am here to get your permission to be involved in my research', reproduced alienating teacher-student relationships that students were already wary of, and there was the suggestion that there was already consensual agreement about attending form and participating. Therefore, in order for the process to be meaningful, the research processes thereafter had to maintain the uniqueness of the students' and my culture systems (Mkabela, 2005). Our cultural variation, and at the same time our cultural 'in-betweenness', preserves notions of self, but self as part of a community where even though speaking order was approached hierarchically, everyone participated and contributed equally to the consent process and mutually reached consensus. That the students were in a position to make the immediate decision not to participate in the research highlights that students' agency and the possibility for students to position themselves as agentic was only possible because of our mutual acceptance and reinforcement of the research participant's role in decision making.

Much reflection on the part of the African-centred researcher is important. Self-reflexivity in this instance was used to question the impact of researcher positioning on students' decisions to participate in the research project. While incorporating consensus building in the consent process, an important step was the recognition that the individuality and plurality of consent-seeking and -giving can coexist in the same time and space. Through agreement, myself, the students and their home and college communities constructed a shared meaning of consent in relation to the research project. Thus, the consent process first met the needs of the students before those of the researcher and their institution.

Given that the proposed research participants were sixth-form college students engaging in their own independent research as part of their study programme, discussion about the researcher's project led to the students' own understanding and interpretation of their own research and where consent might fit into a research project. The discussion was focused first on the various research projects the students were working on and what the researcher/researched role is in the research process. Together, we were then able to draw on the students' own experiences as researchers working with secondary data to find commonalities between our responsibilities as researchers. This process facilitated an emerging researcher/researched relationship built on mutual acknowledgement and respect for each other.

Another complexity that was potentially problematic in this study was the African concept of respect for elders. Calling your teachers or familiar adults by their first names in Nigerian culture is seen as a mark of disrespect. This perspective might be the result of entrenched codes of respect deeply rooted first in years of colonial rule that demanded obsequious respect from the colonised to the coloniser (the British) and later in power distances between younger people/subordinates and elders/superiors deeply rooted in traditional norms. However, in some colleges in England, students can address their tutors and familiar elders by their first names. In my study, the students in England felt conflicted about being on a first-name basis with me, and the students in Nigeria neither asked nor expected to call me by my first name. In the interest of openness, the students were informed that those in England did and that they could if they wanted to.

However, when invited they were insistent that they would not call me by my first name. An important aspect of the consent process, then, was establishing that they had the option to determine how they wished to address me. When there is no harm involved, young people should be able to exercise a degree of control in determining how they see themselves in their interaction with adults, and by extension, how they see themselves in the consent process.

Anglo-Western research ethics protocols emphasise competency and 'sufficient understanding' as requirements for assessing whether a 16-year-old can provide consent in their own right irrespective of a parent's wishes (Heath et al., 2007). In Nigeria, the laws set out that the age of consent is 18 years and that a young person between the ages of 12 and 18 is regarded as a child who can assent to participate in research studies but with the consent of a parent or legal guardian (NHREC, 2016). Nigerian students attending sixth-form college in Nigeria and England are likely to be enmeshed in wider welfare and support groups in which ethical issues go beyond parents; as such, consent issues are articulated in terms of community/collective consent. Adequate consultation with the students' parent, guardian, college administrators, college resident guardian, form tutor and personal tutor then becomes an important part of developing the research ethics protocol to ensure appropriate acknowledgement of the student's cultural context. However, I had to also consider whether one or all levels of consent was appropriate given the nature of my research. Therefore, I was careful that my background knowledge of the age of consent in both Nigeria and England contexts did not prejudice my assumptions about each student's unique cultural identity. Therefore, initial consultations with each student individually enabled me to establish whether or not individual or community/collective consent was appropriate.

Overall, the challenges of consent in my research process were navigated following a relational process and a cultural in-betweenness. In relational consent, consent was understood and enacted in relation to connections that I had with the students, the students had with their community and all that these relations entailed – namely, an acknowledgement of our shared memories, experiences, cultural and linguistic behavioural patterns (Ibrahim, 2008, p. 240) as Nigerian students in diaspora. Consent was thus premised on the belief that the students are individual yet connected in a set of relationships with everything and everyone around them.

In reflecting on my personal challenges as a researcher in this context, it was important that I see consent not as something that may be sought and given by an individual but in relational terms – shared by all who were part of the research. I did not perceive knowledge about consent as something owned by myself or as just interactions involving the students I was working with. I saw consent as a process that involved relational knowledge about what it means to produce knowledge, seek and give consent, and in which I expected to be held to account by all my relations in the research process.

Accountability in this process was on the basis of my belief that the consent process is not an isolated part of the research; the research for me was perceived in relational terms and in the belief that as researcher I am answerable to all the relatable parts. The values I held during the consent process involved including, listening to, paying attention to and facilitating space for the surfacing of knowledge systems of the students and their community about the consent process. In so doing, consent was mutually beneficial as the students were afforded ownership of the research process and the knowledge surfaced therein. Another aspect of accountability that was demonstrated in this process was that as researcher, I was committed to collaborating with the students on how best to seek consent for their part in the research. In this research project, my commitment generated a lot of suggestions in the form of questions from the students that ultimately reflected on other aspects of the research. Questions such as: 'why is my consent important?'; 'will I own the narrative?'; 'will the vlogs portray me accurately?'; 'how will the research portray me?'; 'will the vlogs capture my experiences in a way that is true to my reality?'; 'will others see me as I see myself?'.

Consent centred on recognition and respect for the young person, requires engaging with unconventional models of consent-seeking. It requires new modes of the researcher/researched relationship which seek to address the imbalance of dominant ethical frameworks that ignore knowledge and value systems of the researched while privileging the privileging deficit ways of knowing and seeing historically oppressed and marginalised groups of people. The Afrocentric framework for ethical research seeks to transform the researcher as a responsible *healer of self* – one who questions the role of the researcher and evaluates the researcher/researched relationship as a starting point for ethical considerations in any research process. The concept of African-centred ethics offers firm grounding of this relationship to facilitate an ethical consent process such that the researcher's reflexivity is heightened and an inextricable bond between the researcher and the researched is formed as part of the research journey.

An ethical framework from an African perspective centres on the recognition of the hierarchies of power between the researcher and the research participant(s). It questions and addresses normalised hierarchies of knowledge systems that accept and reinforce Anglo-Western ways of doing ethics. An African-centred ethical framework involves transformative thinking and action on the part of the researcher; starting with self, embarking first on a deep reflection on researcher/researched relationship in the ethics process and ultimately praxis that is informed by a desire to take individual-community-collective consent-giving and consent-taking decisions. While being an African-centred researcher may not always be straightforward, there is much exploration of the potential for conducting almost any research study with an African-centred purpose. Furthermore, researchers working with young people have an opportunity to reexamine the challenges of existing ethical practices and engage in rigorous debate and discourse about the relevance of a broader range of knowledge systems in fulfilling central ethical obligations in their research.

Note

1 The area made up of the ethnic group native to Southeastern and South Southern Nigeria.

References

Alderson, P. and Morrow, V. (2011) *The Ethics of Research With Children and Young People: A Practical Handbook* (London: Sage Publications).

Alkebulan, A.A. (2007) 'Defending the Paradigm', *Journal of Black Studies*, 37(3), 410–427.

Asante, M.K. (1987) *The Afrocentric Idea in Education* (Philadelphia: Temple University Press).

Asante, M.K. (1988) *Afrocentricity*, 2nd ed. (Trenton: Africa World Press).

Asante, M.K. (1990) *Kernet, Afrocentricity, and Knowledge* (Trenton: Africa World Press).

Asante, M.K. (2003) *Afrocentricity: A Theory of Social Change* (Chicago: African American Images).

Asante, M.K. (2016) 'Afrocentricity: Toward a Critical Bibliography of a Concept', in M.K. Asante and C. Ledbetter (eds.), *Contemporary Critical Thought in Africology and African Studies* (Lanham: Lexington Books), 31–61.

Baugh, E.J. and Guion, L. (2006) 'Using Culturally Sensitive Methodologies When Researching Diverse Cultures', *Journal of Multi-Disciplinary Evaluation*, 3(4), 1–12.

Bourke, R. and Loveridge, J. (2014) 'Exploring Informed Consent and Dissent Through Children's Participation in Educational Research', *International Journal of Research and Method in Education*, 37(2), 151–165.

Chawane, M. (2016) 'The Development of Afrocentricity: A Historical Survey', *Yesterday and Today*, 16, 78–99.

Chilisa, B. (2009) 'Indigenous African-Centred Ethics: Contesting and Complementing Dominant Model', in D. Mertens and P. Ginsburg (eds.), *The Handbook of Social Research Ethics* (Thousand Oak: Sage), 407–425.

Chilisa, B. (2012) *Indigenous Research Methodologies* (Thousand Oaks: Sage).

Chilisa, B. and Koloi, O. (2007) 'The Politics and Ethics of Collaborative Research', *Seminar Series on Responsible Conduct of Research, Office of Research and Development, University of Botswana, Gaborone*.

Chilisa, B. and Ntseane, G. (2010) 'Resisting Dominant Discourses: Implications of Indigenous, African Feminist Theory and Methods for Gender and Education Research', *Gender and Education*, 22(6), 617–632.

Chilisa, B. and Preece, J. (2005) *Research Methods for Adult Educators in Africa* (Cape Town: Pearson/UNESCO).

Costandius, E. (2008) 'The Role of Stereotyping in the Post-Colonial and Post-Apartheid Context of an Afrikaans University', *38th Annual SCUTREA Conference, 2–4 July, University of Edinburgh*.

Harcourt, D. and Conroy, H. (2011) 'Informed Consent', in D. Harcourt, B. Perry and T. Waller (eds.), *Researching Young Children's Perspectives: Case Studies of High Quality Research With Young Children* (Abingdon: Routledge), 38–51.

Heath, S., Charles, V., Crow, G. and Wiles, R. (2007) 'Informed Consent, Gatekeepers and Go-Betweens: Negotiating Consent in Child and Youth-Orientated Institutions', *British Educational Research Journal*, 33(3), 403–417.

Howe, S. (2008) 'Imperial and Colonial History', in *Making History: The Changing Face of the Historical Profession in Britain*. Available at: https://history.ac.uk/makinghistory/resources/articles/imperial_post_colonial_history.html (Accessed 15 June 2018).

Ibrahim, A. (2008) 'The New Flâneur: Subaltern Cultural Studies, African Youth in Canada and the Semiology of In-Betweenness', *Cultural Studies*, 22(2), 234–253.

Louw, D.J. (2006) 'The African Concept of Ubuntu', in D. Sullivan and L. Tifft (eds.), *Handbook of Restorative Justice: A Global Perspective* (New York: Routledge), 161–174.

Mazama, A. (2003) *The Afrocentric Paradigm* (New Jersey: Africa World Press).

Mkabela, Q. (2005) 'Using the Afrocentric Method in Researching Indigenous African Culture', *The Qualitative Report*, 10(1), 178–189.

Morreira, S. (2012) 'Anthropological Futures'? Thoughts on Social Research and the Ethics of Engagement', *Anthropology Southern Africa*, 35(3–4), 100–104.

Morrow, V. (2008) 'Ethical Dilemmas in Research with Children and Young People About Their Social Environments', *Children's Geographies*, 6(1), 49–61.

National Health Research Ethics Council. (2016) 'Policy Statement Regarding Enrolment of Children in Research in Nigeria', *PS2.1016*.

Ngara, C. (2007) 'African Ways of Knowing and Pedagogy Revisited', *Journal of Contemporary Issues in Education*, 2(2), 7–20.

Nyamnjoh, F.B. (2006) *Insiders and Outsiders: Citizenship and Xenophobia in Contemporary Southern Africa* (London: Zed Books).

Owusu-Ansah, F.E. and Mji, G. (2013) 'African Indigenous Knowledge and Research', *African Journal of Disability*, 2(1), 1–5.

Shrag, Z. (2010) *Ethical Imperialism: Institutional Review Boards and the Social Sciences, 1965–2009* (Baltimore: Johns Hopkins University Press).

Thomson, P. (2008) 'Children and Young People: Voices in Visual Research', in P. Thomson (ed.), *Doing Visual Research With Children and Young People* (Abingdon: Routledge), 1–19.

Chapter 9

Working with complexity

Between control and care in digital research ethics

Philippa Collin, Teresa Swist, Carmel Taddeo and Barbara Spears

Introduction

In 2019, it was revealed that Facebook had been recruiting people aged 13–35 to a 'paid social media research study' in which they download a 'Research App' (Constine, 2019). Under the terms of the app, users consent to the collection of smart phone data including all information and content within loaded apps, data about how others interact with users via these apps and even those that use encryption (Constine, 2019). While access to user data can usefully inform research agendas and enable better user experience, the collection and treatment of data across digital platforms and services such as social media, health apps and streaming services, raises a whole new set of questions about the ethical conduct of research in digital society and its governance. At the other extreme, researchers working with universities and public institutions are experiencing increasing regulation of the ethical conduct of research through ethics review boards, processes and protocols that present many challenges (viz, Fisher and Anushko, 2008; Guillemin, Gillam, Rosenthal and Bolitho, 2012; Hammersley, 2009; McAreavey and Muir, 2011; Pitt, 2014; Sikes and Piper, 2010). Navigating between the fundamentals of sound ethical principles and the increasingly risk-averse nature of university ethics boards – which position the social sciences as 'risk-producing endeavours' (Haggerty, 2004, p. 392) – is constraining contemporary scholarship and hindering its ability to progress knowledge. Nowhere is this more evident than in interdisciplinary, participatory, digital research involving young people.

Central to this discussion across Australian universities, is the notion of risk and how it is applied: risk *to* the participant, risk *for* the researcher and risk *avoidance by* the university/overseeing body. As such, university-led and industry-engaged research is often inhibited due to ethical concerns principally focused on issues of *controlling* the parameters of research risks. An ongoing set of challenges and tensions emerge for university-based researchers and ethics boards faced with having to predict and develop strategies for dealing with ethical concerns they may not yet know exist. Moreover, these concerns are often focused on issues of risk, harm, privacy and consent: whose definitions were established in a pre-digital era, and thus are ambiguous in current digital climates. We argue that central to these problems are ethics processes which require reframing for contemporary researchers, young people and their digitised social domains, particularly as intensifying university regulatory processes and protocols seemingly position risk management as the prime consideration for committees and boards charged with overseeing contemporary scholarly research – in contrast to the premises upon which the ethical principles originally arose: 'to assure that research involving human subjects would be carried out in an ethical manner' (Belmont Report, 1979, p. 2).

To explore these issues, we utilise the term 'digital research ethics' to define three key areas of focus. First, we understand the digital as a *sociomaterial context* that is constituted through associated mobile devices, software systems and sensors, linking cultural practices and flows, through local and global networks. This digitisation of sociality raises new challenges and opportunities for research, not only in terms of scope but also for methods and ethical considerations. Second, we refer to research that is being *conducted by universities*, and which is increasingly conducted *in partnership* with other organisations. These partners are increasingly from industry – compounding the challenges and tensions as industry operates in the shadow of 'Facebook-type scandals' and in relation to so-called 'industry standards' which are not responsible to university ethics boards. Third, the ethics of research itself is a focus of this chapter: specifically, the ways in which young people are constructed and formal guidelines are interpreted and managed by ethics boards. As such, this chapter explores the entanglement of research ethics, youth, and digital technologies in the Australian context. Specifically, we interrogate how coevolving digital, social and spatial intermediaries enable and constrain young people's participation in digital research. Instead, we argue for a conceptual framework that can help researchers work ethically *with* the ongoing and often unfolding complexities arising with young people in the digital society.

From subjects to participants to 'situatedness' in research ethics

Historically, research ethics frameworks and codes have been shaped by the need to protect people from exploitation and harm. Outlining the evolution of research ethics, Dhai (2014) describes how these codes were made in response to scandals and atrocities: for example, children subjected to vaccine experiments (Institutional Review Board), human research experimentation in WW2 (Nuremburg Code) and recognition that the safeguards in the Nuremburg Code were insufficient and not being observed (Helsinki Code). These codes have been fundamental to articulating principles *for* and *about* research, setting out standards for research conduct in order to meet certain ethical benchmarks. For instance, 'respect for persons', 'beneficence' and 'justice' constitute the three key principles of the Belmont Report (1979) and continue to form the basis of ethics guidelines in many countries. These principles also underpin initiatives to support researchers and administrators to consider and adapt ethical approaches to local contexts. For example, the UNICEF-sponsored project, Ethical Research Involving Children (ERIC), is a compendium of guidance and resources for 'researchers to engage with the complexity of ethical issues as encountered in their specific cultural, social, religious, political and economic contexts' (Graham, Powell, Taylor, Anderson and Fitzgerald, 2013, p. 3). Despite the importance of these codes historically for advancing research that places the rights and needs of participants at the centre of ethical considerations, we find their application via procedural ethics produces challenges for digital research with young people.

First, there have been significant advances in theory and policy to establish children and young people's rights and agency (the UN Convention on the Rights of the Child (1989); Save the Children Fund submission to the UN Summit on Social Development, (1995); Corsaro's *The Sociology of the Child* (1997); James and Prout's *Constructing and Reconstructing Childhood* (1997) and James, Jenks and Prout's *Theorizing Childhood* (1998). Against Victorian constructions of children as passive recipients of adult knowledges, children became recognised as agentic individuals with rights which adults need to uphold. Spears and Kofoed (2013) argue that these shifts also reflected the move away from research practices where something was *done* to children and young people (subjects) (Woodhead and Faulkner, 2000); to something that can be *conducted with* them (as informed consenting participants) (Alderson, 2000; Alderson and Morrow, 2004); and to contemporary practices which are *enabling* of young people *as knowledge brokers, co-constructors of knowledge* and undertaking research codesigned *by* them (Boyden and Ennew, 1997; Spears and Zeederberg, 2013). Simultaneously, an increasing recognition of the power of youth voice has emerged (Fielding, 2001; Hart, 1992; 2008). Yet, despite advances in the theorisation of young people as *social* actors, intersecting with and shaping their environment (Corsaro, 1997; James and Prout, 1997) and the broader notion of 'youth' as a relational category, there are insufficient theories and practical means by which to recognise the digital as a setting for the experience of youth. Young people (under the age of 18) have agency and operate within a social reality in which they do not separate online from offline (Spears and Kofoed, 2013). However, digital research with minors is routinely reviewed by ethics committees as though youth have none of this agency which has emerged over time. The control logics of ethics procedures reengage a deficit lens of youth which effectively infantilises young people, constraining their rights to participation.

Second, these codes often take an individualistic, or linear approach. For example, the Helsinki code (World Medical Association, 2013) established that the researcher's first concern must be the effects on the individual research subject. There is less clarity on what the group or collective risks or benefits might be – and how they should be weighed up in relation to one another in any given situation (see also, Alderson and Morrow, 2012, p. 29). As such risks and benefits are almost always conceptualised from the perspective of individual 'research subjects' – and planned and assessed on this basis. One of the effects of this for youth research is that young people – while diverse – are regularly grouped as 'vulnerable' or without the capacity to provide their own informed consent to participate in research.

Third, efforts have been made to standardise the purported best interest of the (individual) research subject, often from a medical model perspective. Yet, as Lahman, Geist, Rodriguez, Graglia and DeRoche (2011) highlight, this has rested on notions of minimalist 'do no harm' or 'procedural' ethics – in contrast to 'aspirational ethical codes'. While important, this focus on risk management can lead to linear, tick-box compliance rather than an openness to complexity – which is often uncertain. Consequently, in practice, ethics boards tend to concentrate narrowly on the protection of young people, emphasising normative definitions of privacy and consent and therefore imposing particular relationships between youth, digital technologies and research (Gubrium, Hill and Flicker, 2014). Such tendencies inadvertently disempower young people. Recognising this we argue that, while valuable, dominant frameworks (Belmont Protocol, Child Rights, Research Impact) are increasingly implemented in the context of 'top-down' processes underpinned by a risk management culture, whereby all possible risks must be identified and addressed before a project commences. This fundamentally limits the role research can play in surfacing and addressing the specificities and contextual nuance of research projects in the digital age – especially young peoples' views on data and its use. The effect is to prioritise the 'protection' of young people in research at the expense of their rights to 'provision' (of research and new knowledge that is pertinent to their lives) or 'participation' (in research that reflects their experiences and needs).

As such, we argue that the procedural form of ethics that dominates university research exercises a 'control logic'. Continuing in this vein can restrict how research is conducted and with whom – and importantly can compromise quality, relevance and benefits to young people. Just as code, algorithms, apps and platforms reflect the perspectives and biases of those who create them, so it is with research – which does not objectively narrate what is happening 'out there' but is also 'world-making' (Michael, 2012). When legacy frameworks are applied through risk management approaches, research produces data about 'known knowns': reflecting questions that we can already gauge about the relationship between digital technologies and the experience of youth. To generate *new knowledge* and new responses to the *new problems and opportunities* of digital society, we need a new ethics of care in research that can cope with complexity, allow risks and dilemmas in research to reveal themselves, and support scholars, young people and other research partners to negotiate and develop responses for dealing with new questions and challenges as they unfold.

Aligned with a feminist research ethics, some research and practice has developed critical standpoints and approaches to the ethics of research with children and young people (Alderson and Morrow, 2004, 2012; Gubrium et al., 2014). This work argues that there are no simple ethics rules or skills that can manage the ongoing, unfolding and increasingly complex set of relations that shape the experience of youth. Rather, the ethical conduct of youth research requires 'deliberation on values, exercise of judgement, and an appreciation of context' (te Riele and Brooks, 2012, p. 15). Reflecting a 'situated research ethics' (Simons and Usher, 2000), such an approach is less prescriptive about rights and foregrounds the relationality of participants. For example, how 'youth' is a concept that is defined and only makes sense in relation to 'adulthood' (Wyn and White, 1997). Situated ethics – grounded in a feminist ethics of care – emphasises the mediation of general ethical principles *in practice*, paying attention to how ethics is shaped by contextual factors (Ebrahim, 2010, p. 290). In research practice, this can be achieved by listening to children and young people and seeking different approaches for defining, creating and accessing knowledge (Preissle and Han, 2006, p. 516) – in an ongoing way throughout a project. A situated research ethics approach can, therefore, reveal advantages and limitations of observing rights in research. To begin with, rights are valuable in terms of embedding key aspects of children's rights to research participation in ethics committee reviews. For example, the Ethical Research Involving Children (Graham, Powell, Taylor, Anderson and Fitzgerald, 2013) report offers a

> broad framework and a tool for generating reflective dialogue, where the starting point is a deep respect for human dignity and a desire to advance the status of children in the way called for by the United Nations Convention on the Rights of the Child.
>
> (3)

However, in practice, regimes of protection still overshadow aspects of provision and participation. So how might more situated and reflexive approaches inform research ethics with young people in the digital age? To unpack some of these tensions and possibilities, in the following section we present a short case study of a participatory and industry-engaged multiyear study of the role of online campaigns for promoting the safety and wellbeing of young people.

Case study: Safe and Well Online

Safe and Well Online (SWO) was a five-year study of the role of online social campaigns for promoting the safety and wellbeing of young people aged 12–18. The project utilised a participatory design approach: collaborating with young people, sector and industry partners in the coresearch and design of four campaigns, delivered one per year. The original project proposed a randomised, longitudinal cohort study using pre- and post-surveys and in-depth interviews, and a novel form of passive online data collection to capture and match young people's real time engagement with the campaigns. Key stakeholders, including schools, sporting, youth groups and parent associations expressed interest in the study and considerable time and resources were invested in building relationships with these stakeholders. Despite extensive and thorough planning and consultation, the project met with a multitude of barriers associated with the many sites and levels of ethics approvals required – spanning three universities and three state education departments, along with the eventual consent required from schools, parents and students participating in the project. The challenges extended beyond the practicalities of conducting such research but rather were indicative of deeper fundamental differences in the way researchers and gatekeepers perceived ethical practices that would enable youth voice and participation. As discussed earlier, a 'situated research ethics' approach aims to identify complexities and possibilities for change, whereas a more traditional 'research subject logic' focuses on the individual. The following discussion highlights what happens when these logics conflict, and where new learnings can emerge in relation to four challenges: unknowability, organisational gatekeepers, ethical contradictions and legacy mindsets.

Unknowability

The required ethics approvals were granted by each of the higher education institutions involved in the SWO study. Given that schools were the primary avenue for recruitment, ethics approvals also were requested from Education Departments. As a national study, this required ethics applications to be submitted to all jurisdictions, each with (at the time) their own unique procedures, timelines and requirements. Although appreciating the importance of the study, concerns were raised by some industry gatekeepers and ethics committees. In particular, there were reservations about the tracking/mapping of young people's online behaviours and the protection of young people's privacy. There also were requests to review the social marketing campaigns young people would be exposed to. However, this was not possible, given the nature of participatory design, whereby the final product comes about through iterative design and feedback loops. This *unknown* provided further cause for concern for some, as approval was being sought to expose young people to a campaign that had not yet been developed. While this proved to be a significant issue for the project, unknowability is a feature of situated research ethics – requiring trust in the research process and being open to an iterative, ongoing dialogue and deliberation with participants as collaborators (rather than only subjects) over the course of the project.

Organisational gatekeepers

Due to restrictions placed by education departments, modifications to the methodology were required, from a randomised, longitudinal study to a cohort design. This resulted in challenges with recruitment and achieving required sample numbers for each of the four rounds of pre- and post-survey data collection. Conversations with key education department personnel and ethics committees subsequently were held to discuss the use of opt-out informed consent options to maximise recruitment possibilities in line with changes outlined in the National

Statement 2007. Unlike opt-in consent procedures, where informed consent is actively sought, informed consent and participation is assumed unless individuals actively communicate their desire to not be involved (opt out) (NHMRC, 2018). However, this consent option was not approved by the education departments, and subsequently, multiple recruitment strategies and contingency plans requiring opt-in informed consent were implemented. This included engaging industry accredited research panel providers, where informed parental consent and young people's assent were collected at the beginning of each round of data collection. In moving forward, it is vital to recognise the role of organisational gatekeepers as part of research situatedness. Challenging simplistic notions of research subjects and applying relationality by considering who we are in relation with – and bringing them into the deliberation process may help to address and work through issues arising with gatekeepers who are risk averse. While conflicts may also surface when enacting relationality, the learnings from this process can guide decisions more directly and also comprise a form of organisational learning for research partners and ethics boards.

Ethical contradictions

Respect for persons, beneficence and justice constitute the three key principles of the Belmont Report (1979) and continue to form the basis of ethical research. However, contradictions arise when considering youth and digital practices and traditional ethical principles. In keeping with the Belmont principles, the overarching aim of the SWO study was to positively impact young people's wellbeing. Processes were implemented to ensure informed consent and fair and just conduct, along with a commitment to duty of care through strategies such as the inclusion of information about help-seeking services. Respect for young people was demonstrated inherently through the study design: young people were invited to participate as co-designers and coinvestigators in the study. Despite these measures, the ethical restrictions which were imposed created contradictions. For example, while youth participation in codesign of the digital campaigns was endorsed, ethics boards were unwilling to sanction the study unless all campaigns were preapproved. This fundamental conflict highlighted the need to ethically de- and reconstruct interpretations of ethical principles when applied to research with young people and technology. Respect for youth, beneficence and justice in the digital space may mean something different when agency and rights are considered. If we continue to restrict youth involvement and impose limitations on the type of data and ways it can be collected in the online space, we may also be compromising the very principles we are trying to uphold, including the quality, rigour and accuracy of the research. When the restrictions imposed prevent respected researchers from conducting authentic studies applying evidence-informed online methodologies in naturalistic settings, then the essence of ethical conduct is compromised. Unlike individualised ethical approaches, ethical contradictions are part and parcel of research situatedness. Acknowledging these and taking steps to deliberate key issues is a movement towards responsiveness and change, away from a narrow approach to research subjects.

Legacy mindsets

If we are to capitalise on the potential of social marketing campaigns to deliver positive messaging that resonate with young people and maximise reach and impact, and if we are to avoid imposing adult notions about what might or might not be effective and relevant in supporting young people to stay safe and well online, then youth involvement as co-designers and coinvestigators is critical. There is an imperative, then, to challenge the risk-averse organisational mindsets that pervade many research settings and ethics departments. With the uptake of mobile and wearable technologies in particular, research with young people in online settings can move forward and remain relevant and innovative if we embrace opportunities to ethically challenge research boundaries, engage with participants in naturalistic settings which extend to the online space and utilise new developments and tools that enable organic and real time collection of data. Legacy mindsets which can stem from a protectionist, risk-averse mentality need to be challenged through research situatedness. While this is not always easy, it helps to foreground the limitations of a research subject approach – and the need for reflexivity and openness to change.

This case study and the tensions outlined sketch only a few of the challenges associated with youth digital research. We do not suggest that the fundamental principles of ethical research are irrelevant, on the contrary, they are still very pertinent to many research contexts. However, we caution that the answer is not 'to play it safe' and attempt to retrofit traditional notions of what constitutes ethical research practices into new research contexts and settings. Without young people more directly informing future directions for digital research ethics, we run the risk of developing and implementing research processes and delivering initiatives that are irrelevant to them and reflect adult biases. There is a need for more – not less – *deliberation* amongst all stakeholders to interrogate new and more efficient ways of conducting online research and to define and discuss the ethical parameters of digital research with minors, particularly for low-risk research studies. This is to enable research processes to more closely align with the behaviours and practices of young people today and to open up – rather than close down – research possibilities in digital society.

Surfacing a networked capability approach

In SWO, we needed a way to surface the digital as a space of interaction and negotiation between different actors – not as a specific research site that is carved off from 'everyday life'. Not positioning them as research subjects but rather recognising and working with the complexity and uncertainty of the *situatedness* of the research. For example, digital technologies are increasingly embedded in everyday life as 'networked publics' (Boyd, 2008), emerging from complex properties (persistence, searchability, replicability and scalability) and dynamics (invisible audiences, collapsed contexts and the blurring of public and private). The complexity inherent in these dynamics is becoming increasing evident as technologies continue to evolve and the dilemmas associated with ethics and digital research are raised, yet accompanying guidance for managing ethical dilemmas is still only emerging.

In retrospectively analysing the ethical issues that arose for this study, we have specifically considered three aspects – social, digital and spatial intermediaries – in attempting to test a new approach. In previous work we have developed a networked-capability approach (NCA) for working with the complexity of youth research in the digital age (Swist and Collin, 2017). A *networked capability approach* (NCA) foregrounds 'the interrelationship between platforms, people and places (digital, social and spatial intermediaries) that influence our freedom to achieve agency and wellbeing (functioning and capability)' (Swist and Collin, 2017, p. 678). Drawing upon media and development studies, the NCA brings together the notion of the 'networked self' (Papacharissi, 2010) and a capability approach (Sen, 2005), thus highlighting that the experience of youth cannot be neatly separated out from technologies in a world where the self and society are articulated across, and in relation to, the digital. We argue that the NCA helps to identify not only complexities in social phenomenon but also openings for change. First, it surfaces the complex relations of social, digital and spatial intermediaries that enable and constrain young people's wellbeing. Second, it proposes a processual approach to respond to tensions and problems that emerge as a result of the relations between these things. When applied to research with young people, the NCA foregrounds the following key aspects: the social power relations of *people* involved in the compliance and resistance of human research ethics, the digital production associated with platforms and data and the new tensions and possibilities arising from permeable *places* – across which interpersonal, commercial and industry relations emerge. These dynamics reveal how current conceptualisations and conventions in ethics are generating more – not fewer – challenges for research on vital questions affecting young people. Unlike current ethics frameworks which seek to make explicit and manage from the commencement of a project the dynamic relationships between people, places and things, the NCA emphasises processes for revealing and working with these tensions along the way.

Social intermediaries

Young people, schools, parents, researchers, sector and industry partners, and ethics committees were all entwined in power relations that enabled and constrained the project. These actors and the relationships between then can be understood as *social intermediaries* in a particular research context. Education departments, schools and parents had power over young people – to decide if the research would go ahead and who could participate. Digital agencies, community partners and scholars were aligned in efforts to create methods and data collection/use protocols that respected young people's agency and privacy. Young people were involved in the research team as collaborators to inform and guide the themes and development of campaigns and – consequently the type of digital platform they were delivered on (e.g., website or mobile app). Nevertheless, the primary concern for ethics boards was with the lack of definition of the campaign topics, delivery platforms and therefore digital data collection and use. Despite all efforts to demonstrate care and collaborate with diverse constituents in the project, ethics boards required researchers to provide a 'solution' to the data power relations before the project started. This procedural ethics – or control logic – is in contrast with a situated ethics to promote processes that ensure dialogue, discussion or even shared decision making with young people about ethical dilemmas.

From our experience of the SWO project, recognising social intermediaries in research can be a way to promote a more 'culturally responsive' approach (Lahman et al., 2011) to digital youth research. For example, supporting young people's engagement with ethics committees in the assessment of applications and throughout research projects can foster intergenerational learning and bring young people's perspectives and values to the debate. Halse and Honey (2005), for instance, call for the need to 'constitute ethics as an ongoing process of critical reflection, action, and accountability throughout the research rather than as an act of compliance and approval at the beginning of the research' (2158). Such receptivity and responsiveness to young people can help resist legacy mindsets and embrace unknowability throughout the course of a research project. To be more culturally responsive requires increased recognition of young people as social actors and enable their consent to participate in research (see Bessant, 2006; Skelton, 2008). This means reworking notions of participation of minors by working *with* them in ethics committees, as well as in defining research questions, approaches and intended benefits at the project level. Whether intentionally or inadvertently, the effect of excluding young people is to reassert power over young people limiting our understanding of what the costs and benefits of research look like from their perspectives. Instead, in a deliberative system they can be recognised as 'actors' in a more empowering sense – not only when adults choose when and how they participate (Nishiyama, 2017).

Digital intermediaries

The role of digital intermediaries was another significant issue of the SWO project – especially relating to privacy and consent around young people's data, though these concepts are not 'fixed'. Often ideas about young people's rights to autonomy, noninterference and privacy are seen as being in conflict with their needs for *protection*. This can lead to greater exclusion – and even potential exploitation or harm if, for example, the research is about whether a practice, service or product is doing good or causing harm.

For instance, in a study of children's data and privacy online, Livingstone, Stoilova and Nandagiri (2018) point to the *contextual* aspects of privacy – rather than a right or means for control. They also highlight the need to distinguish between interpersonal, commercial and institutional contexts. This is even more important in the context of expanding abilities of private enterprise and governments to access and utilise young people's digital data – often given in exchange in the process of utilising services. Further, in acknowledging the importance of situatedness and relationality in constructing relevant notions of privacy we therefore recommend a *digitally reflexive approach* exploring issues of privacy, consent and usage of data and platforms with young people and organisational gatekeepers throughout the course of a research project.

Insights from the SWO project raise specific questions about the way data is understood in research, particularly as we move towards increasing integration, connection and adoption of technologies such as artificial intelligence, machine learning and personalised AI, in our everyday lives. We therefore suggest a digitally reflexive approach may prompt researchers to attend more closely to their own reactions to a research dilemma 'and adapt in a responsive, ethical, moral way, where the participant's dignity, safety, privacy, and autonomy are respected' (Lahman et al., 2011, p. 1403). Floridi and Taddeo (2016) propose 'data ethics' as a branch of ethics which spans three axes of research: firstly, the *ethics of data*, 'including generation, recording, curation, processing, dissemination, sharing and use'; the *ethics of algorithms*, 'including artificial intelligence, artificial agents, machine learning and robots'; and the *ethics of practices*, 'including responsible innovation, programming, hacking and professional codes' (3). While a large proportion of research focuses on data and practices, algorithms are still underexplored. In a review of ethical guidelines for internet-mediated research, Schneble, Elger and Shaw (2018) observed that 'only a small minority of academic institutions has developed guidelines for data science' and most are underprepared 'to perform ethical evaluations of research proposals that make use of vast amounts of data collected from social media, secondary apps and the Internet' (1).

Spatial intermediaries

The SWO project also revealed that many gatekeepers – parents, schools and ethics boards maintain a demarcation between online and offline settings of social life in ways that obscure the permeability and fluidity of digital sociality and data. The physical environs in which young people engaged with the project included home, school, in different states as well as on different digital devices, apps and platforms. The (digital and digitised) data that was produced also moved through and across these different 'places' and into university computers and repositories. The project activities and data were not easily contained to any one space, but always in flux with this ongoing mediation and management of this flow. While we recognise this complexity requires dedicated attention we argue the need for scholars working in academia and associated industries is to not try and compete with commercial research in an ethical way – but to assert and model ethical research with children and young people in a digital society. Alternative approaches, such as that proposed by Schneble et al. (2018) which embrace a 'trusted partnership triangle of social media companies, users and researcher' can be useful in helping all stakeholders to ethically coexist and thrive in research spaces (2). We therefore suggest a spatial and relational approach which recognises the permeability of places and ethical contradictions across the course of a research project.

As SWO demonstrates, whether by design or not, some aspects of research cannot be preempted or resolved until the research is in process: a 'situated practice of ethics' (Gubrium et al., 2014) is therefore required. Yet an openness to relationality, as Lahman et al. (2011) suggest, is 'an internal ethical stance that cannot be regulated by governments or boards' (1402). For example, industry approaches to scale down, test and experiment are valuable but must be undertaken ethically and dynamically. From within the field of business and management studies, Whiting and Pritchard (2017) propose the need for an 'iterative framework' throughout the research cycle that goes beyond 'procedural ethics'. This builds upon previous inquiries of internet research involving vulnerable people and highlights the need to support the dynamics and relationality of 'ethics as process' (Sharkey et al., 2011, p. 753). In addition, the idea of 'ethics as method' (Markham, 2007) invites continual critique and being adaptive to diverse contexts. This decouples concerns around consent and privacy from individual participants and provides a premise for shifting thinking and practices towards situated approaches that consider and respect relations between people, places and platforms. The benefit being to clarify and foreground other principles such as provision of opportunities for research to be conducted on matters which affect them, as well as participation in the research itself.

Conclusion: from control to care

As social life becomes more complex and unpredictable it is even more important that research is undertaken that can explore and adapt to the shifting experiences, affects and complications of digital society. We argue that this requires resisting the reassertion of deficit discourses of youth and reinforcing strengths-based approaches that recognise and enable young people's rights and capabilities. More so, it implies a deliberate turn away from risk management approaches with regard to digital cultures and data towards frameworks for learning with young people. The current preoccupation with the protection of children (and their future selves) diminishes the *provision* of opportunities for young people to shape, participate in and use research – thus denying their rights to informed participation in the present.

By contrast, we have argued that a 'situated ethics' holds real promise for navigating the complexities of research with young people – particularly in digital society. Deriving from a feminist ethics of care, a situated approach should underpin the development and application of more responsive, reflexive and relational ethics processes. Moreover, the NCA offers a way of working with the attentiveness to the interrelations of people, platforms and places and the joint responsibilities that emerge, for this mode of digital research ethics to be applied to complex, multiyear and participatory digital research at scale. This is particularly significant as taking an NCA approach to situated ethics requires receptivity and responsiveness towards young people as deliberators in the present – not as future adults contributing to choices on a predetermined future. Our chapter aims to contribute to the literature by proposing an approach to support ethics processes in research such that they are not seen as separate or siloed but always situated with shifting social, digital and spatial intermediaries. This invites working with the complexity of digital research ethics: that is, not only recognising the novel entanglements of people, platforms and places – but also giving structural weight to the new forms of deliberation we are obliged to consider and address.

References

Alderson, P. (2000) 'Ethics Review of Social Research: Ten Topics for Social Researchers to Consider', *Education On-Line*. Available at: http://www.leeds.ac.uk/educol/documents/00001481.htm.

Alderson, P. and Morrow, V. (2004) *Ethics, Social Research and Consulting With Children and Young People* (Ilford: Barnardo's).

Alderson, P. and Morrow, V. (2012) *The Ethics of Research With Children and Young People: A Practical Handbook* (London: Sage).

Bessant, J. (2006) 'The Fixed Age Rule: Young People, Parental Consent and Research Ethics', *Youth Studies Australia*, 25(4), 50–57.

Boyd, D. (2008) 'Why Youth ♥ Social Network Sites: The Role of Networked Publics in Teenage Social Life', in D. Buckingham (ed.), *Youth, Identity and Digital Media* (Cambridge, MA: MIT Press).

Boyden, J. and Ennew, J. (1997) 'Children in Focus – A Manual for Participatory Research With Children', *Save the Children: Sweden*. Available at: https://resourcecentre.savethechildren.net/library/children-focus-manual-participatory-research-children.

Constine, J. (2019) 'Facebook Pays Teens to Install VPN that Spies on Them', *TechCrunch*, 29 January 2019. Available at: https://techcrunch.com/2019/01/29/facebook-project-atlas/ (Accessed 12 February 2019).

Corsaro, W.A. (1997) *The Sociology of Childhood* (Thousand Oaks: Sage Publications).

Dhai, A. (2014) 'The Research Ethics Evolution: From Nuremberg to Helsinki', *South African Medical Journal*, 4(3), 178–180.

Ebrahim, H. (2010) 'Situated Ethics: Possibilities for Young Children as Research Participants in the South African Context', *Early Child Development and Care*, 180(3), 289–298.

Federal Register. (1979) 'Protection of Human Subjects: The Belmont Report – Ethical Principles and Guidelines for the Protection of Human Subjects of Research', *US Department of Health, Education and Welfare*, 18 April 1979.

Fielding, M. (2001) 'Students as Radical Agents of Change', *Journal of Educational Change*, 2(2), 123–141.

Fisher, C.B. and Anushko, A.E. (2008) 'Research Ethics in Social Science', in P. Alasuutari, L. Bickman and J. Brannen (eds.), *The SAGE Handbook of Social Research Methods* (London: Sage Publications), 95–109.

Floridi, L. and Taddeo, M. (2016) 'What Is Data Ethics?', *Philosophical Transactions of the Royal Society A*, 374(2083).

Graham, A., Powell, M., Taylor, N. Anderson, D. and Fitzgerald, R. (2013) *Ethical Research Involving Children* (Florence: UNICEF Office of Research).

Gubrium, A., Hill, A. and Flicker, S. (2014) 'A Situated Practice of Ethics for Participatory Visual and Digital Methods in Public Health Research and Practice: A Focus on Digital Storytelling', *American Journal of Public Health*, 104(9), 1606–1614.

Guillemin, M., Gillam, L., Rosenthal, D. and Bolitho, A. (2012) 'Human Research Ethics Committees: Examining Their Roles and Practices', *Journal of Empirical Research on Human Research Ethics*, 7(3), 38–49.

Haggerty, K. (2004) 'Ethics Creep: Governing Social Science Research in the Name of Ethics', *Qualitative Sociology*, 27(4), 391–414.

Halse, C. and Honey, A. (2005) 'Unravelling Ethics: Illuminating the Moral Dilemmas of Research Ethics', *Signs: Journal of Women in Culture and Society*, 30(4), 2141–2162.

Hammersley, M. (2009) 'Against the Ethicists: On the Evils of Ethical Regulation', *International Journal of Social Research Methodology*, 12(3), 211–225.

Hart, R. (1992) 'Children's Participation: From Tokenism to Citizenship', *UNICEF Innocenti Essays, No. 4* (Florence: International Child Development Centre of UNICEF).

Hart, R. (2008) 'Stepping Back From "The Ladder": Reflections on a Model of Participatory Work With Children', in A. Reid, B.B. Jensen, J. Nikel and V. Simovska (eds.), *Participation and Learning* (Dordrecht: Springer), 19–31.

James, A., Jenks, C. and Prout, A. (1998) *Theorising Childhood* (Cambridge: Polity Press).

James, A. and Prout, A. (1997) *Constructing and Reconstructing Childhood: Contemporary Issues in the Sociological Study of Childhood* (London: Falmer Press).

Lahman, M.K.E., Geist, M.R., Rodriguez, K.L., Graglia, P. and DeRoche, K.K. (2011) 'Culturally Responsive Relational Reflexive Ethics in Research: The Three Rs', *Quality and Quantity*, 45(6), 1397–1414.

Livingstone, S., Stoilova, M. and Nandagiri, R. (2018) 'Conceptualising Privacy Online: What Do, and What Should, Children Understand?'. Available at: https://blogs.lse.ac.uk/mediapolicyproject/2018/09/07/conceptualising-privacy-online-what-do-and-what-should-children-understand/.

Markham, A.N. (2007) 'Ethic as Method, Method as Ethic: A Case for Reflexivity in Qualitative ICT Research', *Journal of Information Ethics*, 15(2), 37–54.

McAreavey, R. and Muir, J. (2011) 'Research Ethics Committees: Values and Power in Higher Education', *International Journal of Social Research Methodology*, 14(5), 391–405.

Michael, M. (2012) 'Anecdote', in C. Lury and N. Wakeford (eds.), *Inventive Methods: The Happening of the Social* (London: Routledge), 25–35.

National Health and Medical Research Council. (2018) 'National Statement on Ethical Conduct in Human Research 2007 (updated 2018)'. Available at: https://www.nhmrc.gov.au/about-us/publications/national-statement-ethical-conduct-human-research-2007-updated-2018.

Nishiyama, K. (2017) 'Deliberators, Not Future Citizens: Children in Democracy', *Journal of Public Deliberation*, 13(1).

Papacharissi, Z. (2010) 'Conclusion: A Networked Self', in Z. Papacharissi (ed.), *A Networked Self: Identity, Community and Culture on Social Network Sites* (New York: Routledge), 304–318.

Pitt, P. (2014) '"The Project Cannot be Approved in Its Current Form": Feminist Visual Research Meets the Human Research Ethics Committee', *The Australian Educational Researcher*, 41(3), 311–325.

Preissle, J. and Han, Y. (2006) 'Feminist Research Ethics', in S.N. Hesse-Biber (ed.), *Handbook of Feminist Research: Theory and Praxis* (Thousand Oaks: Sage Publications), 583–605.

Schneble, C.O., Elger, B.S. and Shaw, D. (2018) 'The Cambridge Analytica Affair and Internet-Mediated Research', *EMBO Reports*, 2 July 2018.

Sen, A. (2005) 'Human Rights and Capabilities', *Journal of Human Development*, 6(2), 151–166.

Sharkey, S., Jones, R., Smithson, J., Hewis, E., Emmens, T., Ford, T. and Owens, C. (2011) 'Ethical Practice in Internet Research Involving Vulnerable People: Lessons From a Self-Harm Discussion Forum Study (SharpTalk)', *Journal of Medical Ethics*, 37(12), 752–758.

Sikes, P. and Piper, H. (2010) 'Ethical Research, Academic Freedom and the Role of Ethics Committees and Review Procedures in Educational Research', *International Journal of Research and Method in Education*, 33(3), 205–213.

Simons, H. and Usher, R. (2000) *Situated Ethics in Educational Research* (New York: Routledge).

Skelton, T. (2008) 'Research with Children and Young People: Exploring the Tensions Between Ethics, Competence and Participation', *Children's Geographies*, 6(1), 21–36.

Spears, B.A. and Kofoed, J. (2013) 'Transgressing Research Binaries: Youth as Knowledge Brokers in Cyberbullying Research', in P. Smith and G. Steffgen (eds.), *Cyberbullying Through the New Media: Findings From an International Network* (London: Psychology Press), 201–221.

Spears, B.A. and Zeederberg, M. (2013) 'Emerging Methodological Strategies to Address Cyberbullying: Online Social Marketing and Young People as Co-researchers', in S. Bauman, D. Cross and J. Walker (eds.), *Principles of Cyberbullying Research: Definitions, Measures, and Methodology* (New York: Routledge), 166–179.

Swist, T. and Collin, P. (2017) 'Platforms, Data and Children's Rights: Introducing a "Networked Capability Approach"', *New Media and Society*, 19(5), 671–685.

te Riele, K. and Brooks, R. (2012) 'Making Ethical Deliberations Public: Some Provisional Resources for Youth Research Ethics', *Youth Studies Australia*, 31(3), 11–16.

Whiting, R. and Pritchard, K. (2017) 'Digital Ethics', in C. Cassell, A.L. Cunliffe and G. Grandy (eds.), *Sage Handbook of Qualitative Research in Business and Management* (London: SAGE Publications), 562–577.

Woodhead, M. and Faulkner, D. (2000) 'Subjects, Objects or Participants?: Dilemmas of Psychological Research With Children', in P. Christensen and A. James (eds.), *Research With Children* (London: Falmer Press), 9–35.

World Medical Association. (2013) 'Declaration of Helsinki: Ethical Principles for Medical Research Involving Human Subjects', *JAMA*, 310(2), 2191–2194.

Wyn, J. and White, R. (1997) *Rethinking Youth* (St Leonards: Allen & Unwin).

Chapter 10

Informed consent as a situated research process in an ethnography of incarcerated youth in Denmark

Tea Torbenfeldt Bengtsson

Introduction

In this chapter I reflect on the complexities of obtaining informed consent when doing ethnography with incarcerated youth. Through concrete examples, it is demonstrated that it is often impossible to obtaining informed consent through standardised research practice. Thus, informed consent cannot be standardised if we are to conduct ethically grounded ethnographies with vulnerable youth but must be developed as a situated research practice throughout the research process. In the following expert from my interaction with Mark, a new 16-year-old participant in my doctoral thesis examining young people's everyday lives in secure care in Denmark, shows the tension existing between researcher and researched. Mark, has just arrived:

> It is afternoon when Mark comes out of his private room and I approach him to introduce myself and the study. I smile, put out my hand, and say "Hi". Mark looks at the floor and mumbles a "hi" in return, letting my hand hang in the air. When I start to explain that I'm not part of the staff, he looks up briefly and replies with an "oh". I hoped that I could then explain that I'm a researcher and also introduce the project and let him know that he does not directly have to be a part of it. However, before I get that far, Mark moves quickly to the kitchen, leaving me standing there talking to myself in the corridor.
>
> (Field notes from secure care facility, 2009)

While an awkward and unpleasant situation, it made me reflect on the unequal power structure in secure care facilities were young people are locked up against their will and with little or no control over their own lives. At the time I took little notice of this interaction. Having spent more than six weeks at the secure care facility, I was by that time quite accustomed to being ignored and had become used to the young people not generally having great interest in me or my study. The reasons for their lack of interest are complex and, as I have analysed elsewhere (Bengtsson, 2012a, 2012b), predominantly linked to the young person's loss of freedom. The incarcerated young people not only suffered from the pains of imprisonment but also constituted one of the most vulnerable groups in Danish society – all were minors in difficult life situations and marginalised positions, such as suffering from mental health problems, homelessness and substance misuse. A majority of the young people were under suspicion of crime and placed in the facilities as a result of court-ordered remand. Secure care facilities in Denmark are thus used as an alternative to jail in order to meet the statement of the UN Convention of the Child that the confinement of children should be as lenient and limited as possible (OHCHR, 1989, Article 37b).

After having spent more than 350 hours 'hanging out' in secure care facilities,[1] I learned that Mark's rejection, and that of the other young people, was a pushback against the control and domination of the system they were subjected to. Thus, they were not necessarily rejecting me or my study but rather the controlling circumstances defining their situation – that I, as just another adult professional, came to represent. Although over time Mark's and the others' instinctive rejection became understandable, their lack of interest in my study posed a complex ethical dilemma: how could I adhere to ethical standards of obtaining informed consent when the young people that I set out to understand showed no interest in participation?

Informed consent as research practice when studying youth

Informed consent is heralded in youth studies as a key ethical panacea to counter autocratic and harmful research practices and to protect the rights of each young person we encounter. The assumption underpinning informed consent is that it will protect the rights and welfare of the individual young person by offering the opportunity to make free and informed choices. However, the concrete practice of securing informed consent and its obstacles when entering youth-oriented institutions are seldom addressed in any depth (Heath, Brooks, Cleaver and Ireland, 2009). Furthermore, the complexities of what actually constitutes informed consent in practice go mostly unexamined.

Informing and allowing young people choice and the ability to give consent is today seen as an important part of the research process and most researchers strive to do so in as clear a form as possible. To secure consent, diverse tools and approaches are used such as handing out information sheets, discussing the research with young participants and asking them to sign a consent form (Morrow and Richards, 1996; Kendrick, Steckley and Lerpiniere, 2008). However, the understandings of informed consent underlying these approaches are often indirectly premised on a model of the research participant as an autonomous individual who can engage in reflexive decision making on whether to participate when presented with adequate information (Sin, 2005). The unquestioned belief in autonomy draws on notions of a heightened individualism where 'autonomy' is presented as the ability to act and decide freely without constraint or coercion (Corrigan, 2003). However, when drawing on understandings of young people (as well as all other participants) as autonomous individuals we tend to overlook how both the young participant and the researcher are always embedded in preexisting social and cultural contexts within which the process of consent necessarily takes place. Thus, informed consent as a research practice cannot be situated outside the realm of power and the values informing our research field (Mauthner, 2002).

Ethnographers often acknowledge that the setting is relevant for most aspects of the research, and gaining informed consent is often not a straightforward process but dependent on local circumstances (Hammersley and Atkinson, 2007). In sociology, there is a long tradition of conducting covert fieldwork without participants being aware of the researcher's position as researcher and thus that they are part of a research project (Calvey, 2017). This covert tradition is now generally seen as outdated, but as Hammersley and Atkinson write (2007, p. 210), 'even when operating in an overt manner, ethnographers rarely tell *all* the people they are studying *everything* about the research'. Due to the complexity of observing social action as it occurs, most ethnographic research carries unrevealed aspects for those involved (Blackman, 2007). Ideally, the ethnographer becomes part of the field and the culture under study, and here the demand for informed consent carries the risk of hampering the possibility 'from getting "up close" and result in a failure to gain insight into the lives, motives and experiences of people on the margins, or in situations involving risk' (Blackman, 2007, p. 711). An example of this challenge is to be found in studies of young people's engagement with the nighttime economy, where the observing ethnographer cannot meaningfully collect informed consent from everyone passing on the street or everyone entering the bar (Measham and Moore, 2007; Blackman, 2016; Calvey, 2017). However, this challenge also applies in several other settings, including the secure care facility of my study (Bengtsson, 2012c), where gaining informed consent from everyone I encountered and observed was unrealistic. To track people down in the corridor or interrupt their work or conversations and draw their attention towards you and your research not only creates socially awkward situations, but it can also be directly damaging for building the trustful relations necessary to conduct the research (Hammersley and Atkinson, 2007).

The argument here is not that we should give up on seeking informed consent when researching young people, but that we need to be reflexive about how informed consent may best be secured in practice. In my research at the secure care facilities, I started out by unreflexively adapting a standard model of informed consent, thinking it was an ethical code that I had to employ in a formalised way. It has been several years after completing the research before I openly started to discuss how I strayed from the standard model of informed consent to address the full complexity of actually gaining ethically grounded consent from incarcerated young people. While the complexity of adequately informing the young people is noticeably addressed in my field notes, how to adequately address this complex ethical issue was not obvious to me at the time. In the following analysis, I seek to demonstrate that valuable insights can be gained from 'opening up' a more reflexive approach explaining how informed consent in my study was not something to be obtained or collected, but rather it became an integrated part of the relationship I built with the young people and thus an integrated part of the research process.

Gaining access – the role of gatekeepers

In the Nordic welfare states the responsibility to care for children and youth is seen as essential and high levels of public funding and an extensive safety net for those in need are common (Kvist, 2015). Although researchers are generally trusted with access to welfare institutions for children and youth, surprisingly little is known about Danish secure care facilities and the experiences of young people placed there. This lack of knowledge may be related to the fact that the use of confinement for young people is politically contested. While a general political agreement exists to adhere to the UN Convention of the Child in that confinement of children should be as lenient and limited as possible (OHCHR, 1989, Article 37b), little is known about how confinement is used and with what effects (see Bengtsson, 2012c; Henriksen, 2017).

In practice, research involving children and young people conducted in insti-tutional settings (such as secure care facilities, schools and other welfare agen-cies) is not only politically sensitive but also highly dependent on the good will of powerful institutional gatekeepers (Morrow and Richards, 1996). Research in institutional welfare contexts therefore presents well-known challenges, such as the denial of access to the researcher on grounds that the young people are incompetent to make informed decisions or that they need protection from harm (Powell and Smith, 2009). When researching young people in vulnerable life situ-ations, researchers negotiate participation with professionals, which can become an effective denial of young people's agency and thus construe them as incompe-tent (Heptinstall, 2000; Heath, Charles, Crow and Wiles, 2007; Bengry-Howell and Griffin, 2012).

As pointed out by Heath and colleagues (Heath et al., 2007, p. 404), '[T]he right of gatekeepers to give or withhold access is in practice often conflated with the right to give or withhold consent'. For me, gaining access to a secure care facility proved to be surprisingly easy and without the well-known challenges. One reason was that I did not need any formal ethical approval from a university or welfare-state agencies to contact the facilities and launch the study. In Den-mark, the facilities are to a large degree independent units where management decides who should be granted access. Other reasons were the support I had from an experienced professor and the fact that the project received funding from the Danish Research Council, all which could be taken as indirect validation of the project and my qualifications to carry out the proposed fieldwork.

Even though the managers as gatekeepers had the overall power to decide if I could get into the facility and access the young people, they had no formal powers to give consent on the behalf of the young people. However, even when children and young people are allowed to decide for themselves whether to take part in research, important differences remain in the relative status of younger participants who will, to varying degrees, be more or less dependent on their adult caretakers. Under such circumstances it can be difficult for the young people to actively refuse involvement (Hill, 2005; Cahill, 2007; Powell and Smith, 2009; Holland, Renold, Ross and Hillman, 2010), even more so when they, as was the case in my study, are confined and are not free to leave the institutional setting (Kendrick et al., 2008).

Management was from, the onset, positive towards my project and found it important that the facilities were open to different kinds of inspections from the outside. At the meeting the issue of safety was raised – primarily in relation to my personal safety but it was also stressed that I should not pose a security risk for the staff. It was therefore required that I had my own key to the facility to be able to lock myself out if a violent conflict should arise. I worried that the key would be an obstacle when seeking to be, accepted by the young people and that the key would make them associate me with the staff. However, the key was an unconditional premise and I had to agree that I would lock myself out of the facility in if violence erupted. The strong focus on safety at the meeting was not a surprise, but I was surprised to learn that the safety discussed was directed at me and the staff and did not include the young people in any way.

Having so easily been granted access to the facility, I did not put much consideration into how to best ensure that my research was understood and appreciated by the staff, and most significantly the young people, rather than only the managers. Being met with management's interest and generalised trust that my project was relevant, led me to believe that this trust in my project (and subsequently me) was almost automatically guaranteed as soon as I entered the facility. From rereading my field notes prior to entering the facility, I can see that I did not reflect on possible tensions that could arise from efforts to secure acceptance and informed consent in a setting physically controlled and completely dictated by institutional gatekeepers. My reflection was focused on the role of the key, and only indirectly did these reflections concern the young people's subordinate position. However, the complex process of securing acceptance, and with it, informed consent from the young participants, could not be situated outside the realm of power and the unique characteristics of secure care facilities as correctional institutions (Corrigan, 2003).

Finding a role – the process of securing consent

Before entering the secure care facility for the first time I had drafted a letter outlining my study for the young people stressing that they did not have to talk to me and that I would do my best to respect their privacy. I planned to hand them the letter when appropriate, and in this way, they could read about my study and reflect on their desire to participate. I attempted to make the letter short and readable and included my picture to personalise it. However, when trying to hand it over to the first young person willing to talk to me for more than five seconds, I felt perplexed. The young man told me about going to court the next day and the anxiety he felt. He asked me a lot of questions about the legal system that I could not answer; I ended up trying to comfort him by reassuring him of the system's fairness. I never handed my letter to him or to any other young person. It seemed misplaced when meeting a young person for the first time, and in time it seemed irrelevant to inform them of the study on paper. I also learned that a number of them could not read, making the letter even more irrelevant as a source of information.

Instead of the letter I tried to adapt the notion of 'process consent' so that consent became an ongoing part of my relationship with the young people (Heath et al., 2009, p. 25). I identified myself and talked about why I was there, a theme that fit with the conversations already taking place when a new young person entered the facility. The young people were excited to get to know the newcomer and the newcomer was keen to know the 'veterans' to learn whether they had common acquaintances on the outside. In these exchanges, there would often be a little space for me to present myself and sometimes even my study. In these short exchanges, I spent as much time with the young people as possible and would often mention that I was interested in their experiences while letting them know that they did not have to speak with me.

I mostly just 'hang out', and unlike most other adults in the facilities, did not attempt to create special activities with or for them. As discussed by Tani (2014), 'hanging out' has a blurred character because it is not a predefined activity but rather about the importance of 'just being'. Thus, hanging out as a research method 'makes it challenging for a researcher to follow any strictly defined protocol on ethical principles' (Tani, 2014, p. 367). When hanging out with the young people, I obtained a retracted approach that positioned me primarily as an observer and an inactive participant, giving me the in-between role of being neither staff nor young person. I did not try to become 'less adult' but rather to negotiate a non-professional adult position by not using my key to unlock doors or participate in conflicts (see also Bengtsson, 2014). In my field notes, there are a number of episodes where I registered my negotiation of this position, such as in the following:

It is lunchtime and everyone seems to be in a good mood. Two of the young boys are joking with Mickael, a staff member. Mickael leaves the table and once he is out of the room food is flying through the air. I didn't register who threw first but in no time eggs, meat and bread are flying around me. Luckily, they are not aiming at me and I just sit there. Mickael is called back due to the rising level of shouting and screaming. When he enters the room, the boys are all quiet, looking down at their plates, trying not to laugh. Mickael's face turns red and in a frustrated voice, he asked who had been throwing the food around. No one answers, not even me.

(Episode based on field notes from secure care facility, 2009)

From such episodes, the young people came to understand that I was not one of them nor was I a member of staff. The realisation that I was not a staff member appeared to lead to a more general acceptance of my presence. At first, some of the boys challenged me, trying to flirt with or provoke me. In these situations I played ignorant, seeking the identity of 'last-gendered' (Pascoe, 2012): I did not chat, giggle, or wear makeup or tight clothing. After a little while they stopped challenging me, leaving me in a position at the periphery of interactions, which allowed me to closely observe their self-performances (Goffman, 1990). I left the room when the young people began to whisper with each other and did not ask to join them when they were hanging out in their own rooms. Looking back when I reread my notes, I do not, however, believe that the young people were fully informed about what I was doing when positioning myself as a nonprofessional adult spending time hanging out with them. Did they know that the food-throwing incident would not merely be an experience they shared with me but also that it would be written down and potentially used for an academic analysis years later? I doubt it.

The fact that I was a researcher did not carry any specific meaning for the young people (see also Honkatukia, Nyqvist and Pösö, 2003). Their acceptance and willingness to let me hang out with them was not based on their knowledge of research and my study. Instead their participation was linked to the role I had created in the field.[2] Without planning it, I came to position myself as someone who they could rely on – I listened, did not inform the staff of their secrets, had ample time to listen and tried to help them, such as reading letters or explaining the basic workings of the justice system. While this role of assistance and support played a part in the young people's acceptance of me, it did not lead to great confidentiality between us nor did it engender greater interest in participating in my study. The power dynamics between the young people and me as an adult researcher were not dissolved and never could be. Instead, they positioned me as a harmless and ignorant adult: I could keep my mouth shut, but I did not know anything about what it was like to be them (Emond, 2005; see also Heath et al., 2009, pp. 45–50).

When 'hanging out', I would often mention my study – it was not that the young people did not care or lacked the ability to understand my study, but rather the stress of their incarceration eclipsed their interest in most matters beyond it. Unresolved questions about their future occupied almost all of their energy, leaving little room for issues that did not relate directly to their own needs and concerns (see also Bengtsson, 2012a). Their participation in my study was therefore only a minor interest and was increasingly linked to their confidentiality in and knowledge of me as a person, rather than the concrete information that I tried to convey about my study.

Interviewing – the dilemma of participation

The complexities of securing the young people's informed consent were further revealed when I started to invite them to participate in an in-depth interview about their experiences in secure care and their general life situation. Almost half of the young people turned down my invitation. Amongst the 21 who accepted, six could be seen as unsuccessful interviews in that they were short and uncomfortable for both the young person and me. One of these interviews was with 16-year-old Bryan, an otherwise talkative and friendly boy, who I had known for two weeks when I interviewed him in his private room at the facility. In the following passage, I have just introduced the interview and informed Bryan that it is voluntary and that he could terminate the interview whenever he wished.

TEA: I know that you have been here for two weeks now. Do you have any thoughts about being here, about the facility or something else?
BRYAN: No, not really.
TEA: Okay . . . , do you have any idea how long you are to stay [at the facility]?
BRYAN: Hmm, no.
TEA: What do you think about that uncertainty?
BRYAN: It's not a good . . .
TEA: . . . It must be quite stressful, no?
BRYAN: . . . Sometimes.
TEA: Hmm . . . Would you rather not talk right now?
BRYAN: No, it's fine.
TEA: Okay. . . . Could you tell me a little about what you did before coming here?
BRYAN: I just went to school.
TEA: I see. . . . Did you like school?
BRYAN: . . . No, not really.

(15-minute interview with Bryan, age 16 years)

The interview continued for another ten minutes before I ended it. Bryan did not elaborate any of his answers, and I refrained from trying to further coax him to answer. Silence in interviews is not automatically a failure but rather is linked to the power relations that always inform the interview (Bengtsson and Fynbo, 2018). Bryan's short answers and my repeated questioning was thus a direct reflection of the unmet expectations that we both had of what the interview would entail. I hoped the interview would focus on Bryan's detailed reflections on his situation and experiences. However, after the interview when I had turned off the recorder, Bryan revealed that, 'I just hate to sit and talk about myself like that'. When I asked why he did not end the interview, he explained that he felt uncomfortable disrupting the interview because he already agreed to participate. Bryan had thus felt obliged to continue the interview because of our prior relationship hanging out together in the facility, and consequently he did not want to let me down by terminating the interview (see also Kendrick et al., 2008, pp. 89–90). Our unequal positions, which could be temporarily set aside when hanging out, became obvious in the formalised interview situation. I was an adult asking the questions and Bryan was the one who should deliver the answers. Not only was asking questions a shift away from my nonprofessional role but, for some of the young people, such interviews had often been with social workers or police leading to changes in their circumstances.

Following this interview with Bryan I thus realised that although the young people had positioned me as a harmless adult when sharing everyday life at the facility, this role could not automatically be transferred to the interview situation (Heath et al., 2009, pp. 39–57). Here my role shifted from neutral to being more active, with clear expectations of the young person taking on the role of knowing informant. Despite having given his consent to be interviewed, the interview could not be conducted in an ethical and respectful way because it had not been possible for me to inform Bryan about the full extent of his participation. As pointed out by Heath and colleagues (2009), for most researchers there are significant challenges in conveying what research actually entails. They write, '[I]t is questionable if whether a researcher is ever able to *genuinely* secure fully informed consent given the difficulties of explaining the exact nature of the research process'.

While the experience with interviewing Bryan could have led me to give up on interviewing the young people, I did not. But it made me realise that for the interviews to be more ethically grounded, I had to be explicit that I did not *expect* the young people to be interviewed and to be explicit that the interview would also entail me asking more personal questions. My main reason for continuing to interview the young people was that before I interviewed Bryan, some of the young people indicated that the interview was welcome as a rare opportunity for them to tell their story or share their opinions. When I interviewed 17-year-old Ian, he started the interview by declaring:

> It is insane what goes on here. You have seen it. It is a prison for young people that takes away everything we have, and you know they even put children as young as 12 years in here. You should write about that. You really should.
>
> (35-minute interview with Ian, age 17 years)

Ian had clearly understood that, despite my retracted role, I was studying their lives in the facility and that I would eventually write about it. He had reflected on his situation and had a clear point he wanted to get across to me in the interview and through me to a wider audience outside the facility. At the time, I saw the interviews not only as a source of more detailed personal information about individual youths but also as a possible way of giving the young people a voice beyond the facility. I hoped that the interview could be a way of enhancing their agency and promoting a better understanding of their lives. By interviewing and listening to the young people's opinions and their own sensemaking, I hoped to mitigate the demonising of their lives and to empower them in a context where their lives were controlled and scrutinised (Stephen and Squires, 2003). However, the interview with Ian also made me aware of a possible failure in portraying their lives and the unintended consequences of further objectifying them for the outside world. I could not automatically guarantee that anyone would listen to my findings or listen in order to understand or improve. This realisation made me take extra precautions in the following interviews with the young people to stress that although their motivation for participating was to inspire beneficial changes for those confined after them, I could not promise them that my research would actually result in such changes (Emond, 2005). I would explain that the interview was a way for me to learn and an opportunity for young persons to tell their stories and share their opinions. I would actively listen to them with the hope that the interview setting could create a place in time to give voice to their marginalised lives without being judged.

In a few interviews the transformative power of narration did occur, such as when 16-year-old Alex ended the interview as follows: 'Thank you for just listening to me just talking and going on and on'.

Both the young people's rejection of being interviewed and their consent to share their lives in interviews thus relied on the research relationship that I built with them over time. With my knowledge of their everyday lives, I gradually learned to accept the complexities within the research relationship and attune to their reality and needs. By knowing of their suffering and pain but also their joys and stories, I could understand their disinterest in being interviewed but also why some interviews were less successful despite the young person's consent.

Informed consent as a situated research process

As the previous discussion demonstrates, I only slowly realised the importance of my role in ensuring that the young people were as fully informed as possible about the nature of the study. Gaining access and formal consent to carry out the study is often raised as a major obstacle in much youth research. However, my initial access to the field was unproblematic in that I did not go through a special ethics committee nor was I denied access by key gatekeepers. My principal challenge therefore became how to actually conduct ethical research with young people whose autonomy and social agency were so greatly restricted by confinement in secure care. In this setting, the standard procedure of obtaining informed consent became an ongoing challenge, demonstrating that ethics cannot be situated outside the research context and is essentially formed by the values guiding the research.

In time I came to adopt a situational 'ethical strategy' where informed consent was not seen as something I needed to obtain beforehand but rather something that I had to continually secure through my interaction and dialogue with the young people. Informed consent became reconceptualised as an ongoing and inseparable part of the research process where I continually sought to respect the privacy and emotions of the young people and develop a sensibility towards the situational aspects of their wellbeing. I learned, as a number of researchers have pointed out in relation to ethnography with vulnerable youth, that the practice of informed consent is partial, contingent, dynamic and shifting (such as Valentine, Butler and Skelton, 2001; Lumsden, 2013; Blackman, 2016).

In different ways, as discussed here, I aimed to give the young people power to refuse to interact with me and to be aware of whether my presence was unwanted. Even though I tried to give them both direct and indirect power to refuse to be part of the study, their actual power to opt out of participation was limited. Despite the reciprocity of our relationship over time, the inherent unequal power relationship between us influenced our relationship: they were young, I was an adult; I could leave when they were forced to stay. In practice, the young people had no formal power to ask me (or anyone else) to leave the facility. To avoid being with me they could withdraw to their private rooms but only for short periods before they were obligated to take part in the facility's everyday activities. The devastating experiences of powerlessness that I found to be a key characteristic of these young people's everyday lives in secure care (see Bengtsson, 2012a) which also directly influenced the probability of securing that their consent to participate in my study was at all times entirely free and voluntary. Consequently, I had to actively address the assumption underpinning the ideal informed consent that it would, almost automatically once given, protect the rights and welfare of young participants by offering them the opportunity to make free and informed choices about their participation (Corrigan, 2003). As youth researchers, we must be aware of the danger of being obsessive about obtaining formalised informed consent because what appears to be good ethical practice can be damaging for forming ethical relationships based on trust and reciprocity with young participants.

Hanging out with and studying young people whose autonomy and social agency was so highly restricted meant that it was impossible to rely on their autonomy and social agency for purposes of formally securing their informed consent as research participants. Developing a situational ethical strategy as part of the research process made it possible during the fieldwork stage to hang out with the young people and respect them emotionally, socially and physically, and at the same time to create sensibility about the situational aspects of their wellbeing. Later this strategy also helped me to conceptualise informed consent as a situated part of the complexities arising from sustaining relationships with young people for a substantial period (Ramcharan and Cutcliffe, 2001). As youth researchers, we need to develop research processes of informed consent that actively through our use of contextualised method engaged with young people (Mauthner, 2002). We need to actively acknowledge and address the power relations that young people's lives are part of and that our research is embedded in if we are to better understand the ethical implications of our work.[3]

Notes

1 I often arrived in the morning and left at night for several consecutive days. I wrote extensive field notes afterward, recalling the day and used a few notes on pieces of paper that I kept in my pocket. I conducted 21 formal and 19 informal interviews of young people during approximately three months of fieldwork at two facilities.
2 I have elsewhere analysed the challenges of making field notes while inside the facility and the consequences it had for data collection (see Bengtsson, 2014).
3 I would like to thank the participating youth.

References

Bengry-Howell, A. and Griffin, C. (2012) 'Negotiating Access in Ethnographic Research With "Hard to Reach" Young People: Establishing Common Ground or a Process of

Methodological Grooming?', *International Journal of Social Research Methodology*, 15(5), 403–416.

Bengtsson, T.T. (2012a) 'Learning to Become a "Gangster"?', *Journal of Youth Studies*, 15(6), 677–692.

Bengtsson, T.T. (2012b) 'Boredom and Action-Experiences From Youth Confinement', *Journal of Contemporary Ethnography*, 41(5), 526–553.

Bengtsson, T.T. (2012c) *Youth Behind Bars: An Ethnographic Study of Youth Confined in Secure Care Institutions in Denmark* (PhD Thesis, Department of Sociology, University of Copenhagen).

Bengtsson, T.T. (2014) 'What Are Data? Ethnographic Experiences With Young Offenders', *Qualitative Research*, 14(6), 729–744.

Bengtsson, T.T. and Fynbo, L. (2018) 'Analysing the Significance of Silence in Qualitative Interviewing: Questioning and Shifting Power Relations', *Qualitative Research*, 18(1), 19–35.

Blackman, S.J. (2007) '"Hidden Ethnography": Crossing Emotional Borders in Qualitative Accounts of Young People's Lives', *Sociology*, 41(4), 699–716.

Blackman, S.J. (2016) 'The Emotional Imagination: Exploring Critical Ventriloquy and Emotional Edgework in Reflexive Sociological Ethnography With Young People', in S. Blackman and M. Kempson (eds.), *The Subcultural Imagination: Theory, Research and Reflexivity in Contemporary Youth Cultures* (London: Routledge), 65–79.

Cahill, C. (2007) 'Doing Research With Young People: Participatory Research and the Rituals of Collective Work', *Children's Geographies*, 5(3), 297–312.

Calvey, D. (2017) *Covert Research: The Art, Politics and Ethics of Undercover Fieldwork* (London: Sage).

Corrigan, O. (2003) 'Empty Ethics: The Problem With Informed Consent', *Sociology of Health and Illness*, 25(7), 768–792.

Emond, R. (2005) 'Ethnographic Research Methods With Children and Young People', in S. Greene and D. Hogan (eds.), *Researching Children's Experience: Approaches and Methods* (Thousand Oaks: Sage), 123–140.

Goffman, E. (1990) *The Presentation of Self in Everyday Life* (London: Penguin Books).

Hammersley, M. and Atkinson, P. (2007) *Ethnography: Principles in Practice* (London and New York: Routledge Taylor and Francis Group).

Heath, S., Brooks, R., Cleaver, E. and Ireland, E. (2009) *Researching Young People's Lives* (London: Sage).

Heath, S., Charles, V., Crow, G. and Wiles, R. (2007) 'Informed Consent, Gatekeepers and Go-Betweens: Negotiating Consent in Child- and Youth-Orientated Institutions', *British Educational Research Journal*, 33(3), 403–417.

Henriksen, A.K. (2017) 'Confined to Care: Girls' Gendered Vulnerabilities in Secure Institutions', *Gender & Society*, 31(5), 677–698.

Heptinstall, E. (2000) 'Gaining Access to Looked After Children for Research Purposes: Lessons Learned', *British Journal of Social Work*, 30(6), 867–872.

Hill, M. (2005) 'Ethical Considerations in Researching Children's Experiences', in S. Green and D. Hogan (eds.), *Researching Children's Experience: Approaches and Methods* (London: Sage), 61–86.

Holland, S., Renold, E., Ross, N.J. and Hillman, A. (2010) 'Power, Agency and Participatory Agendas: A Critical Exploration of Young People's Engagement in Participative Qualitative Research', *Childhood*, 17(3), 360–375.

Honkatukia, P., Nyqvist, L. and Pösö, T. (2003) 'Sensitive Issues in Vulnerable Conditions', *YOUNG*, 11(4), 323–339.

Kendrick, A., Steckley, L. and Lerpiniere, J. (2008) 'Ethical Issues, Research and Vulnerability: Gaining the Views of Children and Young People in Residential Care', *Children's Geographies*, 6(1), 79–93.

Kvist, J. (2015) 'Social Investment as Risk Management', in T.T. Bengtsson, M. Frederiksen and J.E. Larsen (eds.), *The Danish Welfare State: A Sociological Investigation* (New York: Palgrave Macmillan), 41–55.

Lumsden, K. (2013) 'Survival of the Fastest: Ethical Dilemmas in Research With "Boy Racers"', *YOUNG*, 21(3), 273–288.

Mauthner, M.L. (2002) *Ethics in Qualitative Research* (London: Sage).

Measham, F. and Moore, K. (2007) 'Reluctant Reflexivity, Implicit Insider Knowledge and the Development of Club Studies', in B. Saunders (ed.), *Drugs, Clubs and Young People* (Aldershot: Ashgate), 13–25.

Morrow, V. and Richards, M. (1996) 'The Ethics of Social Research With Children: An Overview', *Children and Society*, 10(2), 90–105.

OHCHR. (1989) 'Convention on the Rights of the Child', *Adopted and Opened for Signature, Ratification and Accession by General Assembly Resolution 44/25 of 20 November 1989.*

Pascoe, C.J. (2012) *Dude, You're a Fag: Masculinity and Sexuality in High School: With a New Preface* (Berkeley and Los Angeles: University of California Press).

Powell, M.A. and Smith, A.B. (2009) 'Children's Participation Rights in Research', *Childhood*, 16(1), 124–142.

Ramcharan, P. and Cutcliffe, J.R. (2001) 'Judging the Ethics of Qualitative Research: Considering the "Ethics as Process" Model', *Health and Social Care in the Community*, 9(6), 358–366.

Sin, C.H. (2005) 'Seeking Informed Consent: Reflections on Research Practice', *Sociology*, 39(2), 277–294.

Stephen, D.E. and Squires, P.A. (2003) '"Adults Don't Realize How Sheltered They Are". A Contribution to the Debate on Youth Transitions From Some Voices on the Margins', *Journal of Youth Studies*, 30(6), 867–872.

Tani, S. (2014) 'The Right to be Seen, the Right to be Shown: Ethical Issues Regarding the Geographies of Hanging Out', *YOUNG*, 22(4), 361–379.

Valentine, G., Butler, R. and Skelton, T. (2001) 'The Ethical and Methodological Complexities of Doing Research With "Vulnerable" Young People', *Ethics, Place and Environment*, 4(2), 119–125.

Theme IV

Voice and participation

The undue burden of methodological warrant on the voice of disengaged young people

Fiona MacDonald

Introduction

The use of voice in contemporary research presents a number of challenges and the purpose of this chapter is to explore the methodological warrant that has been attributed to the collective voices of young people in alternative learning environments in calls for school reform. The discussion explores the critique of voice as a research methodology to investigate how the stories of these young people have been overburdened with methodological warrant (Yates, 2003) in calls to understand the levels of disengagement in Australian schools. Despite contemporary critique, the study of voice continues to be acknowledged as an authentic and youth-friendly method to engage young people in research (Bourke and MacDonald, 2018; Furlong, 2015; Tarabini, Jacovkis and Montes, 2018). The question of how much weight the individual stories of participants in small-number qualitative studies carry (Yates, 2003) is explored in this chapter alongside critique of voice as the most authentic truth in research (Mazzei and Jackson, 2009; St Pierre, 2009). The investigation of the overreading of the collective voice of these young people explored here is situated within the broader concerns around the level of disengagement in Australian schools and to reimagine what schooling might look like for young Australians (Lewthwaite, Wilson, Wallace, McGinty and Swain, 2017; McGregor, Mills, te Riele, Baroutsis and Hayes, 2017; Mills and McGregor, 2014; te Riele, 2009).

Levels of disengagement in Australian schools

In recent years it has been argued that children and young people are disengaging from Australia's learning environments, with as many as 40% of children and young people unproductive in any year and over half of these were showing signs of disengagement (Angus et al., 2010; Goss, Sonnemann and Griffiths, 2017; Quinn and Owen, 2016; Welters, Lewthwaite, Thomas and Wilson, 2018). The most recent international Programme for International Student Assessment (PISA) results shows 'below-average levels of cognitive, emotional and behavioural engagement' amongst Australian students and over a quarter of young people – at least 80,000 students who are not completing Year 12 or equivalent each year (Lamb and Huo, 2017). An increasing number of young people are being excluded, or pushed out, from school because they are being framed as failures or un-motivated to learn (Best, 2015; McGregor, Mills, te Riele and Hayes, 2015; Smyth, 2006; Robinson and Smyth, 2016).

A Western Australian study, *The Pipeline Project* (Angus et al., 2010), tracked 1300 students from Year 2–8, and found that up to 40% of the students were unproductive at any given time. Their study found that over half of those were disengaged, displaying behaviours from being inattentive and lacking motivation through to disruptive, aggressive behaviour (Angus et al., 2010). In 2013, a New South Wales student feedback survey with 78,600 secondary school students, *Student Engagement and Wellbeing in NSW* (NSW Centre for Education Statistics and Evaluation, 2015), identified a range of complex factors that contribute to disengagement. The study identified socioeconomic status, living in nonmetropolitan areas and gender as factors that impact on an individual students' disengagement from school. Research reveals that disengagement from school may be evident in the primary school years or even earlier (Fredricks, Blumenfeld and Paris, 2004) and is the cumulative result of many factors. The gap between high-performing and low-performing students is growing and young people from disadvantaged backgrounds are more likely to be disengaged from school (Sullivan, Johnson, Owens and Conway, 2014). Research with young people in alternative learning environments reveals that they are 'likely to be "carriers" of risk', suggesting that disadvantage may been a contributing factor to their disengagement from mainstream education (Welters et al., 2018, p. 7). However, these are not contributing factors for all children and young people who disengage from education. The early stages of disengagement or passive disengagement are difficult to identify as children and young people may continue to complete their work but gradually lose interest, others may find the work too difficult and others find it too easy (Angus et al., 2010). While measuring some elements of engagement is possible it is difficult to quantify students social, emotional and cognitive engagement (AITSL, 2016; Goss et al., 2017). Even high performing students can be disengaged if they are not motivated to extend themselves. The path to disengagement is complex but keeping children and young people connected to education is recognised as a critical factor for future financial independence, work opportunities, health and wellbeing as well as social engagement with families and community (Lamb and Huo, 2017).

Smyth (2006, p. 288) acknowledges that the reasons children and young people disengage from school and education are multifaceted and complex, but ultimately, he argues, they 'boil down to "political" reasons' when students begin to 'refuse to make the emotional and relational investment necessary' to engage with schools and learning. He argues that there is a 'clash of frames of reference', when 'the school operates with one frame of reference, or maybe more, and students bring their own frames of reference' (Smyth, 2006, p. 290). To overcome this, it is vital to move beyond blaming the individual or the social structures of school and to begin to understand the relationships and processes that play out between the school and young people (Smyth, 2006).

Disengaged from school: the perception of young people

Welters and colleagues (2018) suggest an interdisciplinary approach is required to understand students' perceptions of the learning environments in both mainstream schools and alternative learning environments. They have used a quantitative instrument with Australian students who have reengaged in learning in alternative learning environments to improve knowledge and understanding of disengagement. Their findings indicate that there is no homogenous attitude to the student's experience, particularly in mainstream schools. Even learning environments that young people perceived to be more favourable or effective do not automatically prevent student disengagement and are not always a 'precondition of educational disengagement' (Welters et al., 2018, p. 13).

Many of their participants reflected favourably on their previous educational experience but had 'nonetheless disengaged from mainstream schooling' (Welters et al., 2018, p. 8). A key finding from their work with young people in alternative learning environments was the significance of feeling valued and being able to 're-evaluate and reform their sense of value' (Welters et al., 2018, p. 13, see also Lewthwaite et al., 2017) in alternative learning environments. This contrasted with their mainstream experience where many young people felt devalued. The study is, of course, retrospective and young people were reflecting back to a trajectory that ultimately saw them disengage from mainstream schooling. It is difficult to track this process in real time, as the pathway to disengagement is unique for each student and does not follow a linear path. There are obviously a number of risk factors, and school attendance is a key indicator but disengagement is a gradual process (Welters et al., 2018). Understanding students' emotional and cognitive disengagement is more difficult (ATISL, 2016).

The Grattan Institute (Goss et al., 2017) investigated the level of disengagement in Australian schools and acknowledged the difficulties in identifying students who had disengaged or were in the process of disengaging. Their observations revisited the findings of Galton, Hargreaves, Comber, Wall and Pell (1999), identifying groups of students who they described as passively disengaged, some heading towards a complete disengagement from school. Some were identified as the 'intermittent workers', identified in the earlier research, who worked when they were being watched but moved off task whenever an opportunity arose; others were considered to be 'easy riders', who worked slowly, dragging out tasks for as long as they could; others were described as 'ghosts', who did not attract the teacher's attention and slipped under the radar (Galton et al., 1999; Goss et al., 2017). In both instances, the understanding of disengagement was gleaned from the researchers' voice (Galton et al., 1999) and larger scale, quantitative reports (Goss et al., 2017). The accounts of young people's experience of working only when they were being watched, of dragging out tasks or avoiding the teachers' attention are absent. The 20 years between the two pieces of research demonstrates the challenges of accessing the less readily available, or the difficult to identify, groups of young people who remain in mainstream education but are in the process of disengaging with education. The need for greater insight and to identify more nuanced indicators of student disengagement is as important today as it was at the end of the 20th century.

Student voice

The study of student voice incorporates a long history of practices 'which include student consultation, participation, collaboration, leadership and intergenerational learning' (Quinn and Owen, 2016, p. 70). One field of student voice relates to young people's participation in decision making at the school level (Mayes and Groundwater-Smith, 2013; Mitra, 2018). In this instance, the collective student voice's speaks to concepts of power between 'young people and adults' in the school space (Mitra, 2018, p. 479). There is an acknowledgement in this scholarship that the young people's collective voice comes with an agenda, with experience being framed by their own unique circumstances. The task for the researcher in this field is to 'elicit and demonstrate some patterns of broader significance' from the individual experiences (Yates, 2003, p. 229). Recent studies use student voice as a representation of students' experience of [dis]engagement, connectedness, wellbeing, social exclusion, bullying and school reform (Aldridge et al., 2016; Bourke and MacDonald, 2018; Quinn and Owen, 2016; Robinson and Smyth, 2016; Tarabini et al., 2018). Much of this research is qualitative, focused on individual schools or communities, and the evidence shows that even primary school students can convey their experiences (Quinn and Owen, 2016). Interviews and focus groups are combined with larger scale survey findings to enable researchers to investigate key aspects of student experience. In this scholarship, researchers recognise that each individual's educational experience is unique and 'shaped by the quality of the relationships between individuals at the school, the quality of the teaching and learning that takes place and the physical, social and emotional safety of the students' (Aldridge et al., 2016, p. 6). It has been argued that student voice cannot be separated from the 'role of state regulation and governance' in calls to reimagine education (Arnot and Reay, 2007, p. 311).

Student voice from mainstream schools in calls for school reform has tended to be drawn from large-scale, quantitative research that conducts surveys around student engagement, wellbeing and belonging. These are often conducted by independent youth organisations such as The Foundation for Young Australians, *Unlimited Potential: A data and information resource on young Australians*, Mission Australia, *Youth Survey Report*, the Australian Institute of Health and Welfare, *Young Australians: Their health and wellbeing reports*, Australian Research Alliance for Children and Youth (ARACY) and *Report card: The Wellbeing of Young Australians*, to name a few of the larger annual studies. State education departments also conduct large-scale quantitative research with children and young people. The Department of Education and Training Victoria conducts an annual Attitude to School Survey with all children from Years 4–12 in government schools, measuring levels of student satisfaction, including their connectedness to school. The New South Wales Department of Education and Training conducts the Tell Them From Me suite of surveys with students, parents and teachers and other states' education departments have their own measurement tools. These larger-scale reports provide valuable quantitative data on the experiences of Australian children and young people. They fall short, however, of providing the valuable insights of educational experiences that are captured through the voices of young people.

Collective voice

The concept of collective voice has been used extensively in human resource and business management disciplines as a means of communicating with management and to have meaningful input into decisions and suggestions for innovation and change (Hennala and Melkas, 2016; Mowbray, Wilkinson and Tse, 2015). The concept of collective voice is to present a multivoiced approach that represents an 'interpretation of views' from the voices of many, rather than the individual's perspective (Hennala and Melkas, 2016, p. 63). Collective voice has been interpreted in a variety of ways across these disciplines, but there are two consistent motives: to eliminate employee dissatisfaction and to capture suggestions to improve business performance and introduce innovative practices (Mowbray et al., 2015). Collective voice in the human resource disciplines enables employees to represent conflicting views to management. The approach requires a deeper analysis of the participants' views but is designed to avoid the large-scale surveys that have become popular in contemporary society (Hennala and Melkas, 2016). Collective voice also enables the voice of the user who benefits from the change or innovation to contribute to the discussions and proposal for change rather than those who benefit from the end product or service (Hennala and Melkas, 2016).

There are benefits of learning from the practices of other disciplines and industries, and I argue that collective voice provides a new way to consider the representation of young people's voices in education debates. The young people are the users who benefit from the change or innovation in education while the employers, policymakers and economists are the beneficiaries of the end product or service. In the school reform agenda, the beneficiaries of the end product or service are making the strongest contribution to these debates while the collective voice of the users, children and young people is being represented by the larger-scale surveys and quantitative research with young people and those who have reengaged in alternative learning environments. Neither, I argue, truly represent the collective voices of the young people who remain passively disengaged in mainstream education.

Methodological warrant

The concept of methodological warrant draws on the work of Yates (2003), who reflected on the weight that the evidence from small-number qualitative research subjects may carry. McLeod and Yates (2006) focused on their 12 to 18 Project longitudinal study and their own potential overreading of a research design that highlighted links between their study and broader educational issues. The focus of this chapter is to consider the potential overreading or undue burden of the body of research investigating the experiences of young people in alternative learning environments in the call for education reform in Australia. The aim here is to consider the collective voice of young people which is not included in calls for school reform and to recognise the undue burden on young people's voices in alternative learning environments that others have ascribed in the call for educational reform around Australia. While it may appear dismissive to consider 70,000 voices (te Riele, 2014) a small sample, the scale is relative when you consider that this represents less than 2% of the 3,849,225 students enrolled in Australian schools (Australian Bureau of Statistics, 2017).

Alternative education

Alternative education is a broad term covering a range of educational programs and organisations. For the purposes of this discussion, alternative education is described as 'the flexi, second-chance or last-chance schools' (McGregor et al., 2017, p. 4) that offer young people who are disenfranchised or disengaged from education a chance to reengage in learning environments. Many of these young people have had negative experiences in mainstream education or live with significant social and/or developmental challenges. Many live with challenging life circumstances, including complex family situations, psychological and health issues. A number have been bullied or experienced social exclusion for their perceived difference and inability to fit into mainstream schooling (Tarabini et al., 2018). Others have been excluded or suspended from school and feel that they have been forced out (Robinson and Smyth, 2016).

Many young people enrol in alternative learning environments because they were unable to conform to the policies and expectations of mainstream schooling and the overemphasis on measurement and university entrance scores (MacDonald, Bottrell and Johnson, 2018). The 'neoliberal focus on individual accountability' emphasises the deficit of the individual, blaming them rather than the system for their disenfranchisement (McGregor et al., 2015; Mills and McGregor, 2014). Scholars in the alternative education field work hard to ensure the voices and stories of marginalised or disenfranchised young people are heard (MacDonald et al., 2018; McGregor et al., 2017; Mills and McGregor, 2014; Robinson and Smyth, 2016; te Riele, 2009). This scholarship builds on a body of knowledge that recognises that members of marginalised groups can speak for their own standpoint and 'articulate their own ways of knowing and their own knowledges'

(Arnot and Reay, 2007, p. 313). Sharing their own educational experiences provides valuable insights into the shortcomings of Australia's mainstream education system and the accumulation of 'years of educational "failure" and lack of belonging' (McGregor et al., 2015, p. 611). Research shows that the majority of young people who have reengaged in alternative learning environments view their new learning environment more favourably than that of their previous schools (Hayes, 2012; McGregor et al., 2015; Mills and McGregor, 2014; te Riele, 2009; Welters et al., 2018)

In this scholarship, voice has been privileged as a means of assisting marginalised young people to speak about their own educational journey and to share the experiences that resulted in their disenfranchisement and disengagement with education (McGregor et al., 2017). Their stories demonstrate the value of policies and practices in alternative learning environments. They perceive these as a more holistic approach to education, as it recognises that:

> Education and learning cannot be divorced from a young person's life. This approach to education is holistic, in the sense that it recognises that learning happens in real-life situations (in and outside of school) and also that schooling is part of life. As Dave (staff, St Luke's ESU) put it: "we don't deal with them in isolation as a school student. We deal with them as a person".
>
> (te Riele, 2014, p. 63)

While alternative education environments may not 'deliver the educational capital necessary to subvert dominant relations of privilege and oppression, they do provide some indicators of the ways in which socially just schooling might be achieved' (McGregor et al., 2017, p. 92). Scholars in this discipline argue that there are important lessons to be learnt from their approach, lessons that would 'ensure that all young people can be "educated" rather than "schooled"' providing "individual agency" for all students rather than "conformity"' (McGregor et al., 2017, p 92). The collective voice of these young people when they 'speak (*their*) truth/s to power' (Said, cited in McGregor et al., 2017, p. 9) is, not surprisingly, compelling. Yet it should be remembered that their voices are not 'independently constructed', but rather they are 'the messages' created by '*particular pedagogic contexts*' (Arnot and Reay, 2007, p. 317) that engage with the power relations in schools and the broader call for school reform. These are subjective voices that cannot be used as the only argument for school reform but should be recognised for the valuable insights they provide into the 'inequalities associated with learning' (Arnot and Reay, 2007, p. 318).

My argument here is not to discount the voices of young people in alternative educational environments but to recognise that, as a collective, their voice may be carrying an undue burden. While they may themselves be advocates for change, the methodological warrant (Yates, 2003) attributed to their collective voice falls short of representing the experiences of students who are passively disengaged in mainstream education but choose to remain.

Expanding the collective voice

The concept of collective voice provides a lens to consider the reading of the collective voices of young people in Australia's school reform agenda. The collective voice of young people who have reengaged with education in alternative education environments is making a valuable contribution to the call to reimagine schooling in Australia. Offered up as their own knowledge, the experiences of these young people are shared as evidence of the shortcomings of Australia's mainstream education system, and they make a valuable contribution to these debates. Largely absent from these debates, though, is the collective voice of young people who have disengaged from their education but choose, or are compelled, to remain in mainstream education. Their contribution to debates is largely through large-scale survey findings and investigations, research which limits the opportunity for their voices to speak their own knowledge to power. The different contributions of the two groups of young people demonstrates two key complexities of incorporating young people's voice in research: (1) the genuine representation of experience without presenting an authentic truth for all; and (2) the challenges of engaging vulnerable young people or the difficult to access.

The experiences of young people in alternative educational environments represents the extreme end of educational disenfranchisement and disengagement. The educational experiences of these young people share a narrative of difference, inability to conform, social exclusion, of not fitting in, of disadvantage, blame and the weight of failure. Their collective subjectivity has been described as one of educational rejection from the normative expectations of Australia's education systems (Best, 2015). Collectively, they present a very compelling story to those in power of an education system that is failing many young people. These are different stories to the grander narrative of economists and policymakers who call for a new education system that will develop young people's capabilities and skills for future employment (Australian Government, Department of Education and Training, 2019). Young people's experiences are valuable and the voices of those who have reengaged in alternative educational environments have much to offer in the debate for school reform. How authentic are they though, in representing the voices of the many young people who are passively disengaged with mainstream education but choose to stay or not to take action.

The collective voices of young people in student voice scholarship are often speaking directly to power and calls to change the dynamic between teachers and students and engage in new adult-youth partnerships (Mitra, 2018). By invoking the concept of collective voice from the human resources and business management disciplines, the argument here is to highlight that the collective voices of young people who are disengaged but remain in mainstream education, or are in the process of disengaging, are underrepresented in calls for school reform. There is a place for survey findings in debates for school reform but missing from the research is the capacity for these young people to speak their own knowledge and share their experiences. These young people are difficult to access as the path to disengagement can be the result of multiple cumulative factors over many years. The challenge is knowing which students are in the stage of passive disengagement and at what stage of their educational journey this begins. These may not be the most vulnerable young people in debates for school reform, but their experience is valuable. Without their voices, the collective voice of young people contributing to calls for school reform are not genuinely representative of the full range of disengaged users.

The multivoiced approach of collective voice is designed to provide an opportunity for all users to contribute to discussions and suggestions for change and innovation. In making these contributions, the aim is that users will be more engaged in improved business performance and avoid the dissatisfaction of being asked to undertake change they have not been a party to. The complexities of interpreting the views of all users in the school reform debates omits the collective experiences of a large group of young people. The absence of the collective voice of young people who have disengaged from education but remain in mainstream schools is not an intentional omission but rather one that reflects the complexities of researching with children and young people. There is also a space here to argue that young people are both the users and the beneficiaries of school reform. While the beneficiaries of school reform in the present are employers, policymakers and the economy, young people are the ultimate beneficiaries as they will become the employers, policymakers and economy of the future. Recognising young people while in their school years as the beneficiaries of school reform challenges the concept of collective voice as it stands but warrants consideration in future research.

The challenge for researchers at this stage is how to access young people who are in the process of disengagement, and to know at what stage they might be able to tell their story and contribute to the school reform debates. Ensuring their voices are heard is vital, though, if we consider that 40% of the 3.8 million Australian students enrolled in our schools may be unproductive at any time and over 50% of these, 760,000 students, are at risk of being disengaged.

Conclusion: sharing the load

The reasons that young people disengage with education in mainstream schools are complex, and the pathway to disengagement is often gradual and influenced by multiple factors. Understanding the reasons young people disengage with their education is significant, though, as staying engaged with education is considered to be a critical factor in successful work opportunities, financial independence, health and wellbeing, relationships and social engagement with families and communities. The need to develop better understandings of why, and how, young people disengage with education is evident.

In this chapter I have highlighted the undue burden of methodological warrant on the collective voice of some young people in the call for school reform and to reimagine what schooling might look like for young Australians. The article demonstrates how the collective voice of young people who have reengaged with education in alternative early learning environments has been used to convey the experience of disengagement in Australian schools. While the collective experience of these young people is valuable in the school reform debates, their collective voices speak to the extreme ends of educational disenfranchisement and disengagement, where young people have left the mainstream system and, for some, believe that education is not for, or about, them (MacDonald et al., 2018). Alternative learning environments are valuable learning spaces, but most young people do not consider alternative learning environments until they are forced to do so (MacDonald, Johnson and Bottrell, forthcoming). The collective voice of these young people is valuable and relevant in these debates. The purpose of this chapter is to question their capacity to truly represent the collective voices of young people who are part of the 40% of unproductive or passively disengaged who remain in mainstream schools or the 760,000 who have disengaged but, for often complex reasons, remain in the system (Angus et al., 2010; Goss et al., 2017). Ensuring their collective voice is heard in the call for education reform highlights one of the greatest challenges of researching with young people, accessing the voices of groups who are less accessible because they haven't yet demonstrated the indicators that would flag them as research participants.

While statistical data from large scale surveys provides some evidence of the numbers of young people who are unproductive, passively disengaged or disengaged and still within mainstream education, they lack the poignancy and rich narrative of personal experience that has so successfully been adopted by alternative learning scholarship. Without their voices the collective voice of young people in calls for school reform cannot genuinely represent the full range of users.

The challenge is, of course, how to access these students who may not even recognise their lack of interest in school as being a form of disengagement or have not yet been identified by schools as being unproductive or in the process of disengagement. Overcoming the complexities of accessing these young people, and ensuring their collective voices are heard in school reform debates, is essential if we are to truly understand the intricate, multiple and complex reasons for student disengagement.

Acknowledgement

I would like to acknowledge Dr Dorothy Bottrell for her insightful and constructive comments on an earlier draft of this chapter. I would also like to thank the editors for their valuable suggestions and advice.

References

AITSL. (2016) 'Engagement in Australian Schools', *Australian Institute for Teaching and School Leadership*, Discussion Paper. Available at: https://pedagogysitesyuoe.word press.com/2016/08/22/engagement-in-australian-schools-a-paper-prepared-by-the-aus tralian-institute-for-teaching-and-school-leadership/.

Aldridge, J., Fraser, B., Fozdar, F., Ala'I, K., Earnest, J. and Afari, E. (2016) '"Students" Perceptions of School Climate as Determinants of Wellbeing, Resilience and Identity', *Improving Schools*, 19(1), 5–26.

Angus, M., McDonald, T., Ormond, C., Rybarcyk, R., Taylor, A. and Winterton, A. (2010) 'The Pipeline Project: Trajectories of Classroom Behaviour and Academic Progress: A Study of Engagement', *Edith Cowan University, Perth*. Available at: www.bass.edu.au/files/5413/9925/8294/Pipeline_Report_Dec_2009.pdf.

Arnot, M. and Reay, D. (2007) 'A Sociology of Pedagogic Voice: Power, Inequality and Pupil Consultation', *Discourse: Studies in the Cultural Politics of Education*, 28(3), 311–325.

Australian Bureau of Statistics. (2017) 'The Schools Australia'. Available at: www.abs.gov.au/ausstats/abs@.nsf/mf/4221.0.

Australian Government, Department of Education and Training (DET). (2019) 'A Student Focused National Career Education Strategy: Ready for a World Yet to be Imagined'. Available at: www.schooltowork.education.gov.au.

Best, M. (2015) 'Wellbeing in Alternative Education', in F. McCallum and D. Price (eds.), *Nurturing Wellbeing Development in Education: From Little Things, Big Things Grow* (Abingdon, Oxon: Taylor and Francis), 72–87.

Bourke, R. and MacDonald, J. (2018) 'Creating a Space for Student Voice in an Educational Evaluation', *International Journal of Research and Method in Education*, 41(2), 156–168.

Fredricks, J., Blumenfeld, P. and Paris, A. (2004) 'School Engagement: Potential of the Concept, State of the Evidence', *Review of Educational Research*, 74(1), 59–109.

Furlong, A. (ed.). (2015) *Routledge Handbook of Youth and Young Adulthood*, 2nd ed. (Abingdon, Oxon and New York: Routledge).

Galton, M., Hargreaves, L., Comber, C., Wall, D. and Pell, A. (1999) *Inside the Primary Classroom: 20 Years On* (London and New York: Routledge).

Goss, P., Sonnemann, J. and Griffiths, K. (2017) 'Engaging Students: Creating Classrooms that Improve Learning', *Report for Grattan Institute*. Available at: https://grattan.edu.au/report/engaging-students-creating-classrooms-that-improve-learning/.

Hayes, D. (2012) 'Re-Engaging Marginalised Young People in Learning: The Contribution of Informal Learning and Community Based Collaborations', *Journal of Education Policy*, 27(5), 641–653.

Hennala, L. and Melkas, H. (2016) 'Understanding Users' Collective Voice in Public Service Innovation', *Knowledge and Process Management*, 23(1), 62–72. doi:10.1002/kpm.1498.

Lamb, S. and Huo, S. (2017) 'Counting the Costs of Lost Opportunity in Australian Education', *Mitchell Institute Report No. 02/2017* (Melbourne: Mitchell Institute). Available at: www.mitchellinstitute.org.au.

Lewthwaite, B., Wilson, K., Wallace, V., McGinty, S. and Swain, L. (2017) 'Challenging Normative Assumptions Regarding Disengaged Youth: A Phenomenological Perspective', *International Journal Qualitative Studies in Education*, 30(4), 388–405. doi:10.1080/09518398.2016.1252867.

MacDonald, F., Bottrell, D. and Johnson, B. (2018) 'Socially Transformative Wellbeing Practices in Flexible Learning Environments: Invoking an Education of Hope', *Health Education Journal*, 78(4), 377–387. doi:10.1177/0017896918777005.

MacDonald, F., Johnson, B. and Bottrell, D. (forthcoming) 'Beyond Me-ism: Teamwork, Team Building and Cooperation in Flexible Learning Environments', in B. Shelley, K.

te Riele and N. Brown (eds.), *Harnessing the Transformative Power of Education* (Rotterdam: Brill Publishing).

Mayes, E. and Groundwater-Smith, S. (2013) 'Performing Alternative Positions: Student Voice, Reflection and Reform', in V. Grion and A. Cook-Sather (eds.), *Joining the Movement: Bringing Student Voice to Educational Theory and Practice in Italy* (Milano, Italy: Guerini).

Mazzei, L. and Jackson, A. (2009) 'Introduction: The Limit of Voice', in A. Jackson and L. Mazzei (eds.), *Voice in Qualitative Inquiry: Challenging Conventional, Interpretive, and Critical Conceptions in Qualitative Research* (Abingdon, Oxon and New York: Routledge).

McGregor, G., Mills, M., te Riele, K., Baroutsis, A. and Hayes, D. (2017) *Re-Imagining Schooling for Education: Socially Just Alternatives* (London: Palgrave MacMillan).

McGregor, G., Mills, M., te Riele, K. and Hayes, D. (2015) 'Excluded From School: Getting a Second Chance at a "Meaningful" Education', *International Journal of Inclusive Education*, 19(6), 608–625. doi:10.1080/13603116.2014.961684.

McLeod, J. and Yates, L. (2006) *Making Modern Lives: Subjectivity, Schooling, and Social Change* (Albany: State University of New York Press).

Mills, M. and McGregor, G. (2014) *Re-Engaging Young People in Education: Learning From Alternative Schools* (Abingdon, Oxon and New York: Routledge).

Mitra, D. (2018) 'Student Voice in Secondary Schools: The Possibility for Deeper Change', *Journal of Educational Administration*, 56(5), 473–487. doi:10.1108/JEA-01-2018-0007

Mowbray, P., Wilkinson, A. and Tse, H. (2015) 'An Integrative Review of Employee Voice: Identifying a Common Conceptualization and Research Agenda', *International Journal of Management Reviews*, 17, 382–400.

NSW Centre for Education Statistics and Evaluation. (2015) 'Student Engagement and Wellbeing in NSW Initial Results From a Pilot of the Tell Them From Me Student Feedback Survey', *Department of Education and Communities, Sydney*. Available at: www.cese.nsw.gov.au/images/stories/PDF/LearningCurve7_TTFM_May2015.pdf.

Quinn, S. and Owen, S. (2016) 'Digging Deeper: Understanding the Power of "Student Voice"', *Australian Journal of Education 2016*, 60(1), 60–72. doi:10.1177/0004944115626402.

Robinson, J. and Smyth, J. (2016) '"Sent out" and *Stepping Back In*: Stories From Young People "Placed at Risk"', *Ethnography and Education*, 11(2), 222–236. doi:10.1080/17457823.2015.1040430

Smyth, J. (2006) '"When Students Have Power": Student Engagement, Student Voice, and the Possibilities for School Reform Around "Dropping Out" of School', *International Journal of Leadership in Education*, 9(4), 285–298. doi:10.1080/13603120600894232

St Pierre, E. (2009) 'Afterword Decentering Voice in Qualitative Inquiry', in A. Jackson and L. Mazzei (eds.), *Voice in Qualitative Inquiry: Challenging Conventional, Interpretive, and Critical Conceptions in Qualitative Research* (Abingdon, Oxon and New York: Routledge).

Sullivan, A.M., Johnson, B., Owens, L. and Conway, R. (2014) 'Punish Them or Engage Them?: Teachers' Views of Unproductive Student Behaviours in the Classroom', *Australian Journal of Teacher Education*, 39(6), 43–56.

Tarabini, A., Jacovkis, J. and Montes, A. (2018) 'Factors in Educational Exclusion: Including the Voice of the Youth', *Journal of Youth Studies*, 21(6), 836–851. doi:10.1080/13676261.2017.1420765

te Riele, K. (2009) 'Pedagogy of Hope', in K. te Riele (ed.), *Making Schools Different Alternative Approaches to Educating Young People* (London: Sage), 65–73.

te Riele, K. (2014) *Putting the Jigsaw Together: Flexible Learning Programs in Australia Final Report* (Melbourne: The Victoria Institute for Education, Diversity and Lifelong Learning).

Welters, R., Lewthwaite, B., Thomas, J. and Wilson, K. (2018) 'Re-Engaged Students' Perceptions of Mainstream and Flexible Learning Environments: A "Semi-Quantitative" Approach', *International Journal of Inclusive Education*, published online 8 March 2018. doi:10.1080/13603116.2018.1447613

Yates, L. (2003) 'Interpretive Claims and Methodological Warrant in Small-Number Qualitative, Longitudinal Research', *International Journal of Social Research Methodology*, 6(3), 223–232. doi:10.1080/1364557032000091824

Chapter 12

Critically examining participation, power, ethics and the co-construction of knowledge in a community-based photovoice research project with LGBTQ former foster youth

Moshoula Capous-Desyllas, Sarah Mountz and Althea Pestine-Stevens

Valuing voice, sharing power and co-constructing knowledge

Photovoice methodology is a community-based, participatory research approach that incorporates the arts by providing individuals with cameras to photo-document their lived experiences (Wang and Burris, 1997). By giving cameras to LGBTQ-identified foster youth, photovoice has the potential for increasing youth participation and visually highlighting the voices of LGBTQ former foster youth who may have been unable or reluctant to tell their stories. The five key tenants of photovoice method include: (1) the visual image is a site of learning that has the capability of strongly influencing people's wellbeing; (2) pictures can influence policy; (3) community people should participate in creating and defining images that shape their social and political wellbeing; (4) the process requires that influential community advocates serve as an audience for community people's perspectives; and (5) the process places an emphasis on individual and community voice and action (Wang, 1999). Through this methodology, participants obtain the power to represent their lived experiences through photography. These participant-generated images are then shared within the community beyond academia in the form of art exhibits in order to promote awareness and social change.

Photovoice can be a particularly empowering research method to use with LGBTQ-identified former foster youth because of the power disparities they face, which may make them unwilling to share in more traditional research practices and because the child welfare system does an inadequate job of cultivating spaces for their voices to be heard. Giving marginalised individuals cameras to represent themselves has the potential to shift the power dynamics. Specifically, photovoice has the potential to empower LGBTQ former foster youth through the process of sharing power in the research process through visual self-representation. According to Delgado (2015), youth express forms of empowerment that can be understood in relation to three multilayered aspects of their lives: personal, relational and strategic. This is especially important for LGBTQ youth who are systems-involved, often experiencing marginalisation and stigma related to the intersections of their foster care status and their sexual orientation or gender identity. Arts-based methods acknowledge and value the contributions of LGBTQ former foster youth within the research process and provide a deeper, more meaningful understanding of the complex realities of their lives (Capous-Desyllas, 2014). This can serve to shift the power dynamics and promote empowerment of LGBTQ former foster youth through increasing their participation in the research process.

Introducing our project

Although they have long been a hidden population within the child welfare system, recent research conducted by the Williams Institute confirmed that LGBTQ youth are overrepresented within the child welfare system (Wilson, Cooper, Kastanis and Nezhad, 2014). Specifically, this research found that in Los Angeles County, 19% of youth in the foster care system identify as LGBTQ and the vast majority are also youth of colour (Wilson et al., 2014). This research built upon previous findings by the Williams Institute regarding the experiences of LGBTQ youth in the foster care system, which has indicated that while LGBTQ youth are overrepresented in the foster care system; they are amongst the most poorly treated youth within in it and have a higher percentage of poor outcomes after care. The Williams Institute research study was groundbreaking in that it provided evidence of a long-suspected overrepresentation of LGBTQ youth within child welfare systems at a time when jurisdictions were not collecting this data (most still do not). However, research with child welfare involving young people has overwhelmingly not tended to be participatory nor has it centreed the voices of the young people themselves. As a research team that values the voices of young people and their ability to self-represent their lived experiences and perspectives, we felt that it was critical to engage in research *with* them, not *on* them. Our goal was to place the power of representation in the hands of the LGBTQ former foster youth themselves and co-construct knowledge about their needs, strengths and sources of resilience.

A total of 25 LGBTQ-identified former foster youth living in Los Angeles (hereafter referred to as LA), California, participated in an in-depth interview lasting between one to three hours. These youth, between the ages of 18–26 years old, shared their experiences related to various aspects of their lives (i.e., family history, foster care placements and transitioning out of care, educational experiences, mental health, substance abuse, LGBTQ identity and coming out, romantic and sexual relationships, resilience, mentoring and systemic change). Of these youth, 18 also participated in the photovoice portion of the project. They were given digital cameras and asked to take photographs of their lived experiences before, during and after foster care, keeping in mind the various aspects of their life discussed in their in-depth interview. The participants engaged in a second interview to discuss the meaning behind their photos. They were also invited to attend a group dialogue session to share their images with one another and to plan for a travelling community art exhibit. The section that follows describes the multilayered and complex ethical issues that we encountered in our engagement with the LGBTQ former foster youth within the context of our research project. While we present our experiences in four phases, these phases are not distinct and exclusive, but rather they are interrelated, as we grappled with issues of power, voice, participation and ethics throughout our study.

Unpacking our ethical dilemmas

Phase 1: preparing for institutional ethics approval

Working with institutional review boards (IRBs) can be an ethical challenge to conducting community-based, participatory research (CBPR) (Mikesell, Bromley and Khodyakov, 2013). One of the challenges that researchers often face is that all research projects must receive ethics approval before coming research (Mikesell et al., 2013). This means that projects such as this one must make use of instruments that more often than not need to be amended in the field. This directly contradicts the nature of IRBs, who typically require researchers have a rigid methodology prior to entering the field. Not surprisingly, this was our experience, and the research instrument which we had initially included for approval required amendment based on the feedback we received from our Community Advisory Board members constituted our CBPR methodology.

CBPR is dynamic and often requires continual assessment and ongoing adjustments to research protocols. However, many IRBs are not adequately equipped to 'address the needs of community-engaged researchers' (Mikesell et al., 2013, p. 10); instead, they operate largely within a biomedical framework (Flicker, Savan, McGrath, Kolenda and Mildenberger, 2007). Ethical issues related to human subjects in arts-based research include 'boundaries, recruitment and consent to participate, power of shaping the nature of representation, potential for harm, confidentiality, and release of materials' (Delgado, 2015, p. 148). The Belmont Report, which informs such ethical guidelines, is insufficient to guide arts-based research because it does not consider how to engage communities, or how to provide guidelines for the researcher-participant relationship (Delgado, 2015). Given our research project's goal to share the photographs taken by the LGBTQ foster youth with the community and the general public in the form of a travelling art exhibit and an interactive website, we were advised to omit all discussions of the community art-exhibit in the IRB application. One of the reasons we were advised to omit this was because art pieces, such as photographs, can elicit potential retraumatisation (Delgado, 2015). In addition, the audience might not interpret the photos the way they were intended, which can be disaffirming to the artist rather than empowering. However, arts-based research does have the capacity to provide an outlet to share the pain that participants may not have felt able to share previously (Delgado, 2015). In this context, facilitators should be aware of the potential for these reactions and should be knowledgeable in how to normalise these emotional responses and follow up with participants if and when these reactions do happen.

In order to ensure that we captured any evidence of potential trauma throughout our community-based art exhibits, we provided a journal and a graffiti board for audience members to share their thoughts and emotions about the exhibit. These two spaces were created as a platform of self-expression and processing deep emotions and responses that may have been triggered by the images and captions. The second gallery show was held at the university in collaboration with the Resilient Scholars, a campus-based program for current and former foster youth. Anticipating that this group would have a highly personal relationship and response to the exhibit, we arranged for a private tour of the exhibit prior to its opening to the general public. Afterwards, we engaged in a facilitated dialogue with them. The facilitated dialogue session was led by two research team members, one of whom is a licensed clinical social worker, with experience in working with systems-involved youth and trauma.

Phase 2: engaging with the community advisory board

Community advisory boards (CABs) can fill in some of the gaps where IRBs fail to address all of the ethical concerns of a CBPR project (Delgado, 2015). Utilising a CAB can improve the translational aspect of CBPR, ensuring that the findings will help the communities, not only the researchers (Delgado, 2015). CABs can also help with recruitment and increase the legitimacy of the research in the community (Delgado, 2015). To proactively address any potential IRB concerns and to promote transparency, a formal written agreement of the roles and processes of the CAB should be established (Delgado, 2015).

For this study, we convened a CAB composed of LGBTQ identified former foster youth and practitioners who work directly with LGBTQ identified current and former foster youth under the auspices of the local LGBT Center. This participatory method had been successfully used by one of the researchers in previous research with systems-involved LGBTQ youth (Mountz, 2016). The aim, in this study, was to engage stakeholders in the planning process of the research to facilitate community investment in the research and to ensure that the substantive areas covered by the research, the recruitment methods, the instruments used and the wording of the instruments were all responsive, sensitive and accountable to the community with whom we were engaging (Pinto, Spector and Valera, 2011). The CAB met approximately once a month during the planning stages of the research and every other month once the research was underway. After initiating the research, the CAB was additionally helpful regarding the recruitment of participants, navigating ethical issues that arose in the course of data collection and planning gallery shows featuring the photovoice photos in collaboration with the participants and other systems-involved LGBTQ young people in the community. The CAB initially met at the university where the researchers were either faculty members or students, but a group decision was eventually made to move the meetings to the LGBT Center, which was more centrally located and accessible for most of the CAB members. All CAB members were given a $100 stipend to cover the costs of travel to the meetings, and dinner was provided at each meeting.

In this study, and in the researchers' other experiences with use of CAB in research, the level of participation of CAB members is often mediated by issues of power, privilege and oppression. The closer that the CAB members' identities are to those of the research participants, the more likely that the material conditions of life and struggles associated with marginality interfere with participants' ability to participate. The result, of course, is disparate representation of voice and perspective between currently/previously systems involved young people and the providers who work with them. It is not surprising that this occurs, given our understanding of the ways in which power plays out in groups, and steps that were actively taken to mitigate it (such as facilitating meetings in a way that ensured CAB members held the floor for equal amount of time, offering transportation and so on).

Wagaman (2015) has written about the ways that interlocking systems of oppression played out in group dynamics within a participatory action research project with LGBTQ youth looking at intracommunity bigotry. Within this study, we also observed the ways in which differential access to power and privilege influenced levels of participation within the study. We noticed this especially around gender identity, so that participants and nonparticipant researchers who identified as transgender and nonbinary frequently had lower levels of participation in different phases of the study. We suspect that this phenomenon was interwoven with some participants' housing instability and the daily struggle of survival. One way in which this played out was that one of our CAB members had an extremely difficult time sustaining participation, and they happened to be the member with the most marginalised social status. They had very recently transitioned from foster care, had unstable housing and identified as a transgender young person (it should be noted that while one of the members of the research team identified as nonbinary, this CAB member was the only other transgender or nonbinary young person attending CAB meetings).

This CAB member, whom we will call Derek, identified that transportation would be an issue early on. Like many emancipated foster youth in LA County, after transitioning from care, Derek moved to the Antelope Valley, in the northern most part of LA County, where rent is significantly cheaper. Getting around using public transportation is a struggle even in the heart of LA, but it is doubly cumbersome coming from more remote parts of the county like the Antelope Valley. Derek did not own a car, and early on we made the decision as a research team that we would take turns driving Derek to and from the meetings, approximately an hour each way.

Derek attended the first meeting and was an enthusiastic participant, lending lots of terrific insight and feedback, even helping to name the study. Sadly, this was the only meeting Derek was able to attend in person. The next time we had a CAB meeting, Derek was unresponsive to emails and his phone had been shut off, so we were unable to coordinate transportation to the CAB meeting. Several weeks later, he contacted me and explained that he had hit a 'rough spot' but was still very interested in participating in the group. The following meeting time did not work for him (we set meeting times via Doodle poll based on group members' collective availability), but we deeply wanted to include his perspective, so we arranged to have a conference call with Derek and the research team at an alternative time, to go over the agenda items with Derek. However, Derek was unreachable when the scheduled meeting time arrived. He again disappeared for several weeks and then contacted us to say that he was still very interested in participating and asking if his stipend for participation could be sent to him, which we arranged.

This pattern persisted for much of the study. Eventually, Derek disclosed that he had been in residential substance abuse treatment for portions of this period of time, and that this accounted for his disappearances. While we did not gain any further insight into Derek's situation, we continued to include Derek in all CAB related emails, sending him the notes from each meeting and inviting him to the gallery shows. However, sadly, we never saw Derek in person again; we only knew of his life and wellbeing through social media, where he had initiated contact with us. This experience urged us to consider if our offer of $100 was too generous and thus an undue inducement to participate in a CAB, particularly those who were struggling financially.

Phase 3: recruiting and interacting with the participants

Participatory research methods involve immersion and physical time spent in the community. While the benefits of the sort of intimate contact this affords – with research participants and with the greater community – are many, this intimacy and immersion can also carry certain risks for participants and nonparticipant researchers alike. Moore and Adams (2007) have described the ways in which issues of safety can arise in the participatory research process and delineate precautionary measures that research teams might take to mitigate the possibility of harm. They include: IRB attention to issues of safety within the protocol, researcher-initiated risk assessments, the development of action plans for dangerous situations, making counselling available, debriefing with the research team and/or IRB, appointing an emergency contact who maintains awareness of researchers' whereabouts when in the field and designating a safety word to trigger a prearranged response. While offering some useful strategies, it should be noted that Moore and Adams primarily consider nonparticipant researcher safety in these scenarios and suggestions. But what about safety concerns for participant researchers, who are often most vulnerable by virtue of various aspects of their social identities and by virtue of the vulnerability that occurs when one puts some of the most sensitives experiences of their lives on display within the context of a research study?

As a research team, and in collaboration with our CAB, we attempted to brainstorm and troubleshoot potential safety concerns that might arise in advance of initiating the research. However, a few unanticipated safety concerns did arise in the course of carrying out the research. One of the more shocking incidents happened as we were collecting data in the main branch of the LA public library in downtown LA. Given that LA is vast and can be hard to navigate, particularly when one does not have a personal automobile, we endeavoured to meet participants at a location that was near to or easily accessible for them. We frequently suggested public libraries as meeting spaces for interviews when other locations were not identifiable. They are free to spend time there and often have private rooms or will arrange private spaces for meetings.

However, not every library has a private meeting room, as one participant and her interviewer discovered upon meeting for the first time at the main branch of the LA public library. After discussing alternatives, the participant and interviewer decided to proceed with the interview at a table in a common room with relatively few people in it. They had delved pretty deep into the interview, and the participant was in the middle of describing her experience of accessing governmental benefits after aging out of foster care, when her face dropped and she said 'he showed me his penis'. It took the interviewer a minute to figure out what was happening, as she tried to draw a connection between the experience the participant was narrating, her sudden upset and the words she just uttered. When the interviewer turned to look behind her she found an older gentleman tucking himself back into his pants with a sheepish smirk on his face. The participant was understandably quite shaken and upset. She had just spent the better portion of an hour talking to the interviewer about some of the most vulnerable experiences of her life, including being bullied at school and rejected by her kinship caregivers because of her attraction to other women, placing her first child for adoption and losing her father to an AIDS related illness. The interview was immediately terminated and the participant was asked if she wanted to report what had just happened to the library staff. She did, and so the following 45 minutes were spent tracking someone down and making a report. Before parting, the participant was asked if she wanted to either discontinue the interview altogether or continue it on another day, but she wanted to complete it then. The interviewer and participant moved to a café in the library that was quite noisy and attempted to pick up where they had left off. The next day, the interviewer checked on the participant's welfare via text message and suggested she select the next place for the follow up interview. She chose a bench next to a playground in a park near her home in South LA. She was incredibly anxious about her photos for the photovoice portion of the study, claiming she was not sure if she had captured the right things, and that she was not a good photographer, but we as a team wondered how much of her anxiety stemmed from what had happened back at the library.

This experience raises questions about what constitutes a 'safe space' in which to conduct an intimate qualitative interview that covers topics including past experiences that may be distressing to recall, and that places the person narrating them in a position of considerable vulnerability.

Issues of interpersonal boundary transgressions can be delicate to negotiate within the context of the researcher-participant relationship. Transgressions of these boundaries can, at times, require the need to (re)stablish unequal power relations between participant and interviewer and at times may mean the need to terminate a participant's involvement. The following case, involving sexual advances by a bisexual, cisgender male participant, is one such example. The interviewer noted that throughout the entire interview process, the participant's testimonies of being in foster care were guarded, inconsistent and scattered, and a number of inappropriate comments and sexual advances were made by the participant. This evoked within the interviewer feelings of discomfort and unease. In response to his advances, the interviewer tried to redirect the focus of the interview and reestablish participant-researcher boundaries between them. In the next few hours after the interview, he sent a series of elicit text messages, and by the end of the evening he sent the interviewer two photographs of his penis. After managing the shock of these sexual images and words, the team processed the events and decided to discontinue his participation in the study because of the boundary violation. Like us, Pascoe (2007) discusses her fieldwork with adolescent boys and her own experiences of receiving unwanted sexual advances by community members. In order to manage these interactions, she kept professional boundaries without sacrificing rapport or challenging the participants' sexist practices in order to maintain her sense of physical safety. Maintaining professional boundaries includes the reiteration of the distinct roles of the researcher and participant, as well as the purpose of the interview and the overall research project.

A complexity which must be acknowledged, arising from the previous example, is that while a transgression may occur in the context of an interview, knowledge of this may need to be taken outside this context. In the case of the aforementioned young man, there was a concern that reporting this youth's inappropriate behaviour to the LGBTQ youth center might prohibit him from using their services again. However, upon disclosure of this incident to his case manager (who was also a part of our CAB), it was decided that, while he would be warned about the inappropriateness of his behaviour, he would continue to be allowed access to social services at the centre.

The issue of appropriate compensation for time and participation in the research study was an ethical issue that arose with the participants. There were some youth who shared prior to commencement of research that they needed the money and would participate in an interview but not in the group dialogue session or the community-based art exhibit. Some youth were in such dire economic need that they asked for the reimbursements in advance, prior to completing the photovoice portion of the project in order to pay for food. In order to maintain the participant researcher relationship and build trust, we often provided the most marginalised youth with the monetary reimbursement prior to their completion of the photovoice portion of the project. In short, our experiences ties to a broader research concern that such rewards for participation may encourage participation out of need rather than real interest (Marshall et al., 2012).

A further ethical issue that arose for us was that of confidentiality and how much to reveal about our own personal biographies. Although no member of our nonparticipant research team held the precise identity of being an LGBTQ identified former foster youth, many of us held various commonalities with our participant-researchers insofar as our race and ethnicity, class, sexual orientation, gender identity and/or citizenship were concerned. Moreover, some nonparticipant research team members had a history of personal or family child welfare involvement and others had been practitioners working closely with this community or had partners who were. In a community so small and specific, such as the one with whom we were conducting research, any points of commonality are intensified, and this arose in a few different ways over the course of the study. In one case, one of our participants was part of the same social circle and community organising group as one of our nonparticipant researchers. In another case, a nonparticipant researcher's partner worked for a program at the LGBTQ Centre where one of our participant researchers was interning. Generally, as a research team, we did a good job of navigating these sensitive boundaries, acknowledging dual relationships with each other and with participant-researchers, where appropriate, and debriefing where necessary. But the nature of our research and our relationship(s) to it demanded that we build an extra level of reflexivity into our group process. Social science researchers in training are not routinely taught these practices, instead, training tends to centre on quantitative and/or nonparticipatory methods of collecting data and an emphasis on researcher objectivity.

Phase 4: engaging with the community through art

As previously mentioned, the production and display of images can elicit ethical concerns. Some of these concerns include legal complications with confidentiality and anonymity, the display of images, the safety and wellbeing of the participants and mitigating the potential that participants will expose themselves to activities that elicit legal recourse (Gubrium, Hill and Flicker, 2014). For example, many of the participants wanted to use their real names rather than their chosen pseudonyms for the community-based art exhibit. Problematically, this desire meant that while we wanted to honour confidentiality we did not want to be paternalistic. Marshall et al. (2012) point out that some youth may want to use their real names and show their face in projects in order to combat stigmatisation and increase visibility of their community or issue. For example, one participant took a series of self-portraits to represent his intersecting identities (his sexual orientation and struggles as a foster youth). Rather than taking power away from the participants, we chose to place the power of self-representation in their hands. Approximately half of the participant-researchers chose to use their real names rather than their pseudonyms and, many of our participant-researchers brought friends, family members or program staff to the exhibit and were proud of their work.

In terms of legal implications, the following example describes the complexities which can arise from this. One participant included in his series of images, a photograph which included the image of marijuana (a substance not yet legalised in California at this stage). Our concern was that his image of an illegal substance, juxtaposed next to the portraits of his face, would place this youth in a vulnerable position with regard to the law. We struggled with wanting to protect this young person while empowering him to have self-determination and make an informed decision about how he wanted to represent himself to the public. After discussing the possible repercussions of presenting this photograph and its corresponding caption with the participant-researcher, he decided to include this image in the community-based art exhibits.

The previous examples show how photovoice as a methodology can be empowering to marginalised youth. It creates an opportunity for dignity: those being researched are the ones who decide what is photographed and how it is displayed, giving them power over the outcomes of the study (Delgado, 2015). They also have dignity in the process: participants decide how to capture the images and the impressions that the images will give (Delgado, 2015). This also helps to combat adultism by giving them decision-making roles and valuing their perceptions (Delgado, 2015).

We faced one final ethical dilemma in respect to the participant researcher's images; images that featured a reality that perhaps no longer existed. The project included an interactive website displaying the photographs taken by the young people, which would remain on display for a period of one year after the community art exhibit. Yet, the images on display captured one moment in time. What was our ethical responsibility with regard to removing images, which no longer represented a participant-researcher's reality? For example, those who took self-portraits with their romantic partners but were no longer with them. In such instances, Gubrium and colleagues (2014) recommend the negotiation of ongoing consent to release photographs. Special considerations should be made for sharing the research data, especially when displaying the images in a community-based art show or sharing them on a website or via social media (Teti, Murray, Johnson and Binson, 2012). Specifically, Delgado (2015) recommends structuring the authorisation as a one-year renewable agreement, in order to acknowledge that the views and circumstances of the participants may change in the future. This would also allow participants to withdraw their work if they so wished after they have seen what the public domain actually looks like. However, while ongoing consent may be best practice, the transient nature of the lives of some of our participants coupled with the various levels of involvement in the project from our participants over time would have made applying ongoing consent incredibly challenging.

Continuing our engagement

We have attempted to demonstrate in this chapter the ways in which we grappled with both anticipated and unanticipated ethical issues that arose in the course of our study. In some cases, we found answers from amongst ourselves, or from other researchers, practitioners and/or cultural workers. At times, questions were generated that we are still seeking to answer. Our understanding of our own research process and of participatory, arts-based and anti-oppressive research processes in general, is that we strive to renegotiate the power differentials inherent in research and conclude that it is extremely difficult, if not impossible, to outrun the stark imbalances of power between academy-based researchers and research participants, even when they are integrated as stakeholders in the research process and engaged as coresearchers.

While we truly believe and were told by participant-researchers that they benefited greatly from their participation, we anticipate that the conditions of their lives have not been deeply transformed through their participation and recognise that we continue to live lives of relative privilege and abundance compared to our participant-researchers. Moreover, our names are listed on academic publications and presentations arising from this research, while many of our participants, and foster youth in general, struggle to gain access to higher education. As a result, we would like to end with a call to continue to find ways to transform the institutions and structures within which research takes places, which ultimately are as complicit in reproducing inequality as they are capable of expanding access.

Acknowledgements

We want to thank the California Humanities grant, the CSUN College of Social and Behavioral Sciences, the University at Albany School of Social Welfare, our Community Advisory Board Members, our graduate student researchers, the various communities who supported our art exhibits and all of the participants who shared their stories and visions for social justice.

References

Capous-Desyllas, M. (2014) 'Using Photovoice With Sex Workers: The Power of Art, Agency and Resistance', *Qualitative Social Work*, 13(4), 477–501.

Delgado, M. (2015) *Urban Youth and Photovoice: Visual Ethnography in Action* (Oxford: Oxford University Press).

Flicker, S., Savan, B., McGrath, M., Kolenda, B. and Mildenberger, M. (2007) '"If You Could Change One Thing . . ." What Community-Based Researchers Wish They Could Have Done Differently', *Community Development Journal*, 43(2), 239–253.

Gubrium, A.C., Hill, A.L. and Flicker, S. (2014) 'A Situated Practice of Ethics for Participatory Visual and Digital Methods in Public Health Research and Practice: A Focus on Digital Storytelling', *American Journal of Public Health*, 104(9), 1606–1614.

Marshall, Z., Nixon, S., Nepveux, D., Vo, T., Wilson, C., Flicker, S., McClelland, A. and Proudfoot, D. (2012) 'Navigating Risks and Professional Roles: Research With Lesbian, Gay, Bisexual, Trans, and Queer Young People With Intellectual Disabilities', *Journal of Empirical Research on Human Research Ethics*, 7(4), 20–33.

Mikesell, L., Bromley, E. and Khodyakov, D. (2013) 'Ethical Community-Engaged Research: A Literature Review', *American Journal of Public Health*, 103(12), 7–14.

Moore, G. and Adams, M. (2007) 'Participatory Action Research and Researcher Safety', in *Participatory Action Research Approaches and Methods* (London: Routledge), 67–74.

Mountz, S. (2016) 'That's the Sound of the Police: State-Sanctioned Violence and Resistance Among LGBT Young People Previously Incarcerated in Girls' Juvenile Justice Facilities', *Affilia*, 31(3), 287–302.

Pascoe, C.J. (2007) 'What If a Guy Hits on You', in *Representing Youth: Methodological Issues in Critical Youth Studies* (New York, NY: New York University Press), 226–247.

Pinto, R.M., Spector, A.Y. and Valera, P.A. (2011) 'Exploring Group Dynamics for Integrating Scientific and Experiential Knowledge in Community Advisory Boards for HIV Research', *AIDS Care*, 23(8), 1006–1013.

Teti, M., Murray, C., Johnson, L. and Binson, D. (2012) 'Photovoice as a Community-based Participatory Research Method Among Women Living With HIV/AIDS: Ethical Opportunities and Challenges', *Journal of Empirical Research on Human Research Ethics*, 7(4), 34–43.

Wagaman, M.A. (2015) 'Changing Ourselves, Changing the World: Assessing the Value of Participatory Action Research as an Empowerment-Based Research and Service Approach With LGBTQ Young People', *Child & Youth Services*, 36(2), 124–149.

Wang, C. (1999). Photovoice: A Participatory Action Research Strategy Applied to Women's Health. *Journal of Women's Health*, 8(2), 185–192.

Wang, C. and Burris, M.A. (1997) 'Photovoice: Concept, Methodology, and Use for Participatory Needs Assessment', *Health Education & Behavior*, 24(3), 369–387. doi:10.1177/109019819702400309

Wilson, B.D., Cooper, K., Kastanis, A. and Nezhad, S. (2014) 'Sexual and Gender Minority Youth in Foster Care: Assessing Disproportionality and Disparities in Los Angeles', *The Williams Institute*.

Chapter 13

Participation, positionality and power

Critical moments in research with service-engaged youth

Signe Ravn

Introduction

In this chapter I discuss practical and ethical challenges and complexities arising in relation to research *participation*, on the part of (potential) research participants as well as the researcher participation, when conducting empirical, qualitative research with young people. Empirically, I draw on the recruitment challenges in the first phases of an ongoing, longitudinal qualitative research project about the everyday lives and imagined futures of young women in Victoria, Australia, who have left school before finishing Year 12 (upper secondary school) or otherwise have had their transitional pathways interrupted. The project is designed as an interview-based project that focuses on the young women's everyday lives and imagined futures as these evolve over time. Through reflection and discussion of specific experiences from this project, this chapter focuses on three particular aspects of research participation with the aim of illustrating the complex dynamics of this.

The research project focuses on young women on the margins of the educational system and/or the labour market, and not those already in more marginalised positions such as in drug treatment or criminal justice programmes. While the boundary between these categories is often fluid, I deliberately focused my recruitment strategy on the former. Hence, to get in touch with potential participants, I decided to go through work/training-focused service providers to have some form of institutional setting in which to meet participants. I made contact and set up collaborations with selected service providers on the fringes of Melbourne and in regional Victoria. After gaining access to these settings I then 'hung out' in the spaces of the service providers – such as offices and communal spaces – to meet the young people there and introduce the project to them. While the research project as such is an interview-based study, I took ethnographic fieldnotes of my observations and interactions with staff and young people during this initial phase of the project, and these fieldnotes form the empirical basis for this chapter.

Targeting service-engaged youth in this way is not without challenges. While the ethical and practical challenges I will touch upon in this chapter are not confined to this population, they are of particular salience here. Scholars have argued that service-engaged youth is an 'over-surveilled' population (Renold, Holland, Ross and Hillman, 2008) and that research easily becomes 'an act of objectification of an already objectified group' (Aaltonen, 2017, p. 331). In particular, in relation to my focus on 'early school-leavers', Vogt argues that this is a group that may already feel stigmatised and targeted (Vogt, 2018) because leaving school early is perceived as problematic given the strong discursive focus on education as the means to success. These issues have practical implications. As Renold and colleagues argue, common interview approaches asking participants to respond to questions such as 'how do you feel about that' or 'what do you think about that' mirror traditional social work (or other kinds of youth work) techniques or the 'social work gaze' (Renold et al., 2008, p. 432). This can easily make the interview situation feel like 'yet another' of those meetings with system representatives scrutinising their lives, and this may facilitate a repetition of the kinds of narratives that are told in such settings, narratives that often are necessary for gaining access to particular services (Farrugia, 2016). A key challenge is to avoid this by making participants interested in participating and also making them agentic subjects rather than passive research objects.

While I have collaborated with a handful of different service providers to recruit the participants in the study, in this chapter I focus on one particular setting where I spent the greatest amount of time. This is a service provider based on the outskirts of Melbourne, Australia, which supports young people at risk of homelessness with a particular focus on supporting their educational engagement. However, the challenges are not confined to this setting. The chapter is structured around three situations from the initial fieldwork. These three situations are chosen as they shed light on particular concerns central to this project (and most likely to many others) and can be seen as what Guillemin and Gillam (2004) term 'ethically important moments'; moments that are 'the difficult, often subtle, and usually unpredictable situations that arise in the practice of doing research' (2004, p. 262). Here, however, I prefer to approach them from a broader perspective, focusing not solely on research ethics – although this is a central part of these – but seeking to relate these ethical issues to broader questions about fostering participation and constructive researcher-researched relationships. Hence, I approach the three situations as 'critical moments' (Thomson et al., 2002). While this is a concept that is usually used in biographical and/or longitudinal research to focus on 'an event described in an interview that either the researcher or the interviewee sees as having important consequences for their lives and identities' (ibid., p. 339), I here use it to refer to events that I see as having important consequences or being of central significance for the research process. The critical moments that I identify in this chapter are thus moments that caused reflection, doubt and hesitation on my part but eventually also fostered deeper insights into the research process. The first critical moment concerns recruitment and participation, the second concerns researcher positionality in the field and the third concerns the management of relations with participants and reflections on how to leave the field again. All names and places are pseudonyms.

Becoming participant: 'I don't feel like talking about myself right now'

> *I am sitting in the communal areas of the [institution] and some of the young people are going to and from the room. I am looking for one young woman, Bibiana, whom the staff has told me might be interested in the project. I met her briefly the other day with some others and gave her one of my recruitment flyers. Back then she sounded vaguely interested, but I'm not sure if she was just being polite. She has not been in touch since then so I am keen to follow up. Bibiana comes in together with two other young women. She often seems to be at the centre of attention. They are busy chatting about something that happened in the shopping centre. I get a chance to talk to Bibiana on her own as the others go outside to smoke a cigarette and I ask her if she has had time to look at the flyer. She says she has been busy and not had time to read it but will read it. I start explaining what the flyer says and say that what I am basically asking is if she is interested in doing an interview where I ask her about her everyday life and her dreams for the future. Bibiana then looks at me and says she is not interested: "I don't feel like talking about myself right now" and she goes outside to the others to smoke. I am the only person left in the room and the disappointment is overwhelming.*
>
> (October 30, 2017)

Bibiana's response, as frustrating as it was for me in the situation, holds significant information about her own current situation as well as broader recruitment challenges. It also emphasises how choosing *not* to participate in research is, as McGarry writes, also 'a means of self-expression' (McGarry, 2016, p. 343). While I can only second-guess as to the reasons for why Bibiana did not want to talk about herself at the time, reflecting on this 'critical moment' is important for understanding the conditions under which participants take part in the project. Farrugia argues that broader social and symbolic hierarchies are unavoidably reflected in the interview/research encounter. In his case, this meant that participating in a study on youth homelessness involved being positioned as 'homeless youth' (Farrugia, 2016). With this in mind, I considered how to frame the current project in a way that would not necessarily position participants in questionable or stigmatised subject positions such as 'early school leavers' or 'people on benefits'; positions that are commonly problematised in public and policy discourse. However, despite presenting the research as about young women's everyday lives and dreams for the future, I cannot avoid the fact that I am recruiting from service providers targeting young people outside education or employment and that potential participants may still assume the research to ask critically into this, expect ready-made plans, etc. This could be what made Bibiana refuse to participate; that she perceived the interview within the service provision setup and did not want to be 'the servile subject' who willingly speaks about her current and future plans.

In light of such reflections it seems fitting to consider the question the other way around: rather than asking why young people (and others) do not want to participate in our research, we should consider what *does* make some people give up their time and participate (see also Ravn, 2012)? What *has* made the 31 women who, to date, have participated in the first wave of interviews decide to do this? Lohmeyer (2018) suggests thinking of the research encounter as consisting of parallel projects, meaning that alongside the researcher's project there is the project, or the motivations, that the participant brings to the encounter. These can take numerous shapes. Farrugia argues that the interview presents an opportunity to show that one is a 'morally worthy person' (2016), while Järvinen (2001, p. 280) uses the term 'moral tales' to refer to such accounts of oneself. This relates back to the point about framing earlier; if participants feel they are often labelled – by the media, by parents, by professionals, etc. – as questionable subjects, this may make them want to speak against such labels. Such accounts were without doubt part of the present study but not the whole story. Others were curious about the research project and wanted to be part of that. And finally, most participants indicated that they participated for altruistic reasons, either simply to help me with my research as a friendly gesture or because they hoped the research would help others in their situation. This is maybe the dominant reason for why people participate in research in their free time (Seymour, 2012) and emphasises the importance of making clear what the purposes of the research are and what the research findings may be used for.

All participants are given a $30 voucher after each interview as a recognition of their time and efforts. While this is a debated practice (see Seymour, 2012 for a detailed discussion of this), I did this to emphasise that I approached them respectfully as busy people who are ultimately doing me a favour as an 'exchange'. The voucher was mentioned in the 'Details' section at the bottom of the flyer and in the plain language statement to participants, but some still seemed surprised when I gave them the voucher, revealing that they might not have read or remembered every section in detail. In general, the voucher did not seem to be the decisive factor for their participation, and none of the participants mentioned the voucher themselves, before or after the interviews. However, given the financial constraints of many participants – few had regular jobs or a secure income and many struggled with finances – the $30 appeared a welcome contribution to their budgets. Therefore, even if the voucher *was* part of their decision to participate, I do not find this problematic as long as they engage with the interview questions – which they all did.

The actual research design can be more or less inviting for potential participants. Although not set up as participatory research – where participants are actively involved in a varying number of steps along a continuum from study design to dissemination of findings (Mannay, 2016) – the study includes a number of creative methods such as emotional maps, life charts and photo voice, which are sometimes described as participatory methods. Despite differences between them, both approaches share the ambition of giving 'voice' to young people and seek to alter the power relation between researcher and researched (Mannay, 2016, see also this book for chapters discussing the notion of 'voice'). However, creative or participatory methods are not a quick fix. McGarry argues that participatory approaches have become the 'new paradigm of youth research' (McGarry, 2016, p. 339) or a new 'orthodoxy' (ibid., p. 340) in research on young people. While these approaches can be valuable, their use is often too unreflected, she argues (McGarry, 2016). The problem rests in claims that participatory methods give 'voice' to the research participants and hence are depicted as producing more 'authentic' and 'true' findings. However, this is too simplistic, especially if applied within an overall constructivist approach to empirical research, where the methods we use inherently shape our findings. In the present study, the motivation for incorporating these methods are different. Instead, I employ these to break away from the 'standard' interview (Bagnoli, 2009) in an attempt to further distinguish the research interviews from interviews with professionals and service providers. Creative methods have also been described as a way of 'making the familiar strange' (Mannay, 2010, 2016), for instance by asking research participants to draw something as familiar and taken for granted as a party (Ravn and Duff, 2015).[1] This can be helpful in research on taken-for-granted aspects of everyday life but also can be a way of breaking away from repetitions of the already well-known narratives that are useful in the service provision setting. The young women who have participated in interviews so far have been keen to take up different tasks, for instance mapping their neighbourhood on a sheet of paper, and the initial impression is that at least for some of them, these aspects of the research are part of the interest in the project.

Positionality and privilege: 'so where are you going?'

Today was my last day here [in the service provider space] before the Xmas holidays, and I wanted to say happy holidays to the people I have come to 'know'. I did not run into all the girls but managed to find a few and also some of the staff and tell them that I will be away until late January. I have been pondering how to approach this as I have come to realise how most of them have not travelled much, if ever, in their lives, and this in sharp contrast to my privileged, academic life where I travel internationally for either conferences or holiday at least once and often twice a year. But I thought it was important to not just 'disappear' for a month, so my strategy was to say I would be 'on leave' rather than telling them that I am travelling. It seemed to work ok – except when I was chatting to Tommy in the kitchen. I asked him what he was doing and he said he would be spending Xmas at [the institution] and that he might go and see an uncle later on. He did not have plans for January either. He then asked into my plans and what I would do while on leave and I felt the awkwardness surround us as I quietly said I was going to New Zealand.

(December 21, 2017)

As part of the relational work involved in ethnographic fieldwork I wanted to make sure I did not just 'disappear' as I was going on annual leave and hence would be taking a longer break from the fieldwork site. The young man in the quote, Tommy, was one of the young men that I had the most interaction with during the fieldwork phase, either chatting or playing basketball together. However, as the quote illustrates, this conversation created an awkward moment for me, as it emphasised the social distance between us when it became clear that I was in a position to travel to other countries while he was barely leaving the institution. While I do not know if Tommy also felt this distance or reflected on my position, it underscored that I entered the field as a white, middle-class woman employed at a university, with all the symbolic messages this position entails and the distance those can create. First of all, I could be seen as someone who represents the educational system and also as an individual who presumably never had 'school fatigue' but pursued education for as long as possible. This is important to have in mind as this may position me (cf. Davies and Harré, 1990; Harré and van Langenhove, 1999) as the 'ideal' (former) student in relation to participants who for the most part have had their transitional pathways through the educational system interrupted, for some involving negative experiences in school and with the school system as such. Second, my university affiliation also indicated a well-paid job with the associated economic privileges such as travelling on holiday; privileges which none of my research participants had. I feared that these differences, which made me not just a clear 'outsider' (Hammersley and Atkinson, 1995) but also put me in a superior position in the social hierarchy in relation to the participants, could be a hindrance for their interest in the project and later for establishing rapport in interviews.

It was important for me to try and downplay these aspects of my identity to not enhance the distance between us and to be able to establish rapport and generally seem relatable and approachable. I did this in different ways. One way concerned my outfit; I deliberately dressed more casually than my usual work clothes (see also Hammersley and Atkinson, 1995). This was my attempt at countering what I assumed potential participants might associate with a 'researcher', i.e., someone formal and boring. Another way concerned interaction and informal chats. Discussions often touched on money and finances; participants having too little money to participate in activities they wanted or considerations about what to buy and not buy when going grocery shopping to make money last. I tried to not present myself as 'carefree' in relation to money and would, for instance, contribute to stories about saving money, such as buying in bulk or waiting for something to come on sale. However, as the excerpt made clear, I could not hide or ignore my privileged position – and doing so would not only be pretentious but also ethically fraught. Rather, the purpose of these efforts was to interact with participants in a respectful way; a way that did not make, for instance, financial struggles seem embarrassing. There is a difference between *acknowledging* one's privilege and *displaying* one's privilege, and I sought to avoid displaying my privilege without pretending that I shared social positions with my participants.

Despite the potential challenges that emanate from differences in social position, the opposite scenario – sharing social positions – is not necessarily better. In their article about 'class matching' in research on social class, Mellor, Ingram,

Abrahams and Beedell (2014) argue against the assumption that a correspondence between the class background of researcher and participant, respectively, automatically creates greater empathy and rapport in the interview situation. Rather, they illustrate how the social background of the researcher often works in unpredictable ways, sometimes productively and other times less so. This was also the case in the present study. Hence, a key part of introducing myself and the study to participants was to frame this as focusing on 'how it is to grow up as a young woman in today's Australia', i.e., implicitly positioning myself as outsider both in terms of origin and generation. The former position, an 'outsider' to Australian society, was easily accepted and became an unforeseen benefit in the research: as a Dane who had only moved to Melbourne two years before commencing fieldwork, I often had to ask clarifying questions about particular aspects of the social and educational systems, acronyms, etc., and I did not know local geographies in much detail. This ignorance and naivety seemingly helped in distancing myself from being a 'system representative' and allowed me to ask 'silly' questions (se also Hammersley and Atkinson, 1995). The latter position, on the other hand, being from a different generation, was sometimes challenged. Some participants would ask 'what do you mean, you are not that old', indicating that things could not have changed much and I should know about this experience. In those situations, being a woman in my thirties gave me some leeway in terms of building rapport through a sense of shared understanding as 'young(-ish) women'. In that sense, my position vis-à-vis the participants was complex, involving both my relative privilege that could create difference and distance as well as shared gender identities (at least with my interview participants, not necessarily all the young people I met, such as Tommy earlier) that could serve to decrease such distances. In that sense, traditional ethnographic roles such as 'insider' or 'outsider' were not as clear-cut, and while I would be perceived as an outsider in most respects, at times I would inhabit more of an insider position, thereby complicating this distinction between such stable roles (see also Merriam et al., 2001).

Managing researcher-researched relationships: 'I bet you did not expect to be doing this with your PhD'

When I arrive to [the institution] Louisa [one of the young people there] is hanging out in the office area and seems bored. It appears that she is waiting for her exam results to be released later in the day. She is also waiting to meet with her mentor later on. Louisa is nervous and checks her phone constantly for the result, but still seems fairly confident that she will do OK. To kill time, she decides to do a bit of gardening in the communal garden beds. After some weeding she needs help filling new potting mix into the beds and asks for my help to do this. Louisa dryly says "I bet you did not expect to be doing this with you PhD". We both laugh out loud and I am short of any pointy remark. Later when we are in the communal room she receives a text message with the result: she has passed one subject and failed another. Her disappointment is visible

and she starts to cry. I don't know what to do with myself apart from saying that I am very sorry. I want to give her a hug but it does not feel appropriate. A staff member comes over and takes over the conversation and I feel superfluous.
(November 3, 3017)

Louisa is one of the participants I met early on in the research, and she quickly said yes to participating in an interview. I would often meet her when doing field work, and she was a 'regular' in the communal areas of the institution. In the first interview it became clear that her social network is quite limited, both in terms of friends and people to 'lean on' if necessary. This, combined with Louisa's great willingness to participate in the research and chat to me when 'hanging out' there, made me slightly cautious, and I had to carefully balance this relation. On the one hand I did not want to give her the impression that I was a new 'support person' or potentially even 'friend' in her life as I felt this might pose a conflict of interest and involve expectations that I could not meet (Bengtsson and Mølholt, 2016). On the other hand, I was aware that the relation between us was based on some form of exchange – participants giving their time and thoughts in interviews and the need for giving something back, apart from answering the questions about myself they would ask me and the voucher as discussed earlier. Hence, on a couple of occasions, my 'field day' turned into more of a one-on-one study session, assisting with school assignments.

My concerns about the perceived nature of the relation between me as researcher and Louisa as participant were momentarily put to rest when encountering the situation described in the field note extract included here. Louisa included me as her 'assistant' in the garden work she was doing, thereby circumventing the power relations implicit in the researcher-researched relation. I interpret her use of sarcasm and explicit mentioning of my PhD degree as her way of showing her awareness of the unequal relation between us, as given by the research context. Critical social research has investigated how humour is not innocent and that humour used by professionals (e.g., social workers) can be counterproductive given the unequal power relations (see, e.g., Andersen, 2015; Mik-Meyer, 2007). However, in this example it is not the 'authority person' (the researcher) who uses humour but the participant. Coser writes about humour that 'Laughter and humour are indeed like an invitation, be it an invitation for dinner, or an invitation to start a conversation: it aims at decreasing social distance' (Coser, 1959, p. 172 in Mik-Meyer, 2007), and humour is said to have 'a disorganizing effect' on power relations and authority (Mik-Meyer, 2007, p. 15). Hence, when Louisa uses humour sarcastically to direct attention to the 'unconventional' situation, she can be seen as both challenging the power relation and attempting to bridge it, decreasing the distance between us. While this works well and makes us both laugh, it is easy to imagine how this might not have been the case if the joke was presented by me.

However, as the end of the previous excerpt demonstrates, the challenges in managing the relationship returned as Louisa received her marks and reacted to these. I wanted to maintain the professional relations between us and not breach personal boundaries, while at the same time feeling sorry for her and wanting to comfort her. Had the staff member not interrupted the situation I might have had to reconsider my approach, for instance, by asking if she wanted a hug or sitting down to talk through the consequences. As Bengtsson and Mølholt write,

> To become part of the lives of young people in vulnerable life situations is a great responsibility. As researchers, we gain valuable knowledge when following young people through time but we also necessarily become involved in the young informants' lives and build up a relationship with them.
>
> (Bengtsson and Mølholt, 2016, p. 13)

While this relationship is a professional one, it may at times require the researcher to simply be a fellow human who shows compassion or support. Balancing this is an ongoing challenge that requires a situated ethical approach, and the situation described here was critical for becoming aware of these challenges.

Discussion: 'reflexivity' and then?

Turner and Almack (2017) have referred to the process of starting up a research project as a matter of 'grinding a complex machine into action' (p. 488), and suggest that this is a matter of making 'wheels within wheels' work together in the recruitment process, each wheel representing a specific, interpersonal relationship (ibid.). Expanding this metaphor beyond recruitment, interpersonal relationships are critical to the entire research endeavour and Turner and Almack indicate, the researcher is as much a wheel in the process; a highly critical wheel in terms of how the research develops.

Participation in research raises a number of challenges, as the three critical moments presented in this chapter illustrate. While the issue of participant participation is often given the most attention, not least during the oftentimes frustrating and difficult process of recruitment, what the researcher brings into their participation is equally central. But on which terms do we – researchers and researched – participate in the research process? In this chapter I discussed how assumptions about and perceptions of the research(er) play into decisions about participating in the research or not and into researcher-researched interactions in the field. I also emphasised the need for acknowledging and reflecting on the social positions we each inhabit and how these affect the research process as well as the data (not to mention the data that *is* the research process, (cf. Bengtsson, 2014). However, while such reflexivity seems to be constantly called for, engaging in this is not straightforward. Indeed, Gillian Rose has argued that such a transparency and self-knowledge is impossible: 'there is no clear landscape of social positions to be charted by an all-seeing analyst; neither is there a conscious agent, whether researcher or researched, simply waiting to be reflected in a research process' (Rose, 1997, p. 316). Instead, drawing on performative and feminist identity theorists such as Judith Butler, Rose suggests to view the research process as a site for the performance of identities, both on part of the researcher and the researched, as neither 'remains unchanged through the research encounter' (ibid., p. 315). Taking this forward, rather than attempting the impossible, i.e., to 'predict' the research encounter and the positionalities involved in this *beforehand*, when planning the research, we should consider the identities performed in particular research encounters – both by researchers and researched – in hindsight and include this in our analyses.

The challenges discussed in this chapter may be more pronounced because of the longitudinal design of the study. For instance, it adds an additional level of complexity to the process of recruitment and seeking informed consent as a central part of the encounter. Participants were told about the follow-up interviews and that the researcher would be getting back to them a number of times over the following two years before agreeing to the first interview (in the plain language statement), but I emphasised that they only consented to one interview at a time (ongoing or processual consent). The longitudinal nature of the research may have turned off some potential participants, while for others this was appealing. And while managing the relationship with participants is arguably a challenge in all qualitative research, this challenge becomes more pronounced when this relationship is continued over time. While the relationship is critical for the success of the longitudinal design, it is also tricky as it is more likely to come to resemble other types of relationships, such as friendship or mentoring (Thomson and Holland, 2003; Bengtsson and Mølholt, 2016).

Conclusion

In this chapter I have discussed three particular challenges related to conducting qualitative research with service-engaged young people. All three challenges concern participation – on behalf of the potential research participants as well as the researcher. Based on three specific incidents that became critical for my understanding of and engagement in my own research, I have addressed challenges related to recruitment, to researcher positionality and to managing relationships in the field. I have demonstrated how encounters such as the ones described call for reflection to foster greater insight into the research process – what went well and what went wrong, and why did it go wrong – and ultimately ensure ethical research practices. This is critical for all research. It may be even more critical when the social distance between researcher and participants is significant or when engaging with people in vulnerable positions, where there is an additional layer of ethical challenges to navigate. However, as I argued in the discussion section, drawing on Rose's argument, the task does not stop here. Taking these challenges seriously is not simply a matter of establishing rapport and developing 'good' relationships in the field; it is about acknowledging, reflecting on and *analysing* the performative aspects of the research and how the power dynamics that are part of all relationships shape the research. This means that we do not just leave such reflections to the methods section of our texts but weave this into the process of analysing and interpreting the resulting data.

Note

1 In my doctoral research on youth recreational drug use I developed a maptask to produce data on hard-to-access spaces such as small-scale private house parties. Participants were given a piece of paper and asked to first draw the floorplan of the house/apartment where the party was held and then to insert arrows to indicate how they moved between different parts of the house as the party progressed. For more detail, see Ravn and Duff (2015).

References

Aaltonen, S. (2017) 'Challenges in Gaining and Re-Gaining Informed Consent Among Young People on the Margins of Education', *International Journal of Social Research Methodology*, 20(4), 329–341.

Andersen, D. (2015) 'What's So Funny? Towards a Client Perspective on Professionals' Use of Humour in Drug Treatment', *Drugs: Education, Prevention and Policy*, 22(3), 263–271.

Bagnoli, A. (2009) 'Beyond the Standard Interview: The Use of Graphic Elicitation and Arts-Based Methods', *Qualitative Research*, 9(5), 547–570.

Bengtsson, T.T. (2014) 'What Are Data? Ethnographic Experiences With Young Offenders', *Qualitative Research*, 14(6), 729–744.

Bengtsson, T.T. and Mølholt, A.-K. (2016) 'Keeping You Close at a Distance: Ethical Challenges When Following Young People in Vulnerable Life Situations', *YOUNG*, 24(4), 1–17.

Davies, B. and Harré, R. (1990) 'Positioning: The Discursive Production of Selves', *Journal for the Theory of Social Behaviour*, 20(1), 43–63.

Farrugia, D. (2016) *Youth Homelessness in Late Modernity: Reflexive Identities and Moral Worth* (Singapore: Springer).

Guillemin, M. and Gillam, L. (2004) 'Ethics, Reflexivity, and "Ethically Important Moments" in Research', *Qualitative Inquiry*, 10(2), 261–280.

Hammersley, M. and Atkinson, P. (1995) *Ethnography: Principles in Practice* (2nd edition) (London: Routledge).

Harré, R. and van Langenhove, L. (1999) *Positioning Theory: Moral Contexts of Intentional Action* (London: Blackwell).

Järvinen, M. (2001) 'Accounting for Trouble: Identity Negotiations in Qualitative Interviews With Alcoholics', *Symbolic Interaction*, 24(3), 263–284.

Lohmeyer, B. (2018) '"Keen as Fuck": Youth Participation in Qualitative Research as "Parallel Projects"', *Qualitative Research*, early online.

Mannay, D. (2010) 'Making the Familiar Strange: Can Visual Research Methods Render the Familiar Setting More Perceptible?', *Qualitative Research*, 10(1), 91–111.

Mannay, D. (2016) *Visual, Narrative and Creative Research Methods: Application, Reflection and Ethics* (London: Routledge).

McGarry, O. (2016) 'Repositioning the Research Encounter: Exploring Power Dynamics and Positionality in Youth Research', *International Journal of Social Research Methodology*, 19(3), 339–354.

Mellor, J., Ingram, N., Abrahams, J. and Beedell, P. (2014) 'Class Matters in the Interview Setting? Positionality, Situatedness and Class', *British Educational Research Journal*, 40(1), 135–149.

Merriam, S.B. et al. (2001) 'Power and Positionality: Negotiating Insider/Outsider Status Within and Across Cultures', *International Journal of Lifelong Education*, 20(5), 405–416.

Mik-Meyer, N. (2007) 'Interpersonal Relations or Jokes of Social Structure? Laughter in Social Work', *Qualitative Social Work: Research and Practice*, 6(1), 9–26.

Ravn, S. (2012) *Intoxicated Interactions: Clubbers Talking About Their Drug Use* (Aarhus: Aarhus University).

Ravn, S. and Duff, C. (2015) 'Putting the Party Down on Paper: A Novel Method for Mapping Youth Drug Use in Private Settings', *Health and Place*, 31, 124–132.

Renold, E., Holland, S., Ross, N.J. and Hillman, A. (2008) 'Becoming Participant', *Qualitative Social Work: Research and Practice*, 7(4), 427–447.

Rose, G. (1997) 'Situating Knowledges: Positionality, Reflexivities and Other Tactics', *Progress in Human Geography*, 21(3), 305–320.

Seymour, K. (2012) 'Using Incentives: Encouraging and Recognising Participation in Youth Research', *Youth Studies Australia*, 31(3), 51–59.

Thomson, R. and Holland, J. (2003) 'Hindsight, Foresight and Insight: The Challenges of Longitudinal Qualitative Research', *International Journal of Social Research Methodology*, 6(3), 233–244.

Thomson, R. et al. (2002) 'Critical Moments: Choice, Chance and Opportunity in Young People's Narratives of Transition', *Sociology*, 36(2), 335–354.

Turner, N. and Almack, K. (2017) 'Recruiting Young People to Sensitive Research: Turning the "Wheels Within Wheels"', *International Journal of Social Research Methodology*, 20(5), 485–497.

Vogt, K.C. (2018) 'Age Norms and Early School Leaving', *European Societies*, 20(2), 281–300.

Chapter 14

Participatory research and political ecology

An evaluation of research with young Syrian refugees in Turkey

Aslihan McCarthy

Introduction

Under growing emphasis on the significance of youth participation for democratic governance (European Youth Forum, 2013; Pronckute, 2018; European Commission, 2013), inclusive collaborative research practices in social sciences provide a promising framework for researchers who are committed to social justice and change (Cahill, 2007). Participatory research, explored in the following, offers a way to empower vulnerable sections of society, including young people, through giving them opportunity to act towards improving their economic, social and political conditions. Addressing action within the three areas, economic, social and political, not only requires the participation of underprivileged demographic groups, but it also requires a social commitment from researchers, and even then the work is possible only if there is a political framework that allows it.

It is not surprising, therefore, that researchers such as Bergold and Thomas (2012) argue that democracy and safe spaces are the preconditions for participatory research. Only when these preconditions exist, 'participants can be confident that their utterances will not be used against them, and that they will not suffer any disadvantages if they express critical or dissenting opinions' (Bergold and Thomas, 2012, p. 5).

The reasons for involving young people in participatory research directly relate to addressing their right to a voice, a right to be respected (Lawrence, Kaplan and McFarlane, 2013). However, the underlying beliefs of participatory research often reflect a Western ideal of democracy within a state/citizenship dichotomy. When research participants are displaced young people, participatory research adopts added complexity with different dynamics to be considered. Such complexities may well be the reason why there is so little in-depth and detailed participatory literature pertaining to young refugees, despite the fact that 'among many refugee communities, the under-25 category sometimes represents more than 50 percent of the total population' (Chatty, 2007, p. 266).

Involving young refugees in participatory research easily becomes an onerous task, disinclining a researcher who uses standardised research instruments and techniques like interviews, surveys or focus groups. While these instruments and techniques may work when applied within stable democratic settings, with citizens whose rights are protected by the state structures and voices matter due to electoral concerns, such research procedures easily become inaccurate or inappropriate with groups such as young refugees. As these distinct cultural groups do not have the same rights, status and thus political power as their host county's citizens (Block, Riggs and Haslam, 2013).

With such a cohort, power asymmetries come into play. These asymmetries pose challenges such as negotiating appropriately informed consent. Indeed, the very notion of informed consent may have little relevance in some contexts, given that the construct it invokes assumes culturally bound Western values of individual autonomy, self-determination and freedom, as discussed by Ellis and Earley (2006). Additionally, when considering this perspective with a refugee community, Temple and Moran (2006, p. 9) pinpoint that refugee communities may have internal divisions, which means that circumscribing their opinions on a given subject within a single social categorisation might lead to overgeneralised conclusions. These examples demonstrate why research, with refugees, using a participatory framework can result in complex 'methodological' and 'ethical' challenges (Khanlou and Peter, 2005) and show why Ellis, Kia-Keating, Yusuf, Lincoln and Nur (2007) are right in arguing that, 'conducting research with refugee populations demands that researchers think beyond standard recommendations' (p. 460). Indeed, participatory research with young refugees or forced migrants involves different ethical concerns, concerns specific to their residence status and considerate of potential language barriers. These complexities also reflect the sociopolitical contexts of nation-state as well as power asymmetries between citizens and noncitizens (Block et al., 2013; Halilovich, 2013). Since young refugees and forced migrants are noncitizens, not fitting in the nation-state framework, to what extend their voices are valued as outsiders to the present democratic systems is a question of concern.

In fledgling democracies with volatile sociopolitical statuses like Turkey, traditional sociocultural structures and the 'political ecology' (Groundwater-Smith, Dockett and Bottrell, 2014) are important determinants of limitations of research with young refugees. According to Moran, Mohammed and Lowel (2006), when there is no political will nor power to draw down resources for empowering young people, the research outcomes may not necessarily benefit or bring about positive changes for young refugees. How the involvement of young refugees in research processes might help to achieve the intended outcome of empowerment, in countries with huge democratic gaps like Turkey, is a question largely overlooked by literature.

Young Syrian refugees, since the outbreak of civil war and the exodus of millions of Syrian people, have been the target group of many research projects conducted in Turkey, a transit country hosting millions of displaced Syrians. Needs assessments, to improve their conditions and thus contain them in Turkey, have been widely funded by the European Union. Participatory methodologies have been used in research about the issues faced by the young Syrians. However, the political context of Turkey does not reflect the preconditions for participatory research to empower underprivileged demographic groups, as purported by Bergold and Thomas (2012). Therefore, and according to the reasoning earlier espoused, to what extent the ideal of participatory research for social justice and change can be realised in Turkey is questionable. The very fact that young Syrians do not have rights pertaining to citizenship raises important questions about the limitations of participatory research with young Syrians in Turkey.

The highly politicised public discourse on the refugee crisis has turned young Syrian refugee involvement in participatory research, aimed towards the betterment of their lives, into an untimely problem. As Turkey spiralled into an economic crisis, Syrian refugees increasingly became less welcomed by their host communities. Within such a framework and amidst decreasing resources the problem of a participatory approach to research with young refugees grew more complex. For example, the conditions exposed the dependency of a researcher on formal organisational structures to enable access to young refugees, that is, access sought within a political ecology that does not value the empowerment of noncitizens – young refugees – those out of the electoral system. And it is in that context that this chapter investigates the challenges to participatory research with young Syrian refugees in Turkey. This investigation is done by providing a desk review of existing research by international/national institutions and academics addressing the needs, concerns, attitudes and aspirations of young Syrian refugees in Turkey. Here I unpack such complexities through looking into research done with Syrian refugees as a community harbouring ethnic, socioeconomic, cultural and religious differences. I highlight the limitations of Western values in designing participatory research with noncitizen young people in unstable political ecologies.

My work explores research methods utilised to deal with some aspects of the refugee crisis between 2014 and 2018. Research that focuses on how the political ecology affects the attempts to build the capacity of young Syrian refugees to analyse and transform their own lives. In laying out the difficulty of engaging perspectives of young refugees under questionable participatory tradition, I hope to demonstrate how complexities emanating from different social, political and cultural dynamics can be challenged by researchers who use a reflective critical perspective.

Overall, within this chapter I present a review of secondary research in which young Syrian people are involved in research processes about the Syrian community. This desk review explores eight studies conducted between 2011 and 2018 on the mental health, education and the livelihood of Syrian refugees. These studies were selected due to their participatory research methodology, which involved employment of people from the Syrian community in the data gathering and analysis processes, to reflect the viewpoints of Syrian refugees, including those between 14–29 years of age. These studies were accessed using predefined keywords and multiple associated word combinations intended to capture relevant documentation via academic search engines.

What is participatory research?

There is no clear cut, standardised definition for participatory research. However, it can be described as 'a self-conscious way of empowering people to take effective action towards improving conditions in their lives' (Park, 1993). Participatory research can be regarded as a methodology that argues in favour of the possibility, the significance and the usefulness of involving research partners in the knowledge production process (Bergold and Thomas, 2012). Combining research, education and action, most participatory research aims to generate knowledge about and provide actions designed to improve the lives of people facing health, social, economic, political and environmental inequities (Mayan and Daum, 2016). Temple and Moran (2006) argue that participatory research can maximise local participation so proposed projects have a better fit to the needs of local people as it more accurately helps detection of their needs. It is also a way of recognising the existing skills and capacities in the community rather than seeing sections of society as permanently needy. While participatory research can release community development capacities, structural problems intrinsic to politically unstable countries like Turkey can make it difficult to reach the intended outcomes.

According to Bergold and Thomas (2012) there are four fundamental principles for participatory research. First, participatory research requires a democratic social and political context. The participation of underprivileged demographic groups like refugees and young people, and the social commitment demanded of the researchers, are not possible unless there is a political framework that allows it. Second, participatory research requires a safe space to facilitate sufficient openness. Willingness on the part of participants to disclose their personal views of the situation, their own opinions and experiences is necessary for participatory research. Third, who is to participate should be defined clearly. When the research is conducted together with the affected persons, which persons, or groups of persons, should, or must, be involved is a methodologic question to be answered. This question must be addressed, especially because different groups have developed different knowledge in the area under study. Only then can the different types of knowledge be related to each other and a possible practical use be outlined. (Bergold and Thomas, 2012). Last, but not the least, for a project to be classified as participatory research, it is important to define who controls the research. In participatory research the objects of the research should have a say and contribute to the process along with the professional researchers in certain stages, if not the whole process.

The next section focuses attention on what I consider limitations of participatory research as highlighted by using it as a framework for a desk review of research focused on the presence of young Syrian refugees in Turkey.

Turkey and young Syrian refugees

Until recently Turkey has not been exposed to immigration waves that have capacity to bring social diversity and to affect social cohesion. However, as the political instability surged in neighbouring countries in the past two decades, Turkey has gradually evolved into a migration receiving country (Icduygu and Yukseker, 2012). According to Cholewinski and Taran (2010), social cohesion in societies characterised by immigration is only possible in a context of human rights, social justice and respect for democracy. In Turkey, due to the pressure of the EU accession negotiations, new regulations began to take effect (Icduygu and Aksel, 2013) and immigration policies evolved into a seemingly more rights-based approach. However, the presence of Syrian refugees in Turkey often becomes a domestic and foreign policy tool for Turkish governments, manipulated for political interests with little concern for human rights or social equality (Mccarthy, 2019).

Towards the end of 2011, conflict in Syria was declared to meet the criteria of civil war by the international community. As the fighting between government forces and the Free Syrian Army and Sunni Islamic militants intensified, so did the burden on the civilian population. The exodus of Syrian people for secure environments began shortly after the fighting intensified. Turkey was the first of Syria's neighbours to formally respond to the influx of Syrian refugees. The Government of Turkey declared an open border policy and a protection regime in 2011. Turkey retains a geographic limitation to its ratification of the 1951 UN Convention on the Status of Refugees (Refugee Convention), which means that only those fleeing because of 'events occurring in Europe' can be given refugee status. In that context, it is important to underline that the Turkish government avoided using the term 'refugee' for Syrians and instead referred to them as Syrian guests under temporary protection which assures no forcible returns, registration with the Turkish authorities and support inside the borders of the camps for Syrians. Support out of the camps, however, is not guaranteed. Although registered Syrians are given access to health, education and partia; employment, there are many setbacks to meet such needs. Their precarious legal status, linguistic and cultural differences, economic limitations and the scarce resources keep the life opportunities limited for young Syrians in Turkey.

As of June 2018, nearly 4 million Syrian refugees were hosted by Turkey under a temporary protection regime. According to the official statistics, the number of young Syrians aged 14–29 is approximately 1.5 million. According to government sources, in 2018, 60%of 5–17-year-old Syrian refugees attended school. While a small portion of Syrian children attend public schools, a vast majority of them attend the Temporary Education Centres (TECs). On the other hand, only 0.5%of Syrians attended universities. There are no reliable statistics on the employment rates of young Syrians, but it is known that many, including those school aged children, work informally.

More than 97%of Syrians live outside the refugee camps, scattered in bordering cities and metropolitan cities (Multeciler, 2019). Although their number remains modest in the larger cities, 'ghettoization' is on the rise where Syrian refugees overtook several suburbs already occupied by socioeconomically disadvantaged groups. This point is a significant fact not only for the Syrian youth but also for the Turkish state and society itself. In cities such as Kilis, the refugee population has outnumbered the native population, while in other border cities, Syrian refugees constitute an average of 20% of the population. That outcome means young people with either citizen or noncitizen status compete for scarce recourses in education and employment.

Young refugees as a distinct group are, however, often overlooked during humanitarian crises, with their unique concerns and needs seldom prioritised (INEE, MYAN, NRC and RET International, 2017). As the expectation that all Syrian refugees would be repatriated in time faded, along with the prolonged civil war, the number of studies addressing the health, livelihood and education of Syrian refugees increased. In 2018, thanks to the education initiatives by international organisations, there have been studies conducted to assess education of Syrian refugees in Turkey. Although, it is still not possible to hear solely the voices of young Syrians as a marginalised group, participatory approaches have been utilised by researchers interested in exploring issues regarding young refugees. The next section will look into research projects that carry participatory characteristic in their design and discuss the limitations and possibility of participatory research with young Syrian refugees.

Participatory research with young Syrian refugees in Turkey: possibilities and limitations

A study by Simsek (2018) discussing the state of Syrian refugee children's access to education, argues that education determines and is determined by the level of integration of the Syrian refugee community. Simsek argues that access to fundamental rights such as employment, education and healthcare are limited in practice, which consequently hinders the possibility for the integration of refugees. In his research, Simsek used network sampling and reached out interviewees at cafes and restaurants run by Syrian refugees. As a result, most of the interviewees were young men.

The basic limitation revealed though Simsek's sampling method is that young Syrian women as the marginalised section of an already marginalised community are in a very poor position to participate in research projects or to initiate such a project themselves due to the cultural dynamics at play. Giving a chance to them to voice their opinions and positions is a challenging task, especially for male researchers. Thus, in practice, implementing qualitative research with a participatory worldview may not always be possible due to cultural dynamics (Block et al., 2013).

Many research projects about young Syrian women tend to be designed as a study about them rather than a study with them. Exclusionary processes emanating from cultural dynamics may lead to hegemonial knowledge perpetuating male hegemony. As put by Bergold and Thomas (2012), if relevant actors or some field participants are quasi invisible, involvement in a participatory research project may represent a privilege and a distinction. Thus, it is plausible that the professional researchers cannot rely on the utterances of the field participants alone.

In that context, individual researchers or institutions trying to implement participatory research ethics of emancipation, human rights and equality should develop additional measures to ensure that the voices of young Syrians from different sections of the community, especially women who are traditionally confined to the household, are heard.

Different genders, persons, groups and institutions who are affected by the research theme and the expected outcomes should be involved in the research process. When it comes to sampling, however, participatory approaches frequently rely on the utterances of the local participants through inadequate sampling. The limitation of Simsek's sample design also reminds us of the importance of recognising the diversity within refugee communities. Indeed, the views of refugee communities may differ along class, gender, ethnicity and sexuality (Temple and Moran, 2006), and it is crucial to specify the group that is under scrutiny rather than generalising the ideas, attitudes or needs of refugees as a homogenous block. In that context, while doing research with young refugees, it is also important to acknowledge that all groups within refugee classification may not agree on future policy and service development to enhance their rights.

There are implications for the importance of safe space in participatory research in Simsek's work (2018). It is noted that most of the informants were afraid to speak about their experiences in Turkey because they were not registered with local authorities, they worked in the informal economy and/or feared deportation to the country they migrated from. In that context, a critical question arises in research with refugees: is it ever appropriate to conduct research with people in such a 'vulnerable' situation (Gillam, 2013, p. 23), especially those with a questionable legal status? Although I am not able to give a clear answer to that question, it must be considered that social research may have harmful consequences for the young refugees that might be underestimated by the refugees themselves or the researcher in a politically unstable sociopolitical setting. Likewise, it is likely that young refugees overestimate the potential benefits of the research. Some refugees may agree to participate in the research because of their perception that it is likely to bring them material benefits (Alpak et al., 2015).

In line with Khanlou and Peter's (2005) research, using a participatory framework can result in complex ethical challenges, and this complexity is furthered when the research subjects are refugees. Participants who give voluntary consent do not necessarily have an adequate understanding of the possible harm of the research process due to the unfamiliarity with the legal framework and precariousness of the situation they are in. Adequate understanding involves an understating of not only the purpose, methods, demands and benefits but also the possible risk of the research. To convey all the information and make the research aims genuinely understandable is a considerable challenge for the researchers due to language and cultural differences. Of course, researchers such as Simsek (2018) are aware of the need to overcome the language barrier; they used an interpreter, and interviewees were given research consent forms that stated the aim of the research, the protection of the anonymity of interviewees and the confidentiality of all information collected during the interviews. Nonetheless, as discussed earlier, adhering to general ethical standards of research with human participants is not adequate when doing research with young refugees. As argued by Gillam (2013), research with young people needs to go beyond any fixed ethical criteria, especially when researchers do not speak the same language as young refugees, as explanatory statements or brief discussions are hardly sufficient in communicating the possible benefits and limitations of research (Kaukko, Dunwoodie and Riggs, 2017). In that context, language barriers comprise another limitation for participatory research with young refugees in Turkey.

An interview is not only a communication between two partners but rather a part of a much larger system of communication. It is not purely a private conversation between the interview partners, but it is, in a sense, public (Bergold and Thomas, 2012). Making use of young interpreters in research processes constitutes an important aspect of community based participatory research efforts. It should be born in mind that to meaningfully engage with young refugees researchers need to talk to the interpreters and translators about their perspectives on the issues being discussed beforehand to increase their sense of involvement in the process (Temple and Edwards, 2006).

Communicating the relevant purpose, methods, demands, benefits and risks with the research participants is a big challenge for researchers using interviews as a data collection method. Even with the help of an interpreter, due to the greater cultural framework a language exists in, language carries cultural, social and political meanings that cannot simply be read/addressed through the process of translation. Every language speaks of a particular social reality that may not necessarily have a conceptual equivalence in the language into which it is to be translated (Temple and Edwards, 2006). Therefore, gathering data through interviews with young refugees by means of interpreters may not necessarily enable the researcher to comprehend their lives and ideas. As a matter of fact, meaning is always a part of a specific language system (Derrida, 1976), and the researcher who is not a native speaker is an outsider to that system. In such a context, involving young bilingual refugees who have a good sense of both cultures and languages as coresearchers can help establish bridges between the refugee community and the researcher as a part of the host community for the desired research outcomes. However, while doing this desk review, I did not find any research papers which involved young refugees as coresearchers. Rather, young refugees tend to be involved as interpreters, which is not necessarily a shortcoming.

The researchers should aim to engage individuals from the refugee community who are familiar with community members to tell their stories and to help in the interpreting process. This way the cultural and structural barriers framed by the dominant research paradigm of viewing the community as objects of research can be overcome (Ellis, Kia-Keating, Yusuf, Lincoln and Nur, 2007). Furthermore, employing the young refugees as interpreters in research would help empower a generation with little prospects for education and employment due to the legal barriers emanating from their noncitizen status.

Another participatory approach in research is based on valuing community members' knowledge and ability to significantly contribute to the research process. (Ellis et al., 2007). According to Bergold and Thomas (2012), from a methodological perspective, the involvement of field partners as coresearchers in the data collection process has various advantages. One major advantage is that the coresearchers have firsthand knowledge of the field. Therefore, they understand the way people think and may be able to obtain better and faster access to the desired informants. While cultural barriers might impede the contribution of refugees as coresearchers in certain cases, this approach is especially valuable in the field of psychology. For example, in a cross-sectional study examining post-traumatic stress disorder (PTSD) and its relationship with socioeconomic variables amongst Syrian refugees, Syrian coresearchers were employed in data collection and analysis stages (Alpak et al., 2015). The interpreters received detailed training about psychiatric interviewing and how to diagnose PTSD prior to the interviews. Arabic speaking psychiatrists of Syrian descent evaluated the participants. Such research methods recognise the skills and capacities of refugees rather than seeing them solely as the objects of the study. This outcome has the benefit of stripping them of the stigma of being permanently needy (Temple and Moran, 2006).

Many Syrian refugees have the capacity to provide meaningful contributions to the research processes, using their insights into, and interpretation of, the context. Making use of this expertise within refugee communities not only improves relationships and trust between researchers and Syrian people, but it also has an empowerment aspect. Likewise, when doing research about young refugees, employing young Syrian refugees as coresearchers can facilitate the discovery of natural codes due to their empathy and understanding for peers in the field.

Still, it is not easy to involve young refugees in the research processes due to 'gatekeepers' such as parents or professionals, who can intervene to make decisions on behalf of or about their participation in research (Aldridge, 2015, p. 37). The term gatekeeper refers to the adult who controls or limits researcher's access to participants. They are individuals who have the power or influence to grant or to refuse access to a field or research setting (McFadyen and Rankin, 2016). Considering the number of young Syrians that are out of school, it is not surprising to notice that a significant gatekeeper role is often played by employers. Researchers have found that participation of young Syrians in research is denied based on spurious notions of what is deemed to be in the potential participants' best interests, without the young people directly involved ever being asked about their desire or willingness to be involved. A study focusing on young Syrian refugees in Istanbul (INGEV, 2016) faced major challenges during the interviews of the 12–14-year-old Syrians, as these young refugees, who work and live in ateliers (textiles, mechanics, begging activities, etc.), were not denied by their employers' opportunity to speak to the research team. This example demonstrates the existing power structures and inequalities that prevent the participation of young Syrian refugees in research practice in Turkey. In that context, gatekeeper attitudes comprise another complexity, turning participatory research with young Syrian refugees into a wicked problem.

Added to this focus, it is important to note that it is not only the out-of-school Syrian children who are hard to reach for researchers in the Turkish context. At times an inclusionary intention of the researcher, working with young refugees, is curbed by the state institutions. The Ministry of National Education (MoNE) exercises its gatekeeping authority to facilitate or deny access to school children in Turkey. In fact, doing research with students of public schools requires a lot of bureaucratic regulation on top of the bias of the bureaucrats against researchers interested in the Syrian crisis. In 2015, with the fear of spies disguised as researchers, the Ministry of the Interior stipulated approval of the Directorate of Migration Management for all the research to be done with Syrian refugees. This condition was grounded on the Temporary Protection Law and the prohibition of sharing information regarding the Syrian refugees with third parties. Although this condition was later revoked, it is an example of how research can be interpreted as a security concern by the state authorities. Based on this example it can be argued that state institutions constitute the 'political ecology' (Groundwater-Smith, 2014) mandating the regulations for inclusion of young Syrian refugees into research process. In other words, political ecology of research in Turkey is infused with bureaucratic hurdles for access and cooperation.

Bureaucratic hurdles also help explain the scarcity of studies addressing issues relevant to the young Syrian refugees attending public schools as opposed to the plethora of studies on Temporary Education Centres (TECs). TECs were initially established as autonomous education intuitions specifically for Syrian refugees, and they accommodated the vast majority of Syrian children. Without doubt, their autonomous structure made it easier for the researchers to involve young Syrians into their research, unlike public schools with strict regulation and bureaucracy. That is why still little is known about how young Syrians are faring in public schools.

While participatory research with young people is a social contract that honours and values the voices and perspectives of young people, underappreciating the perspectives of young people is already commonplace in a traditional Turkish framework (Gökçe-Kızılkaya and Onursal-Beşgül, 2017; Ontas, Buz and Hatiboglue, 2013; Lansdown, 2010). In fact, a lot of research about the needs of young people has often privileged the adult's view of the world, building upon a perception that the adult, being older and more experienced, must necessarily know more than they may know themselves (Groundwater-Smith et al., 2014). Likewise, there is a tendency in research focusing on the needs of young Syrian people to address questions to adults rather than the young people themselves. For instance, Aydin and Kaya (2017) turn to the teachers and principals in public schools to assess the needs of and barriers faced by Syrian refugee students. Purposeful sampling techniques were used to allow the researchers select adult participants who had the potential to provide information regarding the research question to be addressed. That choice is understandable, despite its limitations, considering the regulations conditioning that the any research to be conducted in public schools must not include any content that is in contradiction with national values. Based on this regulation, conducting interviews with Syrian students might be perceived to provoke discrimination and is thus not welcomed. Aydin and Kaya seem to have avoided creating discontent through selecting teachers and principals as the source of information. However, their methodology falls into the fallacy of excluding the voices of young people in matters that would have an impact on their lives.

Conclusion

Within this chapter, I have discussed the possibility of and challenges to participatory research with young Syrian refugees in Turkey. Involvement of young Syrian refugees, one of the most vulnerable sections of Turkish society, in research processes can be a tool to empower them. It can help develop critical consciousness to transform their realities and generate knowledge through collective self-inquiry and reflection (Mayan and Daum, 2016). That said, highly resourced and labour intensive participatory research is not easy to implement in a volatile developing country like Turkey. Engaging with different sections within the Syrian community to ensure that different young voices are heard is already a very challenging task. Dispersed around different parts of Turkey, young Syrians rarely have the resources, insider knowledge of the system or language used by service providers and academics to be able to act as coresearchers.

There are very few examples of participatory research with young Syrian refugees in Turkey. The professional researcher and the institutions have a tendency to do research about young Syrians rather than doing research with them. There are three main reasons for that as discovered through the desk review of relevant research projects. First, it is not easy for the researcher to break the traditional patriarchal structures that confine young women in the household and underappreciate the perspectives of young people. Second, the nondemocratic, nonaccountable bureaucratic structure, or the 'political ecology', makes working within an institutional basis an excruciating task for the researchers. Bureaucratic barriers coupled with greater political concerns and security issues overshadow the ideal of participatory research to empower young Syrians in Turkey. Third, the language barriers and the power asymmetries limit the research objectives, benefits and setbacks to be understood by the participants.

If policymakers are genuinely planning an inclusive public space that is truly democratic and welcoming to all, including young Syrian refugees, then it is important to ensure the effective participation of young Syrians into the research process. As the future generation, young Syrian refugees have the right to a say in the research agendas, processes and actions. Not only will the distribution of power from the researcher to the research participants help young Syrian refugees reveal their problems, but it will also help them think about workable solutions and actions to be taken. This would only be possible when the current limitations of political ecology are eliminated and fundamental preconditions for participatory research, namely democracy and safe spaces, are achieved.

References

Aldridge, J. (2015) *Participatory Research: Working With Vulnerable Groups in Research and Practice* (Bristol: Policy Press).

Alpak, G., Unal, A., Bulbul, F., Sagaltici, E., Bez, Y., Altindag, D., Dalkilic, A. and Savas, H.A. (2015) 'Post-Traumatic Stress Disorder Among Syrian Refugees in Turkey: A Cross-Sectional Study', *International Journal of Psychiatry in Clinical Practice*, 19(1), 45–50.

Aydin, H. and Kaya, Y. (2017) 'The Educational Needs of and Barriers Faced by Syrian Refugee Students in Turkey: A Qualitative Case Study', *Intercultural Education*, 28(5), 456–473.

Bergold, J. and Thomas, S. (2012) 'Participatory Research Methods: A Methodological Approach in Motion', *Forum: Qualitative Social Research*, 13(1). Available at: http://nbn-resolving.de/urn:nbn:de:0114-fqs1201302.

Block, K., Riggs, E. and Haslam, N. (2013) 'Ethics in Research with Refugees and Asylum Seekers: Process, Power and Politics', in K. Block et al. (eds.), *Values and Vulnerabilities: The Ethics of Research with Refugees and Asylum Seekers*, 1st ed. (Toowong: Australian Academic Press), 3–19.

Cahill, C. (2007) 'Doing Research With Young People: Participatory Research and the Rituals of Collective Work', *Children's Geographies*, 5(3), 297–312.

Chatty, D. (2007) 'Researching Refugee Youth in the Middle East: Reflections on the Importance of Comparative Research', *Journal of Refugee Studies*, 20(2), 265–280.

Cholewinski, R. and Taran, P. (2010) 'Migration, Governance and Human Rights: Contemporary Dilemmas in the Era of Globalisation', *Refugee Survey Quarterly*, 28(4), 1–33.

Derrida, J. (1976) *Of Grammatology* (Baltimore: Johns Hopkins University Press).

Ellis, B.H., Kia-Keating, M., Yusuf, S.A., Lincoln, A. and Nur, A. (2007) 'Ethical Research in Refugee Communities and the Use of Community Participatory Methods', *Transcultural Psychiatry*, 44(3), 459–481.

Ellis, J.B. and Earley, M.A. (2006) 'Reciprocity and Constructions of Informed Consent: Researching with Indigenous Populations', *International Journal of Qualitative Methodology*, 5(4), Article 1. Available at: www.ualberta.ca/~iiqm/backissues/5_4/pdf/ellis.pdf [Accessed 16 September 2019].

European Commission. (2013) 'European Youth: Participation in Democratic Life', *Report*. Available at: http://ec.europa.eu/commfrontoffice/publicopinion/flash/fl_375_en.pdf (Accessed 02 November 2018).

European Youth Forum. (2013) 'Young Voters Are Encouraged to Participate in the Next European Elections, Even From Space!'. Available at: www.youthforum.org/young-voters-are-encouraged-participate-next-european-elections-even-space (Accessed 11 May 2019).

Gillam, L. (2013) 'Ethical Considerations in Refugee Research: What Guidance Do Formal Research Ethics Documents Offer', in K. Block et al. (eds.), *Values and Vulnerabilities*, 1st ed. (Toowong: Australian Academic Press), 21–40.

Gökçe-Kızılkaya, S. and Onursal-Beşgül, O. (2017) 'Youth Participation in Local Politics: City Councils and Youth Assemblies in Turkey', *Southeast European and Black Sea Studies*, 17(1), 97–112.

Groundwater-Smith, S., Dockett, S. and Bottrell, D. (2014) *Participatory Research With Children and Young People* (Los Angeles: Sage, ProQuest Ebook Central).

Halilovich, H. (2013) 'Ethical Approaches in Research With Refugees and Asylum Seekers Using Participatory Action Research', in K. Block et al. (eds.), *Values and Vulnerabilities*, 1st ed. (Toowong: Australian Academic Press), 127–150.

Icduygu, A. and Aksel, D.B. (2013) 'Turkish Migration Policies: A Critical Historical Retrospective', *Perceptions*, 18(3), 167–190.

Icduygu, A. and Yukseker, D. (2012) 'Rethinking Transit Migration in Turkey: Reality and Representation in the Creation of a Migratory Phenomenon', *Population, Space and Place*, 18, 441–456.

INEE, MYAN, NRC and RET International. (2017) 'Desk Review of Programming Guidelines for Adolescents and Youth in Emergencies: Education, Health, Livelihoods and Durable Solutions'. Available at: www.myan.org.au/file/file/Desk%20Review%20 of%20Programming%20Guidelines%20for%20Adolescents%20and%20Youth%20 in%20Emergencies%20-%20Sept2017%20-%20INEE_MYAN_NRC_RET%20International.pdf (Accessed 10 September 2018).

INGEV. (2016) 'Capacity Building in Support of Young Refugees in Metropolitans', *Research Paper*. Available at: http://unhabitatyouth.org/media/uploads/2018/04/Capacity-Building-in-Support-of-Young-Refugees-in-Cities.pdf (Accessed 04 August 2017).

Kaukko, M.M., Dunwoodie, K. and Riggs, E. (2017) 'Rethinking the Ethical and Methodological Dimensions of Research with Refugee Children', *Zeitschrift fuer Internationale Bildungsforschung und Entwicklungspaedagogik*, 40(1), 16–21.

Khanlou, N. and Peter, R. (2005) 'Participatory Action Research: Considerations for Ethical Review', *Social Science and Medicine*, 60, 2333–2340.

Lansdown, G. (2010) 'The Realization of Children's Participation Rights: Critical Reflections', in B. Percy-Smith and N. Thomas (eds.), *A Handbook of Children and Young Peoples Participation: Perspectives From Theory and Practice* (London: Routledge), 11–23.

Lawrence, J.A., Kaplan, I. and McFarlane, C. (2013) 'The Role of Respect in Research Interactions With Refugee Children and Young People', in K. Block E. Riggs and N. Haslam (eds.), *Values and Vulnerabilities*, 1st ed. (Toowong: Australian Academic Press), 103–126.

Mayan, M.J. and Daum, C.H. (2016) 'Worth the Risk? Muddled Relationships in Community-Base Participatory Research', *Qualitative Health Research*, 26(1), 69–76.

McCarthy, A. (2019) 'Turning Crisis into Opportunity? Syrian Refugee Crisis and AKP's Welfare Policy Discourse From a Public Choice Theory Perspective', Unpublished Research Paper.

McFadyen, J. and Rankin, J. (2016) 'The Role of Gatekeepers in Research: Learning From Reflexivity and Reflection', *GSTF Journal of Nursing and Health Care (JNHC)*, 4(1), 82–87.

Moran, R., Mohammed, Z. and Lowel, H. (2006) 'Breaking the Silence: Participatory Research Processes About Health With Somali Refugee People Seeking Asylum', in B. Temple and R. Moran (eds.), *Doing Research With Refugee: Issues and Guidelines* (Bristol: Policy Press), 55–74.

Multeciler. (2019) 'Türkiyedeki Suriyeli Sayısı Temmuz 2019'. Available at: https://multeciler.org.tr/turkiyedeki-suriyeli-sayisi/ (Accessed 29 July 2019).

Ontas, O.C., Buz, S. and Hatiboglue, B. (2013) 'Youth and Political Participation: Case in Turkey', *European Journal of Social Work*, 16(2), 249–262.

Park, P. (1993) 'What Is Participatory Research?', in P. Park, M. Brydon-Miller, B. Hall and T. Jackson (eds.), *Voices of Change: Participatory Research in the United States and Canada* (Westport: Bergin and Garvey).

Pronckute, S. (2018) 'The Importance of Youth Empowerment in the European Union'. Available at: https://futurelabeurope.eu/2018/08/31/the-importance-of-youth-empowerment-in-the-european-union/ (Accessed 13 February 2019).

Simsek, D. (2018) 'The Processes of Integration and Education: The Case of Syrian Refugees and Syrian Refugee Children in Turkey', in M. Pace and S. Sen (eds.), *Syrian Refugee Children in the Middle East and Europe: Integrating the Young and Exiled* (New York: Routledge, ProQuest Ebook Central), 20–33.

Temple, B. and Edwards, R. (2006) 'Limited Exchanges: Approaches to Involving People Who Do Not Speak English in Research and Service Development', in B. Temple and R. Moran (eds.), *Doing Research With Refugees: Issues and Guidelines*, 1st ed. (Bristol: Policy), 37–54.

Temple, B. and Moran, R. (2006) 'Introduction', in B. Temple and R. Moran (eds.), *Doing Research With Refugees: Issues and Guidelines*, 1st ed. (Bristol: Policy), 1–20.

Chapter 15

Youth in voice

The concept of voice

Dona Martin

In this chapter I aim to broaden both the claims of who can and cannot be included in studies about a cohort silenced by circumstance and voice and to disrupt a standard concept of youth by using feminist theory to demonstrate the impact of social and personal factors in determining age. I do this by reflecting on work from a mainstream tertiary education environment. My aim is to offer potentially new perspectives in connecting with marginalised youth by unpacking work with what many may consider a juxtaposed cohort. I focus on a group of first-year mathematics education students, a cohort who on the surface do not fit a marginalised categorisation, especially when compared to those who form the basis of other chapters here, yet a cohort with many participants marginalised by a lack of voice, due to factors such as mathematical anxiety, traditional classroom hierarchy or authority perspectives, uncertainty on who owns the knowledge, how mathematical knowledge is structured and so on.

In setting the scene, I first note that in teacher education research explores influences in practice; my field of research is the classroom. Via employment of a wide array of quantitative and/or qualitative methods, drawn from the behavioural and social sciences, we in teacher education use methods that vary with the nature of the learning and teaching problems being studied as much as by the level of detail at which issues are pursued (National Research Council, 2000). Participation and/or response rates, gaining ethics approval and so on are relatively straightforward, which enables us to focus, via our particular level of engagement, on particular problems and or areas of concern. This opportunity to narrow our attention not only empowers us to offer a valid if not somewhat unique contribution to broader behavioural and social science research but also enables others working with broader issues to isolate particular concepts for greater consideration.

The work presented here, for example, does not lay claim to the provision of valid workarounds or compare outcomes to the multitude of issues peers in this text have contributed, experienced and shared. Rather, the work presented here targets exploration of the factors that contribute to and or impact on a 'young voice'. Not young as in people under a certain age but young as in one who exhibits as being fixed in a culture of accepting external authority, as opposed to having a more mature engagement as a critically evaluative agent (as discussed by Belenky, Clinchy, Goldberger and Tarule, 1986; Cooney, Shealy and Arvold, 1998). As, without prejudice to other definitions, in my work, the idea of having a 'young voice' is determined by a person's sense of self.

For me, the notion of 'a young learner's voice' is depicted through engagement with first-year preservice teachers, who on average present as being either 18 to 22 years of age (around two-thirds of an average cohort) or between 23 and 60 years of age (depicted as 'mature age' and as representative of the other third). In considering the youth of a person through their 'voice' rather than via their age, and aligning this positioning with indicators of how they view the nature of knowledge and the nature of knowing, I find a significant cohort of mixed age students (around one quarter of an average cohort) who lack a sense of voice.

A strong focus in my work therefore is to challenge this group to further develop their 'voice' and as a consequence their sense of self. Indeed, as you read my narrative, I challenge you to draw parallels with those who demand your attention, to use this work as an analogy or a juxtaposition.

Voice

In my work, 'voice' is a term used metaphorically, as in the work by Belenky et al. (1986), to represent a person's perspective on knowledge and truth as personal, private and subjectively known – 'voice', as in an exhibiting of dependence on others and as in denoting what is valued and considered as empirical. For me, when discussing a person's 'voice' it is not their style of communication, verbal/ nonverbal, interpersonal, that I refer to; rather it is what they say, how they say it and what it discloses. Therefore, their 'voice', regardless of age or situation, demonstrates reactions within context and exposes the extent to which a learner considers they have a right to participate in the world around them, which in turn impacts on how engaged they are in their learning.

My work focuses on engaging students through reflective episodes. I aim to build an awareness of the emergence of 'voice' in self and/or peers and to explore these shifts within the learning circumstance, and I draw attention to the changes that come from engaging in and reflecting on learning experiences and accomplishments. My work, like that of Signe Ravn and Paulina Billett in this volume, explores how in giving voice we not only alter power relations, establish rapport, empower participants often via reflections on performative aspects and provide opportunity to shape and interpret research inputs and outcomes, but we broaden avenues of contemplation and add to the general theme of challenging rules, rights and authority. We give voice to the vulnerable, or as Darren Sharpe in this volume notes, we cultivate competent coinquirers and amplify the voice of the young.

Youth

As discussed by Billett (see Chapter 1, this volume), youth is not a natural category but a relatively recent social construct used to define a specific group of people. Billett's overview of the development of youth as a social concept explores the development of the concept of youth. Billett explores youth from being defined as a life stage, via childhood development and evolutionary theory and discusses its association as a psychological and physical life stage using psychobiological explanations of adolescence, where 'youth' is broadened to include the social constructions and conceptualisations of young people and their role in society, to one that rejects youth as a homogenous and unified group. Billett's chapter explores how the concept of youth became tied to accepted or expected periods of transition, which she further unpacks in relation to the impact of global forces. Billett explores how a shift in the landscape, in the transition from school to workplace, came about via workforce casualisation, underemployment, shifts in economics and social changes. Her work notes how these changes in circumstance added timing uncertainty to traditional conceptions of when to expect such transitions to occur, which in turn now cause youth theorists to focus on 'youth' studies from a perspective underpinned by a highly complex set of social constructs, constructs that now form the foundation of defining 'young' people and their role in society.

In my work, for example, the notion of youth is not considered a standalone concept; rather, I see that it denotes a complex system of meanings and inferences about a person and their place in society. Of course, there are as many arguments for as there are against espousing broad definitions of concepts within research, but this is neither the time nor the place to debate contestable points of difference. Rather, I argue a stance that aligns with the following.

- The United Nations Educational, Scientific and Cultural Organisation (2019) contends:

  > Youth is a more fluid category than a fixed age-group . . . "youth" is often indicated as a person between the age where he/she may leave compulsory education, and the age at which he/she finds his/her first employment. This latter age limit has been increasing, as higher levels of unemployment and the cost of setting up an independent household puts many young people into a prolonged period of dependency.

- The *Oxford English Dictionary*, which includes in its definition 'an early stage in the development of something'.

My idea of youth, therefore, demonstrates an international preparedness to stretch what is commonly agreed to while accepting broader cohorts of 'youth' when describing complex social, economic and cultural inequalities.

Others in this text also discuss challenges to preconceived notions of youth. Joel Robert McGregor and David Farrugia's chapter, for example, explores a case management program within the Australian juvenile justice system, where youth is imagined not by preexisting life stages but in terms of what is needed to govern movement out of the juvenile justice system and identified through a 'risk score'. They too argue for an alternate narrative, where youth is a relationally constructed and constantly negotiated fluid and heterogeneous concept. Such a concept serves to further broaden implications for conceptualising youth and offers new components to the framework of the contextualisation of research with marginalised youth.

Challenging epistemological ideals

My particular focus, in relation to students, is on the way they respond to mathematical problems and how it is they engage within the social classroom setting. In mathematics classes, I find that most students have a well-developed idea of what is accepted as good or appropriate behaviour. I find that this sense of morals often impacts their 'voice' in the learning process, as they are swayed by developed understandings of subject and classroom social norms and values. In my experience, being quick and right is what most accept as a model mathematics student. However, in introducing a focus on the value of shared mis/understandings and/or public exposure of knowledge gaps, we build opportunity to see mathematics from different perspectives. We challenge rule-following behaviour, we explore how knowledge is developed or accumulated and we build empathy for wider views and different perspectives on what underpins mathematical knowing and knowledge. In challenging epistemological ideals of knowledge – its structure as well as its acquisition – we explore as a learning community factors that contribute to disengagement and challenge the gap between high- and low-performing students.

While I accept a disconnect with tertiary education students' abilities to reflect the social and personal impact factors that restrict 'voice', prevalent in other studies on marginalised youth as presented within this text, I also recognise and argue a common theme between this cohort and other marginalised groups. By removing the words 'mathematics' and 'teacher education' from the narrative, I claim that my work aligns with research focused on creating opportunity to provide young people a voice. I consider those without 'voice' in tertiary mathematics classes representative of all students who lack the confidence to articulate personal ways of knowing and personal knowledges. I see those without voice as being denied the opportunity to engage in challenges to logic, with its explicit and implicit rules. For example, Fiona MacDonald's work (see Chapter 11, this volume) neatly articulates this idea by taking us through an exploration of the burden of methodological warrant in research on school reform. MacDonald's research focuses our attention on affordances given to young people reengaged with education to speak for those who remain passively disengaged. In my circumstance, I too have access to only those brave enough to attend university classes in teacher education.

From a previous role as selection officer, the person in charge of engaging with potential students and enrolling or not those qualifying for and interested in teacher education, for the Education Faculty, I am fully alert to the number of potential qualifiers for university entrance that change their future direction once they find that mathematics education classes are compulsory for all preservice teachers. While aware that this concern is not the issue for all who enrol, or not, I am aware that I only have access to those uncertain students who have a strong desire to become teachers, those willing to chance staying under the radar, those who see themselves as capable of remaining away from direct scrutiny. This cohort of students have become the focus for much of my research career (Martin, 2016; Martin and Itter, 2014; Thomas, Martin and Pleasants, 2011; Campbell and Martin, 2010; Martin, 2010). Therefore, as discussed by MacDonald, I too share in the challenge to find ways to connect with these students before they become disengaged. I draw attention to MacDonald's work to demonstrate that while I claim here to focus attention on how to give voice to those silenced by circumstance, I too am alert to the point that while I discuss strategies to work, to connect with the vulnerable, with those exposed as lacking confidence, lacking voice, I am aware that I too am missing the weakest cohort, those who do not attend university at all due to feeling inadequate.

My lens

Education, for me, is a process that involves a focus on social equity. I work to reduce access barriers and to encourage participation by providing opportunities for all learners to engage, as I consider classroom inclusivity a fundamental element of lifelong learning. I hold value to all participants being accepted as part of a community of learners and use a framework of inclusive pedagogies, as no one approach, however flexible, fits all circumstances. Social constructivism is the best label I can find to suit my theoretical framework, as it encompasses ways to address inequality or disparity and enables resolutions between experience, knowledge and teacher learner expectations, as further discussed in the work of Florian and Linklater (2010). I came to social constructivism in an attempt to better understand how the influence of others impacts cognitive concepts and problem-solving skills (Ingleby, Joyce and Powell, 2010). It provided me with a framework to consider the impact of influential peers, an impact, it is argued, that stems from social interactions influenced by environmental factors and affected by the culture in which a learner develops. Hence, I have become comfortable with seeing cognitive functions as impacted by the values, beliefs and tools of intellectual adaptation as socioculturally determined. Vygotsky's (1978) influence on my work is evidenced by the constant challenges I set via having to account for my actions against other perspectives of learning. In my classrooms, for example, I encourage discourse and action that builds opportunities for all involved to work together. I build opportunities for each participant to challenge and reflect on the implicit messages of cultural values and personal ways of understanding. This work enables us to explore each learner's perceptions of the very nature of knowing and of knowledge. My work ethic is largely built on work with peers, such as explored in Donnison, Edwards, Itter, Martin and Yager (2009), where, as one of a group of academics teaching into the same year level, I have had the opportunity to experience and value a culture of communication and reflective practice.

Indeed, I have repeatedly found that in articulating and reflecting after and in situ on each participant's existing knowledge and needs – for example, in exploring and exposing teaching strategies and or in making explicit content, curriculum and pedagogical knowledge – every member of a classroom cluster is able to work with those around them to realise common beliefs and attitudes. These opportunities for constructive and critical conversations about how to improve engagement sustains constructive conversations about how a teacher can engage every member of a class. These often unscheduled and informal conversations enable ideas to be shared, as well as opening the environment to scholarly critique. This focus on sharing, which occurs in a spirit of collaboration aimed towards building a common understanding of pedagogical knowledge and skills, facilitates academic language and practices. These opportunities prompt discussions on aspects of student engagement practices, such as the relationship between deep learning within unfamiliar contexts and student anxiety and become an unexpected source of social learning that motivates a sense of ownership and a sense of responsibility towards success.

This work is underpinned by what I call a 'researcher's canon', the near permanent capacity to challenge every decision, outcome and recommendation. I include this brief discussion of my personal pedagogical and philosophical underpinnings, as it is how I view the nature of the learning process. It is my attempt to demonstrate why I place so much value on challenging participants to identify situations of reduced involvement. Why I consider it important to investigate any unwillingness for learners to actively participate, to share emotional and or moral perspectives of learning. Why I place such high value on sharing introspective accounts, encouraging participants to act against what many perceive as public opposition or personal conflict and to suspend inappropriately perceived social codes or attitudes to classroom participation.

All of this foundational information is important, for as an educator, I am constantly alert to hidden complications around bringing about a student's 'voice'. For example, when addressing some of the many anxieties about talking mathematically, I find that not all students are open to a consideration of others' views or who see knowledge as the possession of the intellectual community (Martin, 2010).

'Voice' limitations

While the diversity of mathematical opinions is well documented, as are interesting ways to engage participants in the learning, not so well explored are the reasons that inhibit or limit a student's willingness to engage in discussion. In mathematics education classes, but of course not restricted to them, factors that inhibit or cause limitations often relate to a participant:

- being anxious not to disclose perceived inadequate levels of knowledge
- rejecting any challenge to personal assumptions, often regardless of the negotiated outcomes of the majority of the group

- completely dismissive of alternate views
- refusing to join in discussions
- agreeing with the rhetoric so as not to hold up proceedings
- demonstrating firm notions of what interactions are and are not deemed as acceptable, and the list goes on.

These factors are not so different from other works directed at engaging with young people who exhibit with a reduced 'voice'.

To challenge these young people to engage, I focus on asking questions about knowledge, questions that concern both its structure and its acquisition. These are questions about their theory of knowledge and their epistemology.

Challenging epistemological assumptions

Epistemology is defined by Hofer and Pintrich (1997, p. 88) as 'an area of philosophy concerned with the nature and justification of human knowledge'. Brew (2001, p. 15) further defines epistemological perspectives as 'the ways students interpret or make meaning of their education experience as a result of their assumption about the nature, limits and certainty of knowledge'. An established researcher in this field is Perry (1970). Perry worked with males to develop a scheme of 'abstract structural aspects of knowing and valuing' (p. 14). Perry's work focuses attention on how it is that individuals interpret their educational experiences. His work was further explored by Belenky et al., who used feminist theory to demonstrate how social and personal factors create youth in voice. These two studies underpin the influence I place on epistemological assumptions of reflective thinking and reasoning processes. Perry's work (1970), for example, provides a descriptive account of student's experiences – a scheme of intellectual and ethical development. The stages he proposed are clustered into four sequential categories:

- dualism – knowledge is something received and never questioned
- multiplicity – awareness that there are questions have may not answers and accept that there could be more than one solution to any given problem; here learners see that they can legitimately have an opinion
- relativism – knowledge here is considered contextual
- commitment within relativism – knowledge comes from a combination of sources; learners recognise the acquisition of knowledge as having a personal base; it is an ongoing activity.

These were offered as positions and, as discussed by Hofer and Pintrich (1997, p. 91), provided 'an invariant sequence of hierarchically integrated structures'. While the Belenky et al. (1986) work scheme 'positions the different ways [we] . . . come to know using a metaphor of voice' (Cooney et al., 1998, p. 312), this scheme enables a focus on the epistemological perspectives of individuals and a lens with which to become more proficient at aligning each participant's underlying beliefs, with data gathered during engagement activities.

As further discussed in my earlier work (Martin, 2010), the Belenky et al. scheme (1986), presented here as Table 15.1, uncovers themes and suggests gender designs around power within the way societies define, validate and classify knowledge. Belenky et al.'s (1986) work also offers a useful framework that allows others to identify participants according to their beliefs, as it highlights the crucial benchmark of 'learners valuing their own voice and critically incorporating the voice of others' (1986, p. 312). I note this connection to beliefs simply to highlight that by enabling a focus on preservice teachers' beliefs regarding the nature of mathematics, I am well placed to challenge mainstream disciplinary beliefs and place an equivalent challenge on pedagogical practices, as discussed in the work of Burton (1992). According to Belenky et al. (1986), there are five epistemological perspectives for the extent to which learners rely on authority for knowing. These identifiers relate to those who see authority as dictating truth through to those who see truth as contextual.

In consideration of Belenky et al.'s (1986) work, and in relation to understanding behaviours around how the 'self' is constructed, it is worth briefly exploring changes in the roles and relationships of men and women and some of the impacts of movements away from patriarchal societies. In Australia, for example, we have had the Sex Discrimination Act of 1984, which outlawed discrimination on the grounds of gender, as well as the Equality Act of 2010, also designed towards gender equity. Yet when we apply scrutiny to outcomes, to the conditions of acceptance, we find women's employment remains shaped by family and domestic responsibilities and women in general remain, with some degree of passivity, in jobs with lower pay and fewer prospects. Women continue to be underrepresented in many professions and their average earnings remain well below that of men (WGEA). It can therefore be claimed that while females may participate in a broader array of further study and work opportunities, it remains challenging to shake long established norms. I therefore argue that there remains much merit in the categorisation of participants according to their beliefs, as proposed by Belenky et al. (1986).

In unpacking the constructs of voice, for example, as presented by Belenky et al. (1986), I encourage you to consider where those in your cohort, fe/male, are positioned and what you can learn from the process of positioning them in terms of how you might challenge them to engage. It is important to note that years of data consistently align the majority of my participants within the first two of Belenky et al.'s positions, 'silence' and 'received'. Although having clear differences, I have become comfortable combining them for procedural ease. Consider, for example, the following in relation to the 'silence' and 'receiving knowledge' categories.

I find, as a mathematics teacher in higher education, that many students share concerns about publicly engaging with mathematical work. They aim to attend

Table 15.1 Women's ways of knowing. (Martin, 2019)

Epistemological perspectives	Dialogic relations	Breakdown
Silence (knowing-in-action)	Knowledge	Gets knowledge through concrete experience, not words.
	Mind	Sees self ... with little ability to think.
	Mode	Survives by obedience to powerful, punitive authority.
	Voice	Little awareness of power of language for sharing thoughts and insights.
Received knowing	Knowledge	Knowledge received from authorities.
	Mind	Sees self as capable/efficient learner; soaks up information.
	Mode	Good listener; remembers and reproduces knowledge; seeks/invents strategies for remembering.
	Voice	Intent on listening; seldom speaks up or gives opinion.
Subjective knowing	Knowledge	Springs from inner sources; legitimate ideas need to feel right; analysis may destroy knowledge.
	Mind	Own opinions are unique, valued; fascinated with exploring different point of view; not concerned about correspondence between own truth and external reality.
	Mode	Listens to inner voice for the truth that's right for her.
	Voice	Speaks from her feelings/experience, with heart; journals; listen and needs other to listen, without judging.
Procedural knowing	Knowledge	Recognises different frameworks, realms of knowledge; realises positive role of analysis, other procedures for evaluating, creating knowledge.
	Mind	Aims to see world as it 'really it' - suspicious of unexamined subjective knowledge.
	Mode	(Separate): logic, analysis, debate. (Connected): empathy, collaboration, careful listening.
	Voice	(Separate): aims for accuracy, precision; modulates voice to fit standards of logic or discipline. (Connected): aims for dialogue where self and other are clearly and accurately understood even where different.
Constructed knowing	Knowledge	Integrates strengths of previous positions; systems of thought can be examined, shaped, and shared.
	Mind	Full two-way dialogue with both heart and mind; seeks truth through questioning and dialogue.
	Mode	Integration of separate and connected modes.
	Voice	Adept at marshaling/critiquing arguments as well as empathic listening and understanding; speaks/listens with confidence, balance and care.

class as passive rather than active participants and demonstrate as subject to the judgement of those around them. They are often keen to exclude themselves from direct participation and need direct help, or intervention, to find their 'voice'.

In further consideration of the next stage noted in Table 15.1, the subjective knowledge point, as both a teacher and a researcher I see that becoming a reflective practitioner (Schon, 1983) is of great significance in the development of all learners. As Cooney et al. (1998, p. 312) note, when unpacking Belenky et al., it is at this stage that 'an externally oriented perspective eventuates in a new conception of truth as personal or intuited'. Cooney et al. (1998, p. 312) argue that these 'revolutionary points' emerge in a way, where learners once 'dependent on others become learners who evaluate different perspectives in terms of what he or she values and considers to be empirical evidence'.

For those working in the procedural and constructed categories (Table 15.1), the point that they are the engaged, that they have found and use their 'voice', reflects participants who are suspicious, adept and prepared to engage. This cohort knows how to build knowledge. These learners understand that a strong intellectual voice comes from understanding the impacts of personal beliefs and behaviours on a person's ability to engage. This cohort is involved; they have a strong 'voice' and see program content as organised, systematised and challenging. They see that language exists through thought and structure and effective communication (Freire, 2000).

Exposing voice constructs

What is consistently revealed to me in unpacking Belenky's constructs of voice in unison with Perry's sequential categories of dualism, multiplicity, relativism and commitment within relativism, is a strong sense within each cohort of the diversity and depth of understandings and beliefs. Having this understanding assists me in valuing individual and collective experiences, as it helps position me to challenge collaborative learning exchanges, to challenge assumptions held and to connect with each participant.

In considering, for example, their perception of others knowing, I note that those who exhibit a dualistic perspective rely on remembering ideas and procedures. They see my role as teacher is to pass judgments on answers and methods and their role as learners to simply listen and learn. Yet those who exhibit as more multiplistic see knowledge as applied and contextual. They reflect on and recognise their role in the learning process and make conceptual sense via discussion in construction of meaning. These learners value knowledge not as discrete topic areas but rather as integrated and able to be usefully applied.

In building learner awareness, and along with it their sense of voice, I engage students in discussions on valuing the need to understand, as opposed to simple rule following. I am able to encourage them, to challenge them and to be suspicious of unexamined subjective knowledge. I am able to involve them in exploring the culture of mathematical knowing, a process that takes them away from a focus of knowledge as abstract information, where learning relies on applying sets of rules and procedures. By contextualising problems and alerting them to there being more than one way to solve a problem, I remove the notion of the teacher as the ultimate authority. They begin to recognise different frameworks and realms of knowledge and to realise positive roles of analysis and other procedures for evaluating and creating knowledge. They see the culture of knowledge as interrelated concepts, as intuitive and creative, and they begin to share ideas for criticism and further development.

To me, enabling a public awareness of how oneself and others interpret situations and outcomes not only assists participants to situate themselves as social contributors in discourse but also exposes any reliance they have on external authority. It provides a determiner of truth in terms of valuing personal levels of engagement and/or critically incorporating the work of others. It opens opportunity for each participant to explore their beliefs, to expose how their construct of the nature of knowing is impacted by their construct of the nature of knowledge. This awareness impacts their beliefs and is reflected in their attitude, as in no longer focusing on the need to learn rules they become more flexible as learners. They develop confidence in themselves, exhibited in ways such as revealing misconceptions, and overall, they become more experiential, more open to hearing peers' explanations; they place greater value on their own knowledge as well as that of their peers. They become active learners who value contributions and discourse as opposed to having a reliance on others to communicate knowledge to them, knowledge is no longer independent of culture and contextualisation.

In giving up passivity and being dependent on outside authority, and in becoming more collaborative, these students begin a journey of challenging uncertainty in knowledge. They become empathetic, learn to listen and contribute and begin to work together to construct new meaning. The new environment we create for learning encourages them to question authority as they start to focus on conceptual understanding over rule following. This work has as its core a focus on dialogue, where self and others are clearly and accurately understood, even when different. It is here that their voice begins to modulate to fit standards of logic or discipline. And when a problem is solved in a different way, or an answer is different, the focus becomes one of finding contradictions in the logic of another's thinking. There is a need to understand the reasoning behind unexpected outcomes.

In exposing voice constructs, current and prior conceptions of both the nature of knowledge and that of knowing and by focusing on beliefs held, I find opportunity to challenge and to engage. For example, in establishing the parallels between 'silence' and 'received' categories, and that of the static, bounded nature of the discipline of mathematics, where learners believe that the record of knowledge represents the only knowledge, that their involvement entails absorbing what other people have done, that the role of the teacher is mainly managerial or procedural (Romberg, 1999), I am alert to what to challenge and how to engage. I am armed to explore and expose each participant's sense of voice, to change conceptions and practices, and I am ready to build environments that support participants to question and to be critical of their own experiences. Like the ethnographic fieldwork of Signe Ravn (Chapter 13, this volume), which reflects on ethical challenges to research based on participation of women marginalised in the educational system, and like studies that further broaden the research ethics perspective, I feel that my work demonstrates a focus on what I expect we all believe, that marginalisation is simply not acceptable.

Conclusion

As noted in the work of Belenky et al. (1986), epistemologically a sense of voice, mind and self are fundamental in any challenge to encouraging contributions to the discourse under investigation. My aim here has been to have you consider issues, problems and circumstances that limit engagement from an education perspective. To have you consider if my work in establishing a person's 'voice' could possibly provide you with a way to better characterise the circumstances that silence your target cohort. I see that in having the ability to identify diverse perspectives, I am able to create experiences that both challenge and encourage participants towards developing a greater voice. In sharing my focus, I hope to have provided you with a new way to strategize as to what can be done to give marginalised youth a greater voice and a greater sense of self. As I consider that in having an awareness of how others see the world of knowledge and knowing we are better placed to expand associated values. We are better able to involve others in opportunities that challenge what may be limiting perspectives and to offer them a greater voice, a way to participate in the world around them.

References

Australian Government Sex Discrimination Act (1984) Available at: https://www.legislation.gov.au/Details/C2018C00499 (Accessed 24 May 2019).

Belenky, M.F., Clinchy, B.M., Goldberger, N.R. and Tarule, J.M. (1986) *Women's Ways of Knowing: The Development of Self, Voice, and Mind* (New York: Basic Books).

Brew, C. (2001) 'Women, Mathematics and Epistemology: An Integrated Framework', *International Journal of Inclusive Education*, 5(1), 15–32.

Burton, L. (1992) 'Working Together', *Mathematics Teaching*, 140, 16–19.

Campbell, C. and Martin, D. (2010) 'Interactive Whiteboards and the First-Year Experience: Integrating IWBs into Pre-Service Education', *Australian Journal of Teacher Education*, 35(6), 68–75.

Cooney, T., Shealy, B. and Arvold, B. (1998) 'Conceptualizing Belief Structures of Preservice Secondary Mathematics Teachers', *Journal for Research in Mathematics Education*, 29(3), 306–333.

Donnison, S., Edwards, D., Itter, D., Martin, D. and Yager, Z. (2009) 'Reflecting on Improving Our Practice: Using Collaboration as an Approach to Enhance First Year Transition in Higher Education', *Australian Journal of Teacher Education*, 34(3), 18–29.

Equal Opportunity Act 2010. (Accessed 24 May 2019) https://www.humanrightscommission.vic.gov.au/the-law/equal-opportunity-act.

Florian, L. and Linklater, H. (2010) 'Preparing Teachers for Inclusive Education: Using Inclusive Pedagogy to Enhance Teaching and Learning for All', *Cambridge Journal of Education*, 40(4), 369–386.

Freire, P. (2000) *Pedagogy of the Oppressed 30th Anniversary Edition* (New York: Continuum).

Hofer, B.K. and Pintrich, P.R. (1997) 'The Development of Epistemological Theories: Beliefs About Knowledge and Knowing and Their Relation to Learning', *Review of Educational Research*, 67(1), 88–140.

Ingleby, E., Joyce, D. and Powell, S. (2010) *Learning to Teach in the Lifelong Learning Sector* (London: Continuum).

Martin, D.L. (2010) *Pre-Service Teachers' Mathematical Philosophies and Methodologies: First Year, Pre-Service Primary/Elementary School Teachers' Mathematical Philosophies and Methodologies* (Saarbrücken, Germany: Lambert).

Martin, D.L. (2012) 'Rich Assessment in First-Year Mathematics Education', *International Journal of Pedagogies and Learning*, 7(1), 62–72.

Martin, D.L. (2016) 'Alignment of Theory and Practice: A Cycle of Researching, Teaching, and Learning', *International Journal of Arts and Commerce*, 5(1), 1–13.

Martin, D.L. and Itter, D. (2014) 'Valuing Assessment in Teacher Education: Multiple-Choice Competency Testing', *Australian Journal of Teacher Education*, 39(7), 1–14.

National Research Council. (2000) '11 Next Steps for Research', in *How People Learn: Brain, Mind, Experience, and School: Expanded Edition* (Washington, DC: The National Academies Press). doi:10.17226/9853

Oxford Dictionary (2019) Available at: https://www.lexico.com/en/definition/primitive (Accessed 24 May 2019).

Perry, W.G., Jr. (1970) *Intellectual and Ethical Development in College Years: A Scheme* (New York: Holt, Rinehart and Winston).

Romberg, T.A. (1999) 'School Mathematics – National Policy', in G. Kaiser, E. Luna and I. Huntley (eds.), *International Comparisons in Mathematics Education*. Studies in Mathematics Education Series (London: Falmer Press), 182–199.

Schon, D.A. (1983) *The Reflective Practitioner: How Professionals Think in Action* (New York: Basic Books).

Thomas, G., Martin, D. and Pleasants, K. (2011) 'Using Self- and Peer-Assessment to Enhance Pre-Service Teachers' Future-Learning in Higher Education', *Journal of University Teaching and Learning Practice*, 8(1), 1–17.

United Nations Educational, Scientific and Cultural Organisation (2019) Available at: http://www.unesco.org/new/en/social-and-human-sciences/themes/youth/youth-definition/ (Accessed 24 May 2019).

Vygotsky, L.S. (1978) *Mind in Society: The Development of Higher Psychological Process*. Eds. M. Cole, V. John-Steiner, S. Scribner and E. Souberman (Cambridge, MA: Harvard University Press).

WGEA Workplace Gender Equality Agency. (2019) 'Gender Segregation in Australia's Workforce', *Australian Government*.

Theme V

Unexpected tensions

How contradictory friendships disrupted my study of working-class girls' residential instability

Louisa Choe[1]

Friendship as a methodology

This chapter, written in an autoethnographic confessional style (Van Maanen, 1988), evokes mixed emotions when discussing on research with young people. Like many researchers pushing beyond their comfort zone, I came to the realisation that in order to persuade some of my young participants to talk freely, I needed to consciously 'do rapport' with them and to reach out to them while offering friendship (Duncombe and Jessop, 2002). Friendship as a methodology is described as a synthesis of interactive interviews (Tillmann-Healy and Kiesinger, 2000) and collaborative witnessing (Ellis and Rawicki, 2013). Within qualitative studies, particularly during fieldwork, building friendships as an approach allows the researcher to get to know others in meaningful and sustained ways (Owton and Allen-Collinson, 2014). Rapport, on the other hand, is often employed by researchers as a tactic used to establish successful interviews, one in which participants are willing to share and divulge information (Karnieli-Miller, Strier and Pessach, 2008). In my case, I did not intentionally nor specifically conceptualise my work to be adopting friendship as a method, but as the research progressed and relationships with the girls and their families were formed, I quickly learnt that friendships with participants both enhanced the data collection but also created ethical pitfalls and challenges. The fact I was from a different culture (Asian) and social class and age (24) from my cohort of girls established distance that needed to be managed.

I tried various ways to get closer to the girls. In the spirit of reciprocity (Harrison, Macgibbon and Morton, 2001), and recognising that my role as a researcher and mentor was a form of resource to the girls, I held workshops for participants on resume writing and cooking classes at the youth centres. These initiatives acted as a strategy for young people to acquire life-skills – skills that were not only relevant to participants but were useful and beneficial beyond the scope of the project. Despite my will to balance out the power imbalance of relationships resulting from my position of privilege with the girls, I ran the risk of commodifying strategic emotion work (Hochschild, 1983) to secure access and to continuously maintain this access for my research field. Friendship and rapport can sometimes become a kind of emotional labour, where at the heart of an outwardly friendly rapport lies an emotive dissonance between the researcher persona and the 'authentic' self (Blix and Wettergren, 2015). Throughout this research, especially throughout the time I sat by myself in the car following the weekly meetings with the girls, this dissonance was never far away.

This chapter reflexively explores three aspects of my friend relationships with the girls. First, I align my interactions with the girls with what Duncombe and Jessop (2002) highlighted as the contradictory relations that result when a researcher is both a friend and an interviewer. The second aspect of friendship examines autonomy and what consent means. I ask, 'consent to whom?', questioning if it is possible for the girls to differentiate my role as a researcher from my roles as a friend or volunteer. Was their consent to take part in this research given to the 'researcher-friend'? Or were their stories meant only for the friend they had made. A third aspect of autonomy evaluates the nature of consent; what I term 'consent to what?'. Here I question if consent is limited to information disclosed during an interview, or does it also include other spontaneous updates during fieldwork? Online chat conversations or meetings at the supermarket, for instance, drew spontaneous updates. It is within all these fluid boundaries that I share my experience – these are what created the most challenges for me and are not discussed in research methods textbooks.

Unstable reciprocal friend boundaries

Duncombe and Jessop's (2002) recollection of their early experiences of 'faking rapport' captured the instability of researcher-participant relations when participants are made to feel good about themselves, thus leading to insincerity and inauthenticity. Jessop felt troubled with the realisation that, in order to gain a 'good' interview, she frequently had to 'smile, nod, and appear to collude' with views that she sometimes opposed, all of these to help build a 'faked rapport' and only used to 'betray' participants into revealing valuable information (Dumcombe and Jessop, 2002). The failure to reflexively question the hypocrisy of 'faking friendship' exposes researchers to a disturbing ethical naivety which can marginalise the relationship shared between the participant and researcher.

While the empowerment of participants as collaborators should be celebrated, their new roles as friends can add to the ambiguity of the shared relationship. Many researchers have pointed out that the boundaries between a researcher and a friend, real and fake friendship, and between trust and rapport, all become blurred, especially with time invested in the field (Dickson-Swift, James, Kippen and Liamputtong, 2006). Some ethnographers have generated a considerable amount of literature that emphasised the usefulness of establishing close empathetic relationships between researchers and participants, advocating much personal investment in the research progress (Coffey, 1999; Taylor, Bogdan and DeVault, 1998). However, blurred boundaries between the researcher and participant can lead to an array of ethical issues – for example, emotional attachment by the informants

(Duncombe and Jessop, 2002) and participants disclosing information which may be beyond the scope of the research or beyond the capacity of the researcher to handle (Dickson-Swift et al., 2006).

When Jessop asked one participant what she had gained from participating in a ten-month long research, with a total of five interview sessions, the participant replied saying that she had 'made a friend' (Duncombe and Jessop, 2002). Not only was this proclamation one-sided, the claimed friendship highlighted the underlying falseness of the situation – Jessop was only 'doing her job' as a researcher – something which the participant was unaware of. Jessop's personal discomfort with the fake friendship was compounded when she failed to recall the participant's name when they met coincidentally in public (Duncombe and Jessop, 2002).

On reflection, there is much in my research that Jessop describes. It is now with some embarrassment that I recall the initial days of data collection in these two data sites. I recall giggling and nodding along to whatever my participants had shared with me during the initial meetings, even when I did not agree at all. One participant commented that I had never said 'no' to the group. Such comments always provoked an intense uneasiness within me. Reflexively, I question my intention in obliging their requests. I confess that my willingness to follow their lead is akin to those emotions similar to 'peer-pressure', although in this case a pressure was derived from the desire to gain access to the participants' worlds. I wanted to fit in and be seen to fit in.

Despite researchers' efforts to build rapport through methods such as self-disclosure, empathising and showing respect for participants (Dickson-Swift et al., 2006), these strategies in creating a 'level playing field' can still end up being instrumental, hierarchical and nonreciprocal (Oakley, 1981). The power imbalance between researcher and participants is further accentuated when involving young people. Despite drawing heavily on children-centred research (Smith, Monaghan and Broad, 2002; Alderson, 2001), and with practical efforts of acknowledging the young people involved as research-collaborators (Ergler, 2015), the ethical issue of power imbalance was still evident in my research project, especially on the issue of reciprocity.

I know this reciprocity from my own experience. Some years ago, I stumbled upon the infamous "Starving Child and Vulture" photograph taken by Kevin Carter (1993) on the internet. While Carter ended up earning himself a Pulitzer Prize with this piece, I often ponder on the outcome of the child depicted. Relating this to my fieldwork, an ethical question which frequently emerged was 'how can "they" gain from this (project)?' Such a question heightened the inequality within the research setting; while I was able to gather data and information about the lived experience which would contribute towards a doctorate degree, and hopefully a career pathway, my participants, having shared their valuable stories – an intimate part of themselves –would most likely gain little or, if not, nothing at all. As a novice sociologist, the perpetuation of inequality within research settings left me feeling disturbed. Such an awareness added guilt to what was already a complicated web of emotions.

Three examples demonstrate the complexity of these friendships as a methodology conundrum. The focus here is not on my relationship with the girls but the girls' relationship with me. In cases with the headphones and the McFlurry ice cream, I felt that the girls were taking advantage of me, and this is something I had not read in the literature. The case of my reaction to witnessing bullying was more straightforward.

The headphones created an unexpected puzzle. While walking around a retail store with three of my participants, one of them picked up a brand-new pair of headphones ($18) and asked if I could buy that for her. I was stunned into silence. On one hand, I had prioritised maintaining a good relationship with the girls, while on the other, I had identified an immediate need to set boundaries. The true challenge however was learning how to say 'no' in a manner such that they would understand my reasons for declining. I apologised and explained that I did not have that kind of money. She responded with a sulk and walked away. Previously, my studies in ethics had always focused on not putting my participants in a position of vulnerability or discomfort. Never once had I been warned that the table could be turned on me such that I would become potentially exploitable or vulnerable. I felt uneasy and cornered in my options to respond and was emotionally unprepared and unequipped as a novice researcher. While I felt anxious declining her request, I did however feel that it was the 'right' (ethical) thing to do. The episode had a sequel. Upon leaving the store, I noticed that the atmosphere became tense. Two of the girls had kept an obvious distance between themselves and the girl who had requested that I purchase the headphones. To maintain the cohesiveness within the group, I walked over to her, and it was then I noticed she was wearing the headphones, jacked to her cell phone. Not knowing how to react, I too withdrew into silence. The other girls confronted her about the headphones; as they expressed their frustration, the girl denied, saying that the headphones she possessed were an older pair she had brought from home. Immediately, I felt my stomach drop. It became clear she had stolen them. I started panicking and became concerned with mainly how this incident might implicate us. My imagination ran wild; I could be accused of being an accomplice or slapped with a no trespass order. Like the other two girls, I felt unprepared and compromised.

While the literature warned against the ethical issues of fake friendships and their impact on participants, few discussed the emotional impact they have on researchers (Duncombe and Jessop, 2002; Birch and Miller, 2000; Finch, 1993; Oakley, 1981). Traditional boundaries described by Jessop only warned of the vulnerability of participants (Duncome and Jessop, 2002); but in this instance, the roles were reversed. None of the literature I was exposed to prepared me for such an ethically challenging moment – should I say anything to anyone? But I did not witness the event – maybe she was telling the truth? Not knowing the 'ethically' right thing to do was unnerving, and I sought help by bringing such ethical and moral conflicts to my supervisors in hopes of being enlightened. In the case of the headphones incident, I had chosen to accept my participant's account of the incident. Although not bound by any professional code of ethics, like those of lawyers' or social workers, I recognised a need for me to reciprocate the trust which my participants had in me (Bell and Nutt, 2002). This duty of care allowed me to embrace the reality that I needed to initiate trust in order to establish and reciprocate a credible and reliable relationship.

The group had fallen out. The three girls and I never got together as a group again. While I still maintained contact with the girl at the centre of this issue, this incident became the elephant in the room; neither of us spoke of it in subsequent conversations. It is imperative for researchers to consider how boundaries are mitigated when adopting friendship as a methodology, and a need to be reflexive when evaluating and reflecting on the authenticity and impact of the relationship formulated.

The McFlurry was a second incident that upended my rapport with the girls when I felt 'pressured' into agreeing to buy a participant a McFlurry ice-cream during a chance encounter at a local fast food restaurant. Prior to this encounter, I had completed an interview session with her, a session which I felt was success-ful in achieving rapport and trust. However, when I contacted her for a second interview it was the beginning of a number of failed attempts. My third attempt to establish contact had failed, and a slight hunch told me that it was best to stop 'trying', that she was no longer interested in participating in the project. When we met by chance at the restaurant, I was almost shocked when she came over and greeted me with enthusiasm and eagerness. She initiated the conversation, smiling and nodding, and expressed her interest in the project. As a motivated researcher who wanted to complete her project, having someone who was willing to (re) participate in the research project was important. Just as I responded excitedly, she paused and asked if I could purchase a McFlurry for her as she had not eaten all day. Feeling concerned for her wellbeing, I agreed without hesitation. And just as I was making the purchase over the counter, she tapped me on my shoulder and told me that if I was to get her something to eat, I should get her friend a McFlurry too. Her question left me feeling bewildered. I felt 'compelled', as I saw that as an opportunity to build rapport. I nodded and obliged. I handed over the ice creams and left the restaurant. After that encounter, I never heard from her again. Look-ing back, I felt almost embarrassed by my ethical naïveté. Succumbing to my participant's requests left me feeling guilty, especially when I knew for a fact that I had only done so to encourage her participation. Gaining and securing consent was a fraught process.

Negotiating consent

The research field presents itself as an ethical 'landmine' for inexperienced researchers, making it more critical to practice ongoing reflexivity during the research process (Guilleminm and Gillam, 2004). Part of being reflexive required me to acknowledge the responsibilities which comes with the role of a researcher (Guilleminm and Gillam, 2004). A familiar problem many novice researchers must unravel is a workable definition of informed consent (Thompson, 2002) and its three facets of capacity, voluntary and information (Turnbull, 1977). The researcher's responsibility is to ensure that participants have the capacity to make an informed choice, that is, that participants have the ability to select and communicate their decisions through a rational decision-making process (Tymchuk, 1997). Voluntary participation means their decision to participate is free from coercion or constraint (Holloway and Wheeler, 1995). Last, it is important for participants to be fully advised of the elements of the research project, which includes their rights and the nature of the research project (Tolich, Choe, Doesburg, Foster, Shaw and Wither, 2017). Researchers must recognise the complexity of informed consent when engaging with young participants because when participants are asked intimate and personal questions about their lives, relationships and difficulties, they render themselves vulnerable as soon they start sharing (Watson, Irwin and Michalske, 1991).

Researchers are in a unique position. In many instances, we become the few people to whom an isolated and vulnerable participant can speak openly and freely. In my research, I have had girls who even thanked me for 'listening'. It was almost as though the interviews served as a therapeutic opportunity for participants (Birch and Miller, 2000). These conversations can transcend beyond civil cooperation to one of therapeutic alliance (Usher and Holmes, 1997), thereby achieving beneficence through the research process.

On the other hand, the characteristics of qualitative research conceal the huge power differentials that exist between the researcher and participant (Kvale, 1996). Conscious of this dual role, I disclosed my role as a researcher to the girls during our initial meeting. To further heighten my researcher identity, I had ensured that a university pullover was always worn when meeting with participants.

During the initial meetings, a girl even teased me for attending social meetings in a 'uniform', one which was marked with an obvious emblem (the university logo covered three-quarters of the front). It is only through her tease that I learnt why the girls were reserved when talking to me; there were rumours going around about this foreign (Asian) university student who would not change out of her uniform. My hopes to remind participants about my role as a researcher deterred the process of rapport building with them. However, it did act as a prompt for them to be mindful about what they would like to share with me. Although such a prompt was visible, its effectiveness deteriorated over time.

To further disrupt the researcher-friend dichotomy, the girls and I formulated ways which allowed them to tell their stories and perspectives freely. For example, the girls would voice their opinion on how the researcher should conceptualise or approach the research project. They had a say on what was important to them, and they were also invited to help with the design of the interview guide. Their perspectives helped dictate the general direction of the researcher project, validating their roles as collaborators (Ergler, 2015). For example, a couple of girls told me that my overpoliteness or formality made them feel awkward and that I should have a more straightforward approach when asking them questions. Instead of saying 'Could you please tell me more about . . .', they wanted me to go straight to the point, asking 'what do you mean?'. Or more simply, 'What?'. After all, the girls were on 'home turf'; they were the experts in the field who were more knowledgeable (Usher and Holmes, 1997).

To further empower their new roles as collaborators, I would always hand them the audio recorder at the start of each interview, thus sharing with them the power of control over how the interview begins or ends (Gollop, 2000). Traditionally, the control over research processes lies in the hands of the researchers, who dictate how the research was introduced and communicated to the participant. Some might even argue that the amount of information offered regarding the research was at the researcher's discretion (Bravo-moreno, 2003). The negotiation of control over interviews between the researcher and participant could help correct the power imbalance between researchers and participants and also empowers the role of participants as collaborators. For example, when I first started my interviews with the girls, I would always ask them to describe their current 'house' for me. I would then proceed to ask them about their previous house. However, one of the participants pointed out that I had been asking the question the 'wrong way' because in her case she had not moved houses, but each week she would couch surf at her friends' places or at times sleep in a car. My inability to 'engage' with my participants suggested that my questions were not relevant or relatable to their experiences of housing instability. The girls' comments also pointed out another facet of the power differentials of researching with young people. My interview questions relied heavily on my personal reflections on how and what questions should be asked, meaning there was an almost exclusive focus on my opinion on how to manage the interview. The participant suggested that I asked them to 'tell me about the place they are currently living', instead of specifying 'house' in my question, as this limited the scope of my interview question. The inclusion of young collaborators' perceptions on how the interview should be prompted suggest other ways in which collaborators could be engaged in research interviews. It also demonstrates young people's agency and ability to contribute to all stages of the research process. My collaborators' reflections guided my interview questions, as well as their 'tips and tricks' on suggested alternative styles for interviewing (Knapil, 2006). This process of learning from their feedback and comments was a crucial part in ensuring equality between the researcher and the inclusion of young people in the research context (Smith et al., 2002), resolving the tension of my dual role.

Through multiple discussions with the girls, we formulated ways which mitigated power imbalances and helped elevate their roles as collaborators. For example, they had a choice over where they would like to have their interviews, be it a café which they had never been to before or at a different room at the university library. Few chose to be interviewed in their homes. Adopting the girls' suggestions, we agreed that the interview sessions were also accompanied with a light meal or a beverage. The researcher would communicate the budget which she had allowed and the agenda for each session, and this ensured consistency between interviews and cultivated mutual understanding (Taylor, 2011). Having understood my background, research and agenda, the girls were able to approach me voluntarily and openly discuss the purpose and design of my research project. The question about 'where you lived' is an exemplar. I attempted to empower the girls by explaining how there is a lack of information on young people's experiences of housing movements, and their stories were therefore important. Although the girls would joke about how 'boring' writing a thesis seemed to be, they were always happy to help me out during the process, playing their role as a collaborator. In fact, during my initial process of recruiting participants, many of the girls referred their friends to participate in the project. Through this, I learnt that the disclosure of my agendas and intentions helped negotiate boundaries and readdress the power imbalance between myself as a researcher-friend and the girls as participant-collaborators (Taylor, 2011).

Irregular consents

Research involving young people is particularly susceptible to consent irregularities given that information is exchanged spontaneously outside of interviews when the audio recorder is off. For example, when the girls and I met unexpectedly at the supermarket we would share a brief chat ranging from greetings and what they were doing that night, to information which I deemed relevant to my research. These conversations produced data about them not having enough in their budget to purchase household items or how they were sleeping on a friend's couch. Here, another ethical question surfaces: 'What' were they consenting to? More specifically, is consent just about participation in the research interview, or does it go further (Miller and Bell, 2012)? Problems were created due to the multiple roles which I took on. Meeting the girls by chance sometimes forced me to question my role – when I asked them how they had been, was I asking as a friend, a researcher or a shopper? The tension between my role and what should or should not be included in my research led to yet another ethical dilemma; even when the terms of participation were clearly explained, agreed upon and consented to at the beginning of the study, nothing can warrant that these do not change, especially within an everchanging ethnographic field (Hobbs and May, 1993).

Unexpected tension ensued when I met one of my participants, accompanied by her family, in a bank. There, I was introduced by the participant to her parent as the researcher-friend whom they had been talking too. This overwhelmed me with anxiety. I even confessed to my supervisor that the nervousness probably stemmed from the awareness that the characteristics of a researcher and a friend might at times clash. It was perhaps the guilt and the lack of confidence that I might not at all be the 'friend' that the girls had hoped for me to be, or the fear that my lack as a friend might destroy the trust we had built. It became clearly necessary that I needed to take initiatives to sustain the trust we shared.

To practice consideration and respect for my girls, I would seek (ongoing) permission for the information I could include. For example, for anything shared outside the interviews, I would clarify with the girls if they were comfortable elaborating more when the audio recorder was next turned on. Though most would agree to discuss the matter further, there were times when they politely declined – a decision which I would respect. For example, the girls would hold back on the discussion of their friends or family as they had recognised that those stories might not be theirs to share. The negotiation on what or what was not consented to with my participants allowed me to ethically navigate myself when executing (ongoing) informed consent. McCarthy (1998), in her study on sexuality of women who have learning disabilities, demonstrated that involving participants in the research process is further likely to maximise their understanding of and willingness to participate the project. The management of ongoing informed consent should therefore be taken seriously when researching with young people.

Although the research was framed as youth-centred research that acknowledges the social agency of young people within research settings, the constructed meanings unintentionally prescribed to my collaborator's experiences signalled my deviation from my original intentions. For example, when asked about their opinions about moving, what I termed 'housing instability', some girls would describe their feelings as 'alright'. Without giving these too much thought, I took their response as a literal meaning and interpreted "alright" as somewhat positive. It was only during the second round of my interview that a girl explained that 'alright' meant that she knew the move to a new house was not good, but since she had no choice or say in the move, by claiming that it was 'alright' it made her feel better. Recognising that there were gaps in my interpretation of their experiences, I began to involve my participants in the analytical components of the research; they were consulted about the meanings of their expressions and the interpretations of their narratives. Through clarifying how and what the girls interpreted as 'alright', I came to learn that that was their way of avoiding the question, and that they did not wish to give a 'definite' answer. To ensure that the girls' narratives and voices were accurately presented, they were encouraged to be part of the interpretation and evaluation throughout the research project. Here these young people were recognised as 'social actors', meaning they were capable of carrying out meaningful interactions that make 'a difference to a relationship or decision' (Mayall, 2002), and this applies to all aspects of life, including research settings.

Liebenberg et al.'s (2018) research on the influence of physical and relational space on young people's sense of civic engagement in the indigenous communities of Atlantic Canada offered other forms of inclusion. They gave young people the opportunity to use their real name or to show their faces in some of the visual research materials. This decision was informed by their previous research with young people where the researchers were informed by youth that 'they feel empowered by giving voice to their opinion and experiences' (Liebenberg et al., 2018). Hoping to empower my collaborators in the same way, and to give them their deserved 'credit' for their thoughts and ideas, I consulted the girls in the format and manner through which their stories were told. More specifically, I focused on whether their stories were presented in a manner they had intended. For example, one of the girls urged me to clarify in my thesis that although she was aware of the negative connotations that came with housing instability, and living in a lower socioeconomic status neighbourhood – what the Maori call 'Pōhara' – she felt that it was important to highlight her opinion correctly. She said:

> I would say its pōhara . . . it is a Maori word to describe where poor people live. But that's what others would say. I actually don't feel it.

Her request on how she would like her story to be told was one I gladly obliged in order to retain its authenticity. Apart from going back to the girls for validation on the information collected, participants were also reminded that their right to withdraw was valid at all times. I would always remind them of this before and after our interviews. Seeking process consent had therefore helped reaffirm the girls' roles as collaborators and coresearchers. However, there were occasions where before I could ask them for permission they were already telling me what should or should not be included. I see these 'instructions' as guidance from my collaborators, helping all of us (the young people and myself) in carrying out a more ethically sound project together.

Conclusion

The mixed experiences evident in my three confessions suggest only one certainty; that is, the complexities of researching with young people in the field will always be personal and partial. As researchers, we have no handbook or manual to follow, no 'one-size-fit-all' method of orchestrating engagements with participants to ensure a mutually beneficial outcome. It takes time sitting in a car alone after these meetings in the liminal space to realise the gulf between my participants' worlds and my own and the gulf between the textbooks I read preparing me for this research and reality.

The adoption of friendship as a methodology and building rapport with young participants raised ethical dimensions to my research that extends beyond the usual scope of what is considered important in research ethics. The three confession tropes (to whom is the consent for, consenting to what and faking friendship) have the researcher navigating through the complexities of researching with young individuals and formulating creative strategies with participants to disrupt what can sometimes be a considerable power imbalance between the researcher and young participants. To make up for my lack as a friend, my role as a researcher-friend had to also encompass the ethic of care for all of the participants (Miller and Bell, 2012). It was their wellbeing which I had to prioritise. I had an obligation which I needed to constantly remind myself and my participants of.

Note

1 I want to acknowledge my supervisor, Associate Professor Martin Tolich, for his assistance on the first draft of this chapter.

References

Alderson, P. (2001) 'Research by Children', *Social Research Methodology*, 4(2), 139–153.

Bell, L. and Nutt, L. (2002) 'Divided Loyalties, Divided Expectations: Research Ethics, Professional and Occupational Responsibilities', in T. Miller, M. Birch, M. Mauthner and J. Jessop (eds.), *Ethics in Qualitative Research* (London: Sage Publications), 76–93.

Birch, M. and Miller, T. (2000) 'Inviting Intimacy: The Interview as Therapeutic Opportunity', *International Journal of Social Research Methodology*, 3(3), 189–202.

Blix, S. and Wettergren, Å. (2015) 'The Emotional Labour of Gaining and Maintaining Access to the Field', *Qualitative Research*, 15(1), 688–704.

Bravo-Moreno, A. (2003) 'Power Games Between the Researcher and the Participant in the Social Inquiry', *The Qualitative Report*, 8(4), 624–639.

Carter, K. (Director). (1993) *A Little Girl, Weakened From Hunger, Collapsed Recently Along the Trail to a Feeding Center in Ayod. Nearby, a Vulture Waited* [Photograph].

Coffey, A. (1999) *The Ethnographic Self: Fieldwork and the Representation of Identity* (London: Sage Publications).

Dickson-Swift, V., James, E., Kippen, S. and Liamputtong, P. (2006) 'Blurring Boundaries in Qualitative Health Research on Sensitive Topics', *Qualitative Health Research*, 16(6), 853–871.

Duncombe, J. and Jessop, J. (2002) '"Doing Rapport" and the Ethics of "Faking Friendship"', in M. Mauthner, M. Birch, J. Jessop and T. Miller (eds.), *Ethics in Qualitative Research* (London: Sage), 10–122.

Ellis, C., and Rawicki, J. (2013) 'Collaborative Witnessing of Survival During the Holocaust: An Exemplar of Relational Autoethnography', *Qualitative Inquiry*, 19(5), 366–380.

Ergler, C. (2015) 'Beyond Passive Participation: From Research on to Research by Children', in R. Evans, L. Hold and T. Skelton (eds.), *Methodological Approaches* (Singapore: Springer).

Finch, J. (1993) '"It's Great to Have Someone to Talk To': The Ethics and Politics of Interviewing Women', in M. Hammersley (ed.), *Social Research: Philosophy, Politics and Practice* (Thousand Oaks: Sage Publications), 160–180.

Gollop, M. (2000) 'Interviewing Children: A Research Perspective', in A. Smith, N. Taylor and M. Gollop (eds.), *Children's Voices: Research, Policy and Practice* (Auckland: Pearson Education NZ Ltd.).

Guilleminm, L. and Gillam, L. (2004) 'Ethics, Reflexivity, and "Ethically Important Moments" in Research', *Qualitative Inquiry*, 10(2), 261–280.

Harrison, J., Macgibbon, L. and Morton, M. (2001) 'Regimes of Trustworthiness in Qualitative Research: The Rigors of Reciprocity', *Qualitative Inquiry*, 7(3), 323–345.

Hobbs, D. and May, T. (1993) *Interpreting the Field: Accounts of Ethnography*, 18th ed., Vol. 74 (Oxford: Clarendon Press).

Hochschild, A. (1983) *The Managed Heart: Commercialization of Human Feeling*, 18th ed. (Berkeley: University of California Press).

Holloway, I. and Wheeler, S. (1995) 'Ethical Issues in Qualitative Nursing Research', *Nursing Ethics*, 2(3), 223–232.

Karnieli-Miller, O., Strier, R. and Pessach, L. (2008) 'Power Relations in Qualitative Research', *Qualitative Health Research*, 19(2), 279–289.

Knapil, M. (2006) 'The Qualitative Research Interview: Participants' Reponsive Participation in Knowledge Making', *International Journal of Qualitative Methods*, 5(3), 77–93.

Kvale, S. (1996) *InterViews: An Introduction to Qualitative Research Interviewing* (Thousand Oaks: Sage Publications).

Liebenberg, L., Wood, M. and Wall, D. (2018) 'Participatory Action Research', in R. Ed. Iphofen and T. Tolich (eds.), *The SAGE Handbook of Qualitative Research Ethics* (London: Sage), 339–353.

Mayall, B. (2002) *Towards a Sociology for Childhood: Thinking from Children's Lives* (Great Britain: Open University Press).

McCarthy, M. (1998) 'Interviewing People With Learning Disabilities About Sensitive Topics: A Discussion of Ethical Issues', *British Journal of Learning Disabilities*, 26, 140–145.

Miller, T. and Bell, L. (2012) 'Consenting to What? Issues of Access, Gate-Keeping and "Informed" Consent', in T. Miller, M. Birch, M. Mauthner and J. Jessop (eds.), *Ethics in Qualitative Research* (London: Sage Publications), 61–75.

Oakley, A. (1981) 'Interviewing Women: A Contradiction in Terms?', in H. Roberts (ed.), *Doing Feminist Research* (London: Routledge and Kegan Paul), 30–61.

Owton, H. and Allen-Collinson, J. (2014) 'Close But Not Too Close: Friendship as Method(ology) in Ethnographic Research Encounters', *Journal of Contemporary Ethnography*, 43(3), 283–305.

Smith, R., Monaghan, M. and Broad, B. (2002) 'Involving Young People as Co-Researchers', *Qualitative Social Work*, 1(2), 191–207.

Taylor, J. (2011) 'The Intimate Insider: Negotiating the Ethics of Friendship When Doing Insider Researcher', *Qualitative Research*, 11(1), 3–22.

Taylor, S., Bogdan, R. and DeVault, M. (1998) 'Introduction to Qualitative Research Methods a Guidebook and Resource', *Introduction to Qualitative Research Methods: A Guidebook and Resource*, 18th ed. (New York: Wiley).

Thompson, S. (2002) 'My Research Friend? My Friend the Researcher? My Friend, My Researcher? Mis/Informed Consent and People With Developmental Disabilities', in W. van den Hoonaard (ed.), *Walking the Tightrope: Ethical Issues for Qualitative Researchers* (Toronto: University of Toronto Press), 95–106.

Tillmann-Healy, L. and Kiesinger, C. (2000) 'Mirrors: Seeing Each Other and Ourselves Through Fieldwork', K. Gilbert (ed.), *The Emotional Nature of Qualitative Research* (Boca Raton: CRC Press), 82–106.

Tilmann-Healy, L. (2003) 'Friendship as Method', *Qualitative Inquiry*, 9(5), 729–749.

Tolich, M., Choe, L., Doesburg, A., Foster, A., Shaw, R. and Wither, D. (2017) 'Teaching Research Ethics as Active Learning: Reading Venkatesh and Goffman as Curriculum Resources', *International Journal of Social Research Methodology*, 20(3), 243–253.

Turnbull, H. (1977) *Consent Handbook*, Vol. 1 (Washington: American Association on Mental Deficiency).

Tymchuk, A. (1997) 'Informing for Consent: Concepts and Methods', *Canadian Psychology*, 38(2), 55–75.

Usher, K. and Holmes, C. (1997) 'Ethical Aspects of Phenomenological Research With Mentally Ill People', *Nursing Ethics*, 4(1), 49–56.

Van Maanen, J. (1988) *Tales of the Field: On Writing Ethnography*, 15th ed. (Chicago: Univeristy of Chicago Press).

Watson, L., Irwin, J. and Michalske, S. (1991) 'Researcher as Friend: Methods of the Interviewer in a Longitudinal Study', *Qualitative Health Research*, 1(4), 497–514.

Chapter 17

The Multicultural Youth Australia Census

Reading complexity and migrant
youth citizenship into survey methods

Rimi Khan

Introduction

One of the key themes of this book has been a concern with locating young people's autonomy within social and cultural research methods. The growth in interest in participatory, self-reflexive or 'action-based' methods attest to this methodological problem and a desire to avoid objectifying and marginalising young people through methods that are imposed on them from institutions of power. Such methods have historically been reliant on categories that do not give young people space for the expression of cultural complexity. Traditional survey instruments, for example, ask young people to define themselves in terms of preexisting identity categories and forms of classification that come from policy discourses and institutions of government. These research approaches offer little space for young people to contest these forms of institutionalisation. However, the need for research categories which make the experiences of young people intelligible to these institutional worlds persists. The survey has a long history as an administrative instrument for managing populations, particularly in colonial regimes where classifying and categorising difference has been a key governmental objective (Dirks, 2001). Today, the survey instrument continues to be a privileged tool used by governments and policymakers for understanding populations. In Australia, a range of institutions and government agencies draw from survey data in order to support 'evidence-based decision making' (AIFS, 2012). The idea that policies are informed by research that is objective, represents community needs and is produced by experts, continues to shape narratives about government decision making, even if decisions are rarely made in this way (Belfiore, 2009).

This chapter describes the use of survey methods in a research partnership between university researchers and a number of community organisations and government institutions working with young people from migrant backgrounds. The Multicultural Youth Australia (MY Australia) project is a national study of migrant and refugee youth aged 15 to 25, producing data on their cultural, social and economic 'status'. The survey method used in the MY Australia Census (the Census) raises challenges for how we understand this cohort because of its reliance on categories of identity that emerge from multicultural policymaking. The method raises questions about how the term 'multicultural youth' is produced and employed. On the one hand, it risks simplifying hybrid identities and homogenising diversity, while on the other, it creates the basis for collective identity, citizenship and advocacy. This ambivalence reflects the complexity of official discourses of multiculturalism themselves. Such discourses have been met with significant critique for simplifying categories of identity (Noble, 2011) and for supporting managerial contexts which reinforce hierarchies between White Australia and its others (Hage, 1998). However, the term continues to have both policy currency and an everyday resonance in the lives of migrant and nonmigrant Australians, which means that it is hard to do without the language of multiculturalism. This world of multicultural policymaking from which the project emerges raises significant challenges for the research.

The chapter begins by describing the background to the MY Australia project, the governmental spheres from which it emerged and the political narratives it seeks to intervene in. It discusses the institutional context of the research and how its methods were shaped by the need to give the study credibility in policy worlds. The second part of the chapter discusses the history of the census as a method for knowing populations. In this section I draw on the theoretical literature on the 'social life of methods' to examine how the research methods used in this project (re)produce the category of 'multicultural youth'. The policy world which motivates this research informs the choice of method, but the method, in turn, produces particular categories for knowing this social world, specifically that of 'multicultural youth'. In this way the census method is not simply reductive but also generative. In the final section of the chapter I ask how these research methods and categories create challenges and limitations but also particular possibilities for identity and citizenship amongst multicultural youth. The focus of this chapter is not on the census findings themselves but what is revealed when we look at the data from 'inside the method' (Law, Ruppert and Savage, 2011). In this last section I pay close attention to the materiality of the survey instrument itself and investigate the ways in which young people have engaged with the census. Young people contest and complicate survey classifications and engage in forms of citizen making through their participation in the Census. Despite the ways that rigid identity categories such as 'CALD' or 'migrant' might work to discipline young people, the research data reveals how they try to articulate the specificity and complexity of their identity, despite these methods and categories.

Given these tensions between governmental agendas for data collection, and the interests of youth researchers in cultural complexity, this chapter asks what we might do with the MY Australia Census. It proposes new approaches for reading census data and the relationships between the survey instrument and its research subjects. While the survey has the potential to 'flatten out' the experiences of its respondents, it is also a crucial way of producing knowledge that makes the complexity of refugee and migrant young people's lives comprehensible to researchers, policymakers and young people themselves. I argue that if we pay greater attention to the governmental lifeworlds in which the research findings circulate then the census can be understood as a lively method that has the potential to produce new social and institutional relations and critical modes of civic participation for migrant youth. In this respect the MY Australia Census can be understood both as a research method and as an advocacy strategy for migrant youth.

Multicultural Youth Australia: how the social constitutes the method

In Australia, young people from migrant backgrounds comprise about half of the nation's youth (ABS, 2017). This cohort includes migrant young people who have arrived in Australia as children with their families, international students, humanitarian migrants and second or third generation migrants who are Australian-born. This range of trajectories and reasons for migration, as well as the hugely diverse language and ethnic affiliations of migrant youth in Australia make them a complex and dynamic research cohort. While there are numerous reports on the status of Australian youth (Mission Australia, 2017; Stanwick et al., 2013), there is no comparable research which provides a national snapshot of migrant youth as a distinct population group. At the same time, political anxieties about the supposed threat of migration, and media panics about migrant youth violence and radicalisation in Australian cities, make such research increasingly urgent. In the context of these stigmatising discourses, migrant youth enact complex practices of belonging, identity and resilience which are not adequately understood by policymakers. Research examining how migrant youth are faring in relation to their 'local' counterparts is lacking. However, there are good reasons why migrant youth are not easy to know, and why they are difficult to access through social science research methods seeking to produce a 'snapshot' of their lives. Varying levels of English language proficiency, socioeconomic disadvantage or institutional exclusion all contribute to a lack of data about this cohort.

This chapter draws from an Australian Research Council-funded Linkage Project that aims to address this gap, by conducting a census of Australian migrant youth.[1] The MY Australia project forms part of a research collaboration between university researchers, government agencies and community-based organisations working with migrant and refugee youth around Australia. The institutional context from which this study emerged produced significant challenges and limitations for how we were able to research and 'know' multicultural youth. Given these challenges, it is worth describing the institutional and social worlds that motivated the project in some detail. However, while the survey method risked simplifying the complexity of multicultural youth experiences, it also generated new positions for migrant and refugee youth as citizens and advocates in studies about themselves. As the account below highlights, the institutional context of the research made the census a fraught but ultimately necessary and productive method for researching refugee and migrant youth lives.

The MY Australia project developed out of longstanding professional and personal connections between university researchers and stakeholders within the 'multicultural youth' sector. One of the project's key funding partners, the Centre for Multicultural Youth, works closely with migrant youth, offering them a range of support and advocacy services, training and opportunities for consultation that might 'remove the barriers young people face as they make Australia their home' (CMY, 2014). From CMY's perspective, and in light of the ongoing stigmatisation of migrant youth, the research had an important political function: to provide an evidence base for more informed debate about migrant youth lives, to give migrant youth 'a voice' in these debates, and to cast migrant youth in terms of resource and resilience rather than risk and criminality.

It is because of the project partners' research priorities that the study took on a distinct advocacy agenda. As academic researchers on this project we were not detached from the institutional contexts of the research; rather, we were invested in our partners' objectives. We were not external to the social and political worlds we were researching but implicated and embedded in them. This blurring of lines between scholarly research and advocacy has the potential to risk the critical distance that traditionally characterises academic work (Belfiore, 2009). However, as Law, Ruppert and Savage argue, research methods 'don't come into being without a purpose [and] . . . they don't come into being without advocates, or more exactly without forms of patronage' (Law et al., 2011, p. 5). When social researchers are encouraged to seek out these kinds of patronage and institutional partnerships as a condition of their research, clear distinctions between the critical academic and the advocate are difficult to maintain.

Fulfilling this advocacy objective required undertaking the research in ways that would assure its credibility in the institutional settings it would ultimately circulate in. This need for institutional legitimacy created a number of restrictions and challenges for our study of migrant youth. First, the study had to produce quantitative data against social, cultural and economic indicators that could, ideally, be compared to similar studies on the 'status' of young people in Australia. Second, the research also had to adhere to norms of statistical data collection and analysis that would ensure its validity when scrutinised in the mediasphere. This need, for both comparability and rigour, informed the kinds of questions that could be asked of research participants. At the same time, methods were used to ensure that young people themselves had a role in shaping the census instrument. Early photovoice workshops were used to help formulate survey questions and test categories for their relevance to migrant and refugee youth.

Ultimately, decisions to pursue the survey method, and particularly to name our survey the Multicultural Youth Australia Census, can be understood as practices of legitimacy, attaching value and authority to the research. Branding the project a 'census' elevated its importance in the eyes of the thousands of young people enlisted to participate in the research and gave it authority among the organisations and policymakers who might use the research. At the same time, the use of a survey method created some ambivalence because it carried the risk of 'flattening out' the identities of the young people we were hoping to understand. This web of relationships between researchers, policymakers, advocates and migrant youth themselves, contributed to the complexity of the method but also gave the research utility. It is these relationships, the 'administrative conditions' which underpin them, and the research norms that emerge from them, that contribute to how we imagine migrant youth as a population (Ruppert, 2007, p. 9).

The 'social life of methods': situating the census

The discussion of method in this chapter owes much to the literature on the 'social life of methods', which argues against the traditional divisions that have defined social research methodologies. The distinction between 'theory', which produces research questions, and 'method', which is said to provide tools for testing and examining these questions, contributes to a perceived binary between critical and instrumental modes of knowledge (Law et al., 2011, p. 3). Law, Ruppert and Savage suggest that in this view, the task of research is understood as trying to bridge this binary between the empirical and the critical – but that this leads to 'an objectivist concern with "bias" and a humanist response which seeks refuge in an "ineffable" human moment which somehow lies outside this purview of representational methods' (Law et al., 2011, p. 4). Such humanist responses become particularly important in studies of minoritised groups, such as migrant youth, who risk being coopted into instrumentalist strategies for knowing and managing these populations through research. Participatory or self-reflexive methods might be employed as strategies for resisting this instrumentalism. However, these efforts to find the most 'effective', critically informed or reflexive research tools, do not always acknowledge the potential productiveness, and liveliness, of the survey method. Paying attention to this liveliness enables the survey instrument to be a relevant and generative method for researching migrant young people.

The social life of methods literature offers a helpful framework for understanding connections between the institutional worlds that produce research and the social worlds that research produces (Law et al., 2011). Such connections raise challenges for youth researchers because they highlight how research methods are never neutral. Methods perform the social by performing certain realities and not others. Rather than thinking of a population, such as migrant youth in Australia, as an already existing entity waiting to be discovered and represented, such populations are produced through the specific administrative practices that render them an object of knowledge. The institutional relationships that shaped the MY Australia Census methodology, and which worked to make particular narratives about migrant youth lives visible, exemplifies this double action. The census makes certain things visible and not others, partly because of the norms of analysis that go along with quantitative survey methods. In what follows I want to ask whether there are alternative ways of seeing from 'inside the method' (Law et al., 2011, p. 8) which make other realities knowable to researchers.

The census emerged from a historical concern for states to both know their populations and to produce populations as an object and category of government. This objectifying function means that the history of government surveys is also the history of colonialism; to know a population is a practice of power over a population, making it amenable for programs which might civilise or extract value from it. At the same time, when it emerged, the census was seen to offer a more democratic tool for conceiving and acting on the population than was available previously. When the Government Social Survey was implemented in Britain in the 1940s, it marked a shift away from research tools which relied on the privileged voices of a few 'known informants' to the more 'objective' methods of anonymous sampling (Law et al., 2011, p. 5). The census was said to allow a democratic engagement between governments and their populations. Survey instruments continue to form part of a broader ideal that encourages people to 'have a voice' in the processes by which decisions are made about them.

The census constitutes people as individuals at the same time that it situates them as part of a collective: 'It involves classifying, categorising and enumerating people's specific characteristics, and aggregating those individuals and character-istics together to form a governable national population' (Law et al., 2011, p. 5). This dual impulse – to both specify and aggregate individuals – is a form of sub-jectification. As Ruppert argues, the census produces subjects with 'the capacity to recognise themselves as members of a population' (2007, p. 2). The categories defined and circulated by the census become crucial axes by which individual and collective identities are formed. It also means that the practices of identification enabled by being a census subject are connected to the ability to speak to the state – they 'are connected to citizenship and the claiming of social and political rights' (2007, p. 2). The state returns the gaze by which people's self-identification takes place and in doing so legitimates these subjects as citizens.

For the stakeholders who participate in these processes, numbers acquire an affective function. Ian Hacking has characterised censuses as part of an 'ava-lanche of numbers' in the 19th century, a period in which an intense normalisa-tion, codification and standardisation of governmental practices was carried out (Hacking, 1990). Such is the continuing power of numbers that it has been argued, 'the methods of evidence gathering' that produce this data matter more than 'the social scientific results of this evidence gathering' (Campbell, Cox and O'Brien, 2017, p. 50). This is not to say that research findings do not matter, but in the case of the Multicultural Youth Australia project, the validity of its social science methods and its naming as a census shape the meanings and forms of authority that are attached to the research.

These methods also become important ways of establishing trust. Others have argued how relationships of trust are integral to the processes of information exchange embedded in the research process (Wyatt, Harris, Adams and Kelly, 2013, p. 131). Trust in methods must be established in order to persuade those that we seek to influence with the evidence of numbers. This question of trust is particularly significant in the context of youth research. While the quantitative methods of the social science survey have the potential to objectify the youth sub-ject and reiterate hierarchies between the researcher and researched, they can also reassure the youth participant that they are contributing to a process of knowledge production about themselves that is legitimate and important. The MY Australia Census needed to enlist young people in the research process by convincing them to participate. We made a case for the importance of the research through communications with young people, pitching it as an opportunity to 'have your say' and to participate in 'the decisions that affect your lives'. In most respects this pitch was successful – many of the project's respondents were enthusiastic about taking part, leaving notes at the end of the online survey 'thanking' researchers for their efforts. In this way, participation in the census was understood as a practice of citizenship by young people themselves, some of whom we could say felt empowered by the opportunity. Of course, for others, this injunction to participate was a more intimidating one – the census' connections to government and authority meant that some young people responded to the process with suspicion or anxiety.

Despite its limits, a national survey of young people was a strategic response to the particular institutional context and political problem we were intervening in. The MY Australia project had a specific purpose: to construct alternative narratives about migrant youth experiences that would be taken seriously in policy settings. Naming the study a 'census' was an important strategy for ensuring the intelligibility and legitimacy of the research. Law et al. suggest that 'methods inhabit and help to reproduce a complex ecology of representations, realities and advocacies, arrangements and circuits' (Law et al., 2011, p. 13). Elsewhere I have described these circuits and ecologies as the *lifeworlds of policy* to which academic research must find ways to speak (Khan, 2017).

Producing 'multicultural youth': how the method constitutes the social

This section examines how the MY Australia Census produces 'multicultural youth' as a governable population, and the kinds of subjectification and disciplinisation that it entails. One of the starting points for this research project was the conviction that current governmental categories for understanding migrant youth are inadequate. This created a particular kind of pressure for us as youth researchers, to develop ways of knowing young people that do not rely on existing methods and classifications. We were particularly concerned with highlighting the problems with the Australian policy term 'culturally and linguistically diverse', or 'CALD', now the standard descriptor for reporting on migrant or non-White Australians. 'CALD' people are defined as 'those people born overseas, in countries other than those classified by the Australian Bureau of Statistics (ABS) as "main English speaking countries"' (ECCV, 2012, p. 1). The term replaced the previous classification, 'Non-English Speaking Background' or 'NESB' – a category that was perceived to have 'negative connotations' and to homogenise different language and cultural groups (DIMA, 2001, p. 4). However, similar critiques can be made about its successor, CALD, which is 'used broadly and often synonymously with the term "ethnic communities"' (ECCV, 2012). In practice, the term CALD is used imprecisely and inconsistently, and continues to conflate forms of cultural and linguistic difference. Moreover, it has the effect of marginalising those who are referred to as 'CALD communities' rather than positioning cultural difference as central to visions of Australian identity.

One of the risks that our research had to manage was producing a cohort called 'multicultural youth' without homogenising or marginalising them. We were responding to a reality in which 49% of Australians have one or both parents born overseas, and where ethnic, linguistic and religious diversity can no longer be considered minority issues (ABS, 2017). Discussions with the project's stakeholders emphasised that 'diversity is mainstream' and that in contemporary Australia 'we are all multicultural'. At the same time, we needed to acknowledge what was distinctive about those with recent experiences of migration, and the realities of discrimination and exclusion particular to migrant and refugee youth. The project sought to hold on to the specificity of the migrant youth experience without essentialising them, and without conflating the diversity of migrant youth lives.

In this respect, the label 'multicultural' was a useful one. While the term has been rightly problematised as part of a governmental discourse that manages and controls difference (Hage, 1998), in this project it serves a strategic purpose. The term has a very particular policy history in Australia but despite this is used broadly and imprecisely; multiculturalism has become a flexible and provisional policy formation that can be put to work in different ways. In the context of the MY Australia Census, 'multiculturalism' could also be understood as what Ruppert describes as a 'boundary object' that mediates between different communities of practice that are engaged by the research instrument (2007). In the MY Australia project the term is especially useful for constructing a collective identity for young people who participated in the research. In order to participate in the MY Australia Census, potential respondents aged 15–25 had to self-identify as a 'multicultural young person'. The sample of almost 2000 young people was extremely diverse – respondents were born in 91 different countries, lived in different parts of Australia, had a range of reasons for migration and length of time spent in Australia, as well as widely varying levels of English language proficiency. Nevertheless, they identified as 'multicultural youth'. By mobilising this category, the research contributed to a process of self-recognition and self-making that was both individual and communal. In fact, many responses carried a strong civic inflection and reflected the political affiliations and cultural connections amongst this cohort. When asked what they thought were the most important issues facing Australia one participant responded:

> Validated racist rhetoric and the presence of discriminatory parties in government. This [rhetoric] feeds into the disgusting treatment and policy on refugees and asylum seekers. This also affects the everyday interactions and processes we go through. I am a sixth generation Pakistani-Australian but because I look different, speak multiple languages and have a funny name I'm often asked where are you from. . . . [M]yself and a lot of other young

people [feel] as though our voices and skills are not being recognised due to our names on a piece of paper.

Here, the respondent mobilises a kind of collective consciousness, speaking for 'other young people' who are being treated unfairly because of their difference and also connecting this treatment to wider policies on refugees and asylum seekers. The categories of identity and difference set up by the census enable significant forms of attachment and solidarity between different kinds of migrants and 'multicultural youth'. Another respondent writes that the most important national issue is:

Acceptance of people who are not White Australians. Although we claim to be a very multicultural country, which we are, there is still so much racism and discrimination happening.

This young person identifies as 'multicultural', as someone who is affected by Australia's treatment of those 'who are not White Australians' but also as part of the 'we' who is responsible for this treatment. The category of 'multicultural youth', then, enables young people to take on and move between these different locations of citizenship.

Importantly however, while the census helped to produce this self-conscious, collective category of multicultural youth, the category was also one that some respondents expressed ambivalence towards. As well as asking standard questions on country of birth, ancestry and language, the MY Australia Census deliberately sought out flexible and indeterminate terms via which young people could describe their identities. An open-ended question asking respondents to describe their 'ethnic background' encouraged young people to identify the multiple and complex affiliations that shape their identities. Responses included:

'100% Indian'; 'Arabic-Christian'; 'I am half Samoan, half Maori, born in Wellington'; 'I'm awesome'; 'Gaming'.

As well as revealing a rich and detailed picture of hybrid identity, some of these responses can be read as a form of refusal. For some respondents, the question was an opportunity to defy the classificatory schemes informing the census. Claiming 'I'm awesome' or describing one's ethnic background as 'gaming' guards against easy categorisations of migrant youth identity. Such responses deliberately refute the apparent simplicity of the question, 'Where are you from?' and evade efforts on the part of researchers and institutions to 'know' and 'categorise' multicultural youth.

At the same time, others responded to this question by describing their identities in considerable detail, highlighting attachments to languages, group identities and places that are at once partial and multiple. While these responses reiterate the impossibility of being fully 'known' and 'categorised' to researchers, they also express a desire to be understood. These responses perform the complexity of identity for the census and highlight a form of what Nancy Fraser has described as strategic essentialism. Being 'strategically essentialist' involves claiming identity through the available categories, but also complicating and denying the specificity of these categories (Fraser, 1997, in Tyler, 2015). This dual impulse only becomes apparent from reading census results with an attention to the plurality of individual experiences that characterise this cohort. Ruppert makes the distinction between 'macro data' that comprises aggregated, population level statistics, and 'micro data' which captures 'the variability and diversity of individuals that constitute a social space' (2007, p. 4). The latter is often overlooked in the analysis and reporting of survey data. A challenge for the MY Australia project has been to find methods for making this micro data visible.

One technique for working with this micro data has been to cast attention to the materiality of the census itself – for example, by looking to completed, hard copies of the census questions and the myriad ways in which individuals have interacted with them. Doing so reveals the forms of 'classificatory and interpretive struggle' that take place between the individual and institutions of research (Ruppert, 2007, p. 5). Observing the responses that have been crossed out, whited-out, amended or annotated with exclamation marks, smiley faces and sad faces, it becomes clear that respondents have different relationships to the norms of research participation. Their marks and annotations convey an anxiety about these norms. In some cases this anxiety is resolved with a form of refusal. The very last question of the census asks whether 'there is anything else you'd like [the researchers] to know', and many participants responded with a 'no', 'No!' or 'Nope'. These answers might be an expression of frustration or boredom with the census. But they can also be read as an earnest response – participants have nothing further to say but feel compelled to 'complete' the question anyway. These forms of knowledge about how one *should* respond to a survey point to the ways that participation in the census acts to *discipline* subjects. It makes migrant youth governable by training them in a particular practice of citizenship. This is not simply a form of control, however, but as I have suggested earlier, it can also give young people a (qualified) power to speak back to the census; they can express forms of collective identity, agency or refusal of census categories and questions. At any rate, the process of citizen-making enacted by the census is an uneven one, which young people take up in different ways and with different results. Making this plurality, specificity and agency visible requires close attention to the minor material practices through which young people engage with the research instrument.

Conclusion

Historically, the census has stood at the interface between the individual and the state. The census produces populations but does so by producing individual census subjects – as we have seen, by instilling capacities of citizenship that are developed through the census-taking process. In this chapter I have argued that rather than understanding such practices simply as processes of objectification, the census can be characterised as a lively research instrument. The Multicultural Youth Australia Census does not construct 'multicultural youth' as a reductive or essentialising category but opens up a platform in which young people can engage with institutional knowledge production about their lives, in ways that are ambiguous, contradictory, agential and as a tool for expressing collective identity and civic connection. While the census categories and questions reflected the research priorities of academic researchers and their partners in the multicultural youth 'sector', migrant youth responded to these with particular forms of capital or 'knowingness', which show how 'social agents are increasingly aware of the social classifications which they work with, and are increasingly concerned to position themselves with respect to such classifications' (Savage, 2013, p. 11). Others have explained how this capacity to resist or question classification is part of being a citizen; institutional discourses of citizenship discipline people to be loyal and compliant members of a polity, but in liberal democracies, they also grant them the right to disagree or protest (Stevenson, 2003). Struggles over categorisation can work to reinforce, or contribute to, broader collective struggles over identity and inclusion. The census embodies this tension between establishing relations of trust and making visible the ways in which institutional categories and modes of knowing fall short of complex realities.

The liveliness of the research instrument extends to what is done with the census data itself. A quantitative survey method was crucial in this project for giving the research findings institutional authority. However, efforts can also be made to ensure that the findings have value for the youth participants in the research. The project is developing 'youth-friendly' modes of reporting, including visual material for social media and enlisting migrant youth into the reporting process. The census is not the endpoint for this research but the beginning of an iterative process in which the research continues to have a life, incorporating feedback and contestations from the project's partners, from policymakers, the media and migrant youth themselves. The MY Australia Census, in this sense, becomes a participatory and circular method rather than a reductive and linear one. It is through both the 'doing' and the 'reading' of the census that it produces social and institutional relations, but it is also through circulating and remaking the research instrument that it goes on to be useful to different stakeholders in the research.

Note

1 ARC LP150100219 2015–2018 'Defining the Status of Culturally and Linguistically Diverse Young People'.

References

Australian Bureau of Statistics. (2017) '2016 Census: Multicultural', Australian Bureau of Statistics. Available at: https://www.abs.gov.au/ausstats/abs@.nsf/lookup/Media%20 Release3 (Accessed 28 September 2019).

Australian Institute of Family Studies. (2012) 'What Is Evidence-based Policy and Practice?' Available at: https://aifs.gov.au/cfca/2012/07/16/what-is-evidence-based-policy-and-practice (Accessed 2 October 2019).

Belfiore, E. (2009) 'On Bullshit in Cultural Policy Practice and Research: Notes From the British Case', *International Journal of Cultural Policy*, 15(3), 343–359.

Campbell, P., Cox, T. and O'Brien, D. (2017) 'The Social Life of Measurement: How Methods Have Shaped the Idea of Culture in Urban Regeneration', *Journal of Cultural Economy*, 10(1), 49–62.

Centre for Multicultural Youth. (2014) 'About Us', *Centre for Multicultural Youth*. Available at: www.cmy.net.au/about-us (Accessed 10 June 2018).

Department of Immigration and Multicultural Affairs. (2001) 'The Guide: Implementing the Standards for Statistics on Cultural and Language Diversity', D. o. I. a. M. Affairs. Canberra, ACT.

Dirks, N. (2001) *Castes of Mind: Colonialism and the Making of Modern India* (Princeton: Princeton University Press).

Ethnic Communities' Council of Victoria. (2012) 'ECCV Glossary of Terms', *Ethnic Communities' Council of Victoria*. Available at: https://eccv.org.au/wp-content/uploads/2018/07/2-ECCV_Glossary_of_Terms_23_October.docx (Accessed 2 October 2019).

Fraser, N. (1997) *Justice Interruptus: Critical Reflections on the 'Postsocialist' Condition* (London: Routledge).

Hacking, I. (1990) *The Taming of Chance* (Cambridge: Cambridge University Press).

Hage, G. (1998) *White Nation: Fantasies of White Supremacy in a Multicultural Nation* (Annandale, NSW: Pluto Press).

Khan, R. (2017) 'Researchers, Bureaucrats and the Lifeworlds of Cultural Policy', *International Journal of Cultural Policy*, 1–13.

Law, J., Ruppert, E. and Savage, M. (2011) 'The Double Social Life of Methods', *CRESC Working Paper No. 95*. Faculty of Social Sciences, Open University.

Mission Australia. (2017) 'Mission Australia Youth Survey Report 2017', *Mission Australia*. Available at: https://www.missionaustralia.com.au/publications/youth-survey/746-youth-survey-2017-report/file (Accessed 2 October 2019).

Noble, G. (2011) '"Bumping Into Alterity": Transacting Cultural Complexities', *Continuum*, 25(6), 827–840.

Ruppert, E. (2007) 'Producing Population', *CRESC Working Paper No. 37*. Faculty of Social Sciences, Open University.

Savage, M. (2013) 'The "Social Life of Methods": A Critical Introduction', *Theory, Culture & Society*, 30(4), 3–21.

Stanwick, J., et al. (2013) *How Young People are Faring 2013* (Melbourne: Foundation for Young Australians).

Stevenson, N. (2003) *Cultural Citizenship: Cosmopolitan Questions* (Maidenhead: Open University Press).

Tyler, I. (2015) 'Classificatory Struggles: Class, Culture and Inequality in Neoliberal Times', *The Sociological Review*, 63(2), 493–511.

Wyatt, S., Harris, A., Adams, S. and Kelly, S.E. (2013) 'Illness Online: Self-Reported Data and Questions of Trust in Medical and Social Research', *Theory, Culture & Society*, 30(4), 131–150.

Chapter 18

The pressures of building reciprocal relationships in an intergenerational research team

Darren Sharpe

Introduction

This chapter explores the building and maintenance of reciprocal relationships in an intergenerational research team investigating children and young peoples' perceptions of the UK child protection system. The origin of this chapter is a study entitled *Recognition and Telling: Developing Earlier Routes to Help for Children and Young People* (Cossar et al., 2013; Cossar, Brandon, and Jordan, 2016). The study was funded by the Children's Commissioner Office in England and undertaken by two universities, one local government authority and a children's charity. Young people were involved in the research commissioning process and were part of the research advisory group and research team. This chapter focuses on the role of the young researchers who contributed to coproducing the recruitment leaflets, advised on ethical aspects of the research, contributed to the design of activity-based interviews, co-facilitated workshops held with children, young people and adult professionals and helped to produce a children's and young people's version of the final report.

The study aimed to examine young people's perceptions of abuse and neglect and to explore their experiences of telling and getting help from both informal and formal sources. We intended to use this knowledge to make suggestions for practice that would improve access to support following abuse. The study was prompted by the Munro Review of Child Protection, which was established in 2010 in the wake of the Peter Connolly crisis and the subsequent report by Lord Laming (2009). One of the key recommendations in the final report (Munro, 2011) was that more should be done to look at how children's rights, wishes, feelings and experiences are used to inform what help and services they are getting and whether what is provided to children, young people and their families is helping to keep children safe. This chapter focuses on the research team's different experiences in investigating young people's complex lives. Thinking critically about the concept of 'reciprocal relationships' in social research, this chapter argues that we must look beyond the dilemma posed by the policy and practice nexus – which often puts pressures on building trusting relationships – and use the freedoms incumbent in applied social research as a platform to innovate how adult researchers and young researchers coproduce knowledge. The inferences made in this chapter are based on my observations (adult researcher) and monitoring data and feedback from the young researchers during debrief sessions.

Critical reflections on researching with young people

Over the last 18 years, I have had the opportunity to be at the forefront of the young researchers' movement in the UK and Europe, involved in the commissioning and delivery of research with, by and for children and young people in order to help inform and shape policy and practice. My work started in the 1990s, which was a period of high public spending and which witnessed growing interest in user involvement in policy research. Now in uncertain economic times in Europe, the efforts to effectively involve disadvantaged groups of children and young people in policy research is undermined by public cuts. In my view, this fraught sociopolitical environment has provided researchers with the grounds to innovate and find new ways to better involve young people in research to uphold the United Nations Convention on the Rights of the Child. Involving young people in research can focus on issues about children and young people or about other people's issues. They can be involved as peer researchers or coresearchers. They can engage in research projects led by children and young people or those led by adults involving children and young people (see Morrow, 2008; Powell and Smith, 2009; Sharpe, 2009; Graham and Fitzgerald, 2010; Holland, 2010 Törrönen and Vauhkonen, 2012). There are a multitude of different ways and reasons for involving young people in real-world research, but all come with their unique pressures and challenges.

This chapter draws on the concept of 'reciprocal relationships' to help explain the pressures we experienced as an intergenerational research team. The members of the research team shared social work biographies as both 'recipients' and 'providers' of social care, although at the time of the study all the members took on the role of 'researcher'. As alluded to, the study aimed to better understand the enablers and barriers to children and young people using the UK child protection system. In the UK context, local government[1] have the responsibility to protect and support children and young people who are in need or under a protection order. Acting on behalf of local government, the role of social workers is to support, protect and empower people, as well as having statutory duties and other obligations that may be viewed as coercive and restrict people's freedoms. As a result, social work is often thought of quite narrowly in the UK. It is associated with professionalised practices of assessment, management and resolution of individualised 'problems' (see Smith, 2010). In the Munro Review (2011), the social work profession was criticised for excessive bureaucratisation and focus on risk management at the expense of engagement with children and families. The rethinking of social work practice in the UK stresses models of strengthening and improving the relationships in children's lives to better assess risks, need and strengths. Against this backdrop, the intergenerational research team modelled this way of working in order to build trusting and empowering relationships to successfully complete the study.[2]

Young people as 'expert by experience'

It is important to note that the young researchers were not subjects of the study but coinvestigators. Their knowledge was considered to be on a par with the adult researchers but from a different standpoint. They were experts by experience (Clewes, 2014), since they had over time built up knowledge of negotiating and navigating the child protection system. The adult researchers were experts based on practice in delivering child protection services. The recruitment and selection of the young people as coresearchers in the study was narrowly focused on their biographies to match the population under investigation and proximity to the adult researchers and study sites, as well as their willingness and ability to get involved. Table 18.1 illustrates the reasons why we involved young people in this study.

Table 18.1 Reasons to involve young people in the study

Reason to Involve Young People in research

Justification	Description
Producing trustworthy data	A participative approach involving young people as collaborators allows professional researchers to develop a feasible, flexible and adult-facilitated but youth-friendly evaluation plan to accomplish the stated goals of the evaluation specifications.
Insider knowledge	Research conducted with young people provides interesting, noninstitutional knowledge regarding the lives and experiences of young people. Noninstitutional knowledge is more grounded in the interests of the young people themselves. It can complement or even transform knowledge produced from institutional and adult perspectives, and it can be utilised in the ongoing campaigns.
Navigating micro politics	The young people will be familiar with the geography and risk factors that will limit the scope of the evaluation and provide answers to ways of working with or involving other children and young people.
Voice and influence	Active involvement in the evaluation process will enhance the young people's opportunities to influence sociopolitical issues (an overall aim of the programme), as well as having a positive effect on their citizenship, their position in society and their right to be heard.
Moral and legal rights	Listening to what young people have to say is an integral part of social work community. Involving young people actively in the evaluation process is an extension of this, and part of the participation agenda.

This research offered a unique opportunity for care-experienced young people to have a genuine podium to feel more confident about their 'care identity' and less stigmatised and stereotyped by society, as well as to be more understood and respected by professionals and non-care-experienced young people. The team's dynamic (i.e., it resembled the conventional workplace relationship, the experienced colleague mentoring the less-experienced colleague, and the social work client–worker relationship) challenged the underlying negative stereotypes and stigma attached to being social worked. The spider's web of relationships we embarked on needed to be carefully managed so that each person could expect to benefit from exposure to the study and receive the right level of support. In other words, to build reliable relationships, trust and cooperation were essential components. Through reciprocated relationships, the team was forced to confront the thorny issues of ageism, 'racism', masculine hyper-performativity, teenage sexuality, class and ableism linked to inclusion. These issues were complicated further by family crises, pregnancy, exam and coursework anxiety, long periods of silence, insecure housing and unemployment, work demands and personal difficulties that arose over the time of the study. The fluid and changing life circumstances did not stop all of the young researchers from continuing to work. Paradoxically, this dynamic served to strengthen relationships, and in the long term it improved the quality of coproduced knowledge.

Focusing for a moment on the concept of coproduction, the anthropological idea of 'gift giving' (Malinowski, 1922) is a useful concept to use in describing the adhesive that bound us together to form a research team. In this instance, the notion of gift giving was the cultural capital excavated from the young researchers' biographies, which was exchanged economically and morally in the realisation of their voice and influence in the study. Reciprocated relationships can find expression through the idea of 'social capital'. As Billett (2012) suggests, the idea of indicators of youth social capital provides a youth-centric conceptual framework to situate young people with care experience as more than passive recipients of a process or system and instead allows young people to be understood as having assets within the child protection system. Social capital is usually regarded in more clinical terms than assets, but it provides us with a useful way to illustrate how young researchers with care experience have skills and knowledge that can be activated and mobilised for the advancement of others, which is the underlying mechanism of social capital.

Social capital is a contested concept, with many different approaches to how it is defined and analytically applied (Coleman, 1988; Halpern, 1999; Hall, 1999; Putnam, 2000). The concept of social capital was developed, in part, by Bourdieu (2011), who posits that there are three main forms of capital: social, cultural and economic. These forms of capital are related to each other, so that the existence of one facilitates the acquisition of the others. The concept of social capital can be applied on an individual level, starting from personal experiences to evidence personal competencies and leading to theories about trust, resilience and reciprocity (Boeck and Fleming, 2011). In this sense, social capital has been defined as the resources to which a person has access by means of his/her social bonds and relations (Bourdieu, 2005). Social bonds can be more or less institutionalised, such as clubs and groups, but can also be with family, friends or colleagues. Granovetter (1973) and Putnam (2000) found that the quality of social networks can be more important than the quantity. In this sense, Putnam (2000) differentiates between 'bonding' and 'bridging' social capital: bonding social capital supports solidarity within existing tighter groups, whereas bridging social capital creates new chances beyond the group through relations between individuals who occupy distant social positions. This research drew heavily on this resource and reciprocated by providing the young researchers with exposure to new people, networks and environments.

Narrative of reciprocal relationships in social policy research

This section provides background information on the young researchers who applied to be part of the intergenerational research team. We examine how the young people were recruited, trained and supported to contribute to the different strands of the study, and how we hoped to mitigate the complexities and pressures of involving young people who were living with, and working through, adverse childhood experiences and living in socially excluded communities. We set out to make the research strategy as young-person-friendly as possible, without undermining scientific rigour or avoiding the bureaucratic structures and procedures required by the participating organisations. These conscious steps towards inclusivity and coproduction resulted in slippage in time, curtailing the research activities for some of the younger team members and requiring continual reassessment of the team's expectation and ability to cope with the pressures of doing real-world research.

In total, 18 young people from disadvantaged and socially excluded backgrounds responded to our call to be part of the research team; 67% were male and 33% were female, and they were aged 17 to 22. They had in common experiences of foster care, homelessness, autism, racism, being a young parent, convictions and recreational drug use. The minimum age to join the project was set at 16 years due to the sensitivity of the material to which they would be exposed and also the ability to travel independently to and from the training and fieldwork sites. Of the young researchers, 11% needed a risk assessment to be completed to top-up their conventional Disclosure and Barring Service (DBS) check due to recorded offences and pending sentencings. The unconventional backgrounds of the young people did not prevent them from joining the research team but did determine the role they would go on to play in the study. For example, it was agreed with the funder that young people without a satisfactory DBS check could not co-run workshops in schools with primary-age children. Most of the young people responded to advertisements posted by the participating organisations (e.g., 44% children's charity, 39% local council and 17% self-nominated), who served as initial gatekeepers and later provided ongoing support for the research team. It was of paramount importance to the success of the study that we had a well thought through support system in place on par with the research activities. The study would not disrupt the young people's schooling, work or training, or overburden them.

The study attracted 18 young people from the outset, with ten active young people by the mid-point, which reduced to five upon completion. We experienced high levels of churn in the first two quarters while the study was being established. During this period, we coordinated two separate groups, which were based on geography (i.e., semi-rural and ultra-urban), before merging both groups. This approach served two purposes. First, pragmatically, we needed to reach young people in their own local spaces in order to fit around their schedules (e.g., 39% in full-time training, 6% in higher education, 6% in further education, 22% in sixth form, 6% volunteering, 6% on an apprenticeship and 17% NEET), and second, we needed to rapidly build-in knowledge about the study and establish good working relationships to start having authentic conversations. We proactively worked to minimise any disruptive factors that would prevent the young people from being their true 'self' and opening up to other young people with whom they shared local referent points.

The accumulative number of hours worked on the study by the young researchers was 318.55. With three adult researchers, we spent on average just under 32 hours – or four working days over the life of the study – with each of the young researchers. While four days does not sound like a lot of time to build trusting working relationships, when split over two years we shared episodes of highs and lows in each other's lives, which strengthened the team relationships. In practice, the direct contact time between the adult researchers and the young researchers was approximately 14 hours per month or 3.5 hours per week with each young researcher. This level of direct contact time with young researchers was not spread evenly but occurred in bursts aligned to research activities. The downside to periods of nonactivity was that it could result in the young researchers' disengagement from the study. We know the time dedicated to the study because we recorded every activity in order to remunerate the young researchers based on their input. When a direct payment was not possible – due to the young person lacking an active bank account or the necessary paperwork to open an account – we paid them with vouchers of the same monetary value for time worked in the study.

Despite our success in concurrently establishing two young researcher groups, in quick succession we lost young people reportedly due to them feeling out of their depth with the research-skills training or due to personal discomfort following reviewing online threads of abuse and neglect (i.e., posted blog chat), pregnancies and bouts of homelessness. In the start-up phase of the study, not all the young researchers felt comfortable sharing personal information with the team, and they often asked their support workers to explain their withdrawal. We accounted for attrition by overrecruiting at the start of the study. We also learnt that asking the young people to commit for block periods of three months – building pathways for exit and reentry – helped to focus attention and normalise periods of long absences in the study.

With the remaining young researchers, we quickly built up a good rapport and also successfully merged the groups. Merging the groups did not occur without certain risks. For instance, we often experienced discussion that became haphazard – which could be taken as a sign of confidence and comfortability with one another – that led to new lines of inquiry and the refinement in ideas but also rendered team members speechless (detailed later). An example of where conversations worked well and the team members were able to bounce off each other was in an early exercise ranking the seriousness of different types of neglect and abuse gathered from the content analysis (e.g., peer-to-peer violence, abuse at the hands of a stranger and abuse by someone known to you). The young people were asked by the adult researchers to consider the very practical issues of when, where, how and why young people would disclose cases of neglect or abuse to an adult.

The young researchers often described their own lived experience to help them frame and qualify their response. This factor is difficult to reconcile in terms of how much or how little you should encourage open self-reflection to drive debate and discussion. We quickly learnt through deliberative dialogue that telling runs much deeper than the abuse itself. For instance, the young researchers candidly talked about why they might not tell. Young researchers affirmed that 'out of fear' and the 'loss of control' are reasons that prevent some children and young people telling. They suggested that telling eventually happens out of desperation because things have gotten so bad rather than as a result of an informed decision to get early help. The urgency to tell was described as an all-consuming necessity. However, for boys, telling can come with additional barriers, as they might not be believed by peers, especially 'black boys', who might fear that they cannot tell the police about their problems because of historical reasons for mistrust of the UK police force. In other cases, adults might pick up and respond to the symptoms and not the cause of the problem, and young people could be stereotyped simply as a problem teenager. The sharing of biographies interwoven with the discussion on the online threads helped adult team members to better understand the complexities of telling from a young person's perspective and enabled us to go back and refine the analytical framework.

The young researchers also tested the assumptions held by the adult researchers about why certain young people might not tell of abuse and neglect. The adult researchers, whose biographies had been shaped by and large through decades of social work and social policy research, held a different story about why children and young people who do not tell of abuse and neglect might avoid safeguarding structures. They also pointed out and sympathised with the moral dilemma faced by adults who in their work have to make decisions to protect vulnerable children and young people from harm. While deliberative dialogue was productive on the whole, to have their voices heard, the young researchers pushed personal boundaries with the adult researchers and with peers. Their honesty sometimes resulted in an atmosphere of unease in the room that could easily silence members of the team. It tested the adult researchers' resolve to preserve an inclusive and supportive atmosphere.

Moving the team in one direction was partially my responsibility; this undertaking was not always so straightforward. Widening participation to involve young people in research has its inherent challenges, such as planning activities around times suitable for young people and striking a balance between dedicating limited time and resources to the delivery of the study weighed against dealing with the private concerns of the individual young researchers. Conviction in the research goals sustained the team. We each held the belief that something positive would inevitably come out of the study, which kept us all on track. For instance, the safeguarding requirements in the UK made it necessary for all members of the research team to undergo a Disclosure and Barring Service (DBS) check. This requirement left the adult researchers and the young researchers in a state of limbo as DBS checks were compulsory and lengthy to complete. A number of the young researchers did not possess key documentation that would prove their identity (e.g., passport, driver's licence, birth certificate) or where they lived (e.g., utility bill, bank statement, tenancy agreement). We partially resolved this impasse by completing in-depth risk assessments designed by the Youth Offending Team. The absence of personal documentation also prevented some of the young people from being registered and paid as an employee of the university. Due to UK employment law, proof of identity, residency and right to work in the UK for non-British citizens was a requirement, as was having an active bank account. University Human Resources were patient and supported the study as best they could, even though employing school-age children was uncharted territory for them. All the young researchers were paid the minimum wage for a research assistant or vouchers of the same value.

Crucially, half of the young researchers who stayed the full course of the study received vouchers, and some young researchers moved from cash payment to vouchers because of a change in their circumstances. The desire to pay young researchers for their involvement linked to a university pay grade demonstrated the value and trust that the adult researchers placed in the young researchers to coproduce knowledge. Adequate remuneration recognised that the young people's contribution to the study was valued and also served as a motivation to stay involved. It was unlikely that the adult researchers could or would have stayed involved in the study without a salary, so why would we expect young people to stay involved without recognition of their time and expertise?

Returning to the issue of DBS checks, as a result of involvement in the study, all the young researchers entered a child protection vetting system designed primarily for adults. The background checks opened up a Pandora's box for young researchers with care experience. All the young researchers had at some time experienced and moved on from a problematic episode in their short lives, but they were required to revisit this time in the telling of criminal activities. This critical moment in the study could have undone all our hard work to build trust in the relationships. We needed to say 'no' to a number of young researchers to stop them from taking part in all strands of the study upon hearing their disclosures. Ironically, this critical moment served to strengthen trust and cooperation across the team. In practice, this level of scrutiny will typically prevent the most marginalised and vulnerable groups of young people from actively taking part in research because they have a criminal record. The Prison Reform Trust suggests that children aged 10 to 17 in care are more than five times as likely to be in trouble than others. A brush with the law was certainly the case for a few of the young researchers, who had recent convictions. But we creatively found ways around this obstacle that met our funders' and young researchers' needs and expectations. To summarise, by the end of the recruitment phase we had a study team diverse in ages and backgrounds as well as in motivation.

How young people were trained and supported to effectively contribute to the research processes

Providing good research-skills training not only provided the young researchers with knowledge on how to stay safe but also promoted accountability in their decision making. Good research-skills training makes great effort to help young researchers express themselves authentically and empirically. How young researchers then translated those skills and attributes into an ethical code of conduct is dependent on their ongoing support. We worked under the assumption that each of the young researchers had assets to contribute to the development and implementation of the study. For example, the young researchers' knowledge of the daily realities and concerns of the research population helped in the development of the research materials (e.g., consent form and participant information sheets) to ensure that the study was clear and accessible for potential participants.

The young researchers' exposure to research-skills training was not the first or only time they had encountered situational ethics. Most, if not all, of the young researchers have sought answers to their own set of circumstances that involved exploration in the complexities of being young and devoid of adequate support systems. Some young researchers reported that they had had to endure in the past humiliation at the hands of parents and adults who should have been protecting them, as well as harm by their peers. They have been forced to deal with questions of guilt and shame, pleasure and desire, as victims or perpetrators, and witnessed distressing and degrading acts. They have seen the paradoxes of home, school and leisure as spaces of harm and safety, and finally the difficulties in finding responsible adults to confide in. Using the research-skills training, the young researchers were able to bridge their lived experience to make sense of the data collected.

Most, if not all, of the young researchers enhanced and built new skills to become sensitive young researchers. They performed well in the field, consciously applying their training and knowledge to good effect. As alluded to, building trusting and cooperative relationships came with certain challenges, and on the odd occasions young researchers fell back on old patterns of disruptive behaviour in order to control the environment and get their voices heard. Based on my observation, these occurrences came about due to the blurring between social worked young people and social workers turned academics meeting in a research space. For some young and adult researchers, the level of what you could expect from team members went below or above the normal expectations of a study team.

How we overcame significant challenges in the implementation of the study

In child protection studies, finding the right balance for youth engagement is linked to the funding envelope, and this was a constant challenge in our study. Other similar studies, such as by Tucker (2012), adopted a remote way of involving and working together with young people from across the UK, which drastically cut costs to bring young people together, but limited where and how they could become involved in the study. Both studies show that there are different ways to involve young people in sensitive research and that one approach does not fit all. Both studies also demonstrate how the young researchers' insider knowledge of the child protection system was the prime currency in which we traded to strengthen the internal validity of the research findings. Similarly, the role of the adult researcher in both studies fluctuated from being a facilitator, educator, critical friend and principle investigator – periodically and momentarily – in order to ensure the production of high-quality data and to nurture a strength-based environment in which the young researchers could perform at their very best and feel comfortable to take risks and make mistakes. Over time, the maturity in our working relationship effectively accommodated space for risk taking, often leading to the coproduction of knowledge that tested the strength of organisational policies and practices. While there is plenty of training and literature available on diversity in the workplace and interdisciplinary research teams, very little information exists on intergenerational research teams. We made a lot of assumptions about how things would unfold, based implicitly on our shared social work biographies. However, the realities of fusing adults from different academic institutions together and interfacing with adults from the funding organisation was complex enough without the added layer of young people with a highly diverse range of needs. Table 18.2 illustrates the challenges and dilemmas we encountered as an intergenerational research team.

Not everything could be planned for and controlled. For example, we were literally unable to find young people while simply crossing a busy urban road, riding on a bus and minutes before a presentation, despite arriving a day early to present at the conference. When involving vulnerable groups of young people in research, we learnt to expect the unexpected. We learnt that you will always need a plan 'B' and 'C' should the young people deviate from plan 'A'. Events can occur so fast that, as an adult researcher, you can only react to events. Nonetheless, we continued to provide an inclusive research environment and offered a wide range of research experiences that stretched the young researchers, which

Table 18.2 Overcoming challenges in research with young people

The key challenges gathered from the young researchers	Risk	Mitigation steps
Who decides on the research tasks I do?	For young researchers, they might opt-out of the study if they are not involved in choosing and codesigning tasks.	For adult researchers, they must identify all the tasks that will be needed to complete the project. Assign tasks making use of team strengths or areas where development is desired. Carefully manage expectations of roles and responsibilities.
When do I get paid?	For young researchers, feelings of anxiety in submitting timesheets and waiting for payments in their first job.	For adult researchers, there are some things about getting paid they will need to know during their induction. Attention should also be given to payroll to set the right tax codes for casual workers.
Will my pay affect my welfare benefit or my carer's allowance?	Disruption in welfare and housing benefits resulting from the recalculation of payments paid by the study.	Plan an agile remuneration system to ensure that no young person in receipt of state welfare is penalised for being involved in research.
Can I claim twice for travel expenses?	Study risks overspending on its nondirect staff costs.	Understanding the roles and responsibilities of all the organisations involved in supporting the young person and establishing a clear joint protocol on remunerations.
What happens if I am absent or perform below expectations?	Periods of unexplained silences and poor punctuality.	For adult researchers, timetabling research activities/meetings in young-people-friendly times/locations that will make involvement accessible to most, if not all, the young people.
What happens if I experience a family tragedy, pregnancy, court appearance, homelessness and changes and/or loss of mobile phone?	Low performance or concentration resulting in slippage and study deficit.	For adult researchers, person-centred support and mentoring is essential to establish trusting relationships, which goes beyond research-skills training and allows the young person to share what matters most to them.

(Continued)

Table 18.2 (Continued)

The key challenges gathered from the young researchers	Risk	Mitigation steps
What happens if I use 'soft drugs' (i.e., cannabis) in the proximity of adult members of the research team and/ or experience unwelcomed sexual flirtation by fellow young coinquirers?	Unfriendly behaviour (i.e., presentation of loud and antagonistic behaviour) resulting in opting-out.	For adult researchers, setting healthy boundaries is important, especially as employees of an organisation and representing public bodies. We learnt how to navigate and negotiate relationships that can become blurred when forming trusting relationships in practising person-centred support.
Why do I always miss out on opportunities?	Unmet expectations resulting in opting-out.	For adult researchers, they must strive to prevent young people falling into victimhood modes of behaviour and provide equitable opportunities to get involved in the study.
What will happen if I experience pressures in doing my accreditation, school work and being involved in the study?	ASDAN portfolios or other modes of accreditation not being completed by the young person and the task falling on adult members of the team.	For adult researchers, to agree with young people if they want to go down the route of accreditation and if so, how they would balance this with other areas of their lives.
How do you budget for the involvement of young people in the study?	Loss of expenses (e.g., prepaid train tickets not used by young people).	For adult researchers, they should build in loss in expenditure resulting from involvement of young people. Plan as best as possible, but the study will almost certainly incur losses due to prepaid bookings and incur additional expenses such as taxi rides to ensure the timely and safe transport of a young person, a meal or the urgent purchase of seasonal clothing.

was sustained by our 'reciprocated relationships'. The reciprocated relationships formed the safety net to participation in the study. Rather than being reactive, we always deliberated, and solved problems together. We would look at the problem and its implications from a personal and study level before reaching a decision. All the young people that stayed until the end blossomed as young adults because they experienced having an amplified voice and influence.

The flipside to the young researchers' empowerment was, on occasions, an unwillingness to give way, which resulted in strained relations in the team. We feel that the pressures underlying such moments were lessened through our codependency and sense of ownership of the study. As mentioned, issues and concerns were always resolved at a personal and project level, but without an authentic attempt to empower the young researchers, some issues would not have been voiced, leading to misaligned expectations and a failure to meet the needs of the team. For example, the original study plan comprised two focus groups with children and young people in schools. However, adult members of the team decided to drop the second focus group, based on what the data collected had been telling us. A few of the young researchers who were unable to take part in the first round of focus groups due to geographic distance felt unfairly treated. Consequently, they requested that we run a second focus group, which they could cofacilitate. The decision was made to explore this option and to reinstate the second focus group, although it was very unlikely to yield any new insights. This issue dominated several project meetings before the decision was made not to run an additional focus group, which the young researchers finally accepted.

The most challenging or awkward moment in the study came near to its end. A number of the young researchers voiced their concerns over the number of hours being allocated to them. They wanted opportunity to earn equal to their fellow young researchers. They also wanted greater recognition and visibility in the work and cited the broken trust in the relationship. They questioned why the adults had taken on tasks independently, such as writing the main study report. Other young researchers acknowledged that they had never expected to take part in the write-up of the study. In retrospect, we needed to set clearer parameters and not fear saying 'no' when it was required. I feel that the team's social work backgrounds prevented this frank and honest exchange from occurring, and instead we fell into the trap of not speaking in absolute terms out of fear of upsetting and/or setting back the young researchers.

This dilemma is a tightrope that all intergenerational research teams must face. Regardless of high-quality research skills, training young people will always require ongoing support to cope with the pressures of doing applied social research. All social encounters present new and challenging situations, and although safety is a dual responsibility, there will be times when the adult researcher will need to respond to incidents straightaway for the welfare of the young researcher. They might be confronted with threats of physical harm or witness an event that causes them distress. Debriefing and support sessions should always be available, along with individual reviews where exit strategies can be planned, so that time away from the project does not equate to failure. Young researchers should also be reminded not to masquerade as a social worker, counsellor or friend to the study participants. It is perfectly natural to want to help others, but as early career researchers they are finding their role in the team, and lines can often be blurred when you have to collect data with care. Thus, young researchers need clarity around their roles and responsibilities and to know what is to be expected to help them cope with the pressures of walking away from respondents.

Conclusion

This chapter does not rest on a notion of childhood innocence, but it faces up to the reality of working with some of the most disadvantaged and marginalised groups of young people in society. This chapter argues that such young people should not be penalised from taking part in research. On the contrary, they have so much to give in practice and in theory. The trouble arises when there are no clear guidelines on how to disentangle young people and their biographies from a system of scrutiny designed by adults for adults. We advocate that young people should experience high-quality research-skills training to ensure that the research, and the researcher's conduct, are safe and robust. It is about cultivating competent and highly skilled coinquirers but not expecting postgraduate-level performance following one weekend's training. To recap, a number of the young people success-fully used this experience as a springboard into higher education and meaningful employment, whereas other young people gained from the exposure to new people and new ways of doing things, which in turn enhanced their skills, confidence and self-esteem.

> Being part of the recognition and telling study has been an eye-opening experience for me. Not only because it was my first time doing research but knowing that I will help or even save the lives of children and young people has been a great and interesting experience for me.
>
> (Anabel Acheampong, Young Researcher ARU)

> I am proud to have worked on the study as an Associate Research Assistant. The project was unique in its commitment to working with young people in the research process and ensuring that our views and analysis was reflected in the final report.
>
> (Joshua Snape, Young Researcher)

Acknowledgements

I would like to acknowledge the young researchers whose efforts and hard work contributed to the success of the study.

The study, called *Recognition, Telling and Seeking Help with Abuse and Neglect*, was funded by the Office of the Children's Commissioner in England, 2014.

Dr Darren Sharpe was in part supported by the National Institute for Health Research (NIHR) Collaboration for Leadership in Applied Health Research and Care (CLAHRC) North Thames at Bart's Health NHS Trust. The views expressed are those of the author(s) and not necessarily those of the NHS, the NIHR or the Department of Health and Social Care.

Notes

1 Local authority children's services have responsibilities under the Children Act 1989 for the children they look after and who live with foster carers or in residential care on either a short- or long-term basis.
2 The study was qualitative in orientation and employed an 'action research' (Carr and Kemmis, 1986) approach in the data collection and analyses. The study commenced in 2010 and was completed in 2013. Ethical approval was given by the University of East Anglia and Anglia Ruskin University Research Ethics Committees and through the research governance procedures of the participating organisations.

References

Billett, P. (2012) 'Indicators of Youth Social Capital: The Case for Not Using Adult Indicators in the Measurement of Youth Social Capital', *Youth Studies Australia*, 31(2), 9–15.

Boeck, T. and Fleming, J. (2011) 'The Role of Social Capital and Resources in Resilience to Risk', in H. Kemshall and B. Wilkindon (eds.), *Good Practice in Assessing Risk: Current Knowledge, Issues and Approaches* (London: Jessica Kingsley).

Bourdieu, P. (2005) *The Social Structures of the Economy* (Cambridge: Polity Press).

Bourdieu, P. (2011) 'The Forms of Capital (1986)', in I. Szeman and T. Kaposy (eds.), *Cultural Theory: An Anthology* (Oxford: Wiley-Blackwell), 81–93.

Carr, W. and Kemmis, S. (1986) *Becoming Critical: Education, Knowledge and Action Research* (London: Falmer).

Clewes, J. (2014) 'Could Experts by Experience Gain Positions of Real Power?', *Mental Health Today*, 24–27 November–December.

Coleman, J.S. (1988) 'Social Capital in the Creation of Human Capital', *American Journal of Sociology*, 94, S95–S120.

Cossar, J., Brandon, M., Bailey, S., Belderson, P., Biggart, L. and Sharpe, D. (2013) *'It Takes a Lot to Build Trust'. Recognition and Telling: Developing Earlier Routes to Help for Children and Young People* (London: Office of the Children's Commissioner).

Cossar, J., Brandon, M. and Jordan, P. (2016) '"You've Got to Trust Her and She's Got to Trust You": Children's Views on Participation in the Child Protection System', *Child and Family Social Work*, 21(1), 103–112.

Graham, A. and Fitzgerald, R. (2010) 'Progressing Children's Participation: Exploring the Potential of a Dialogical Turn', *Childhood*, 17(3), 343–359.

Granovetter, M. (1973) 'The Strength of Weak Ties', *The American Journal of Sociology*, 78(6), 1360–1380.

Hall, P.A. (1999) 'Social Capital in Britain', *British Journal of Political Science*, 29(3), 417–461.

Halpern, D. (1999) *Social Capital: The New Golden Goose* (London: Institute for Public Policy Research).

Holland, S. (2010) 'Trust in the Community: Understanding the Relationship Between Formal, Semi-Formal and Informal Child Safeguarding in a Local Neighbourhood', *The British Journal of Social Work*, 44(2), 384–400.

Laming, H.B. (2009) *The Protection of Children in England: A Progress Report*, Vol. 330 (London: The Stationery Office).

Malinowski, B. (1922) 'Ethnology and the Study of Society', *Economica*, 6, 208–219.

Morrow, V. (2008) 'Ethical Dilemmas in Research With Children and Young People About Their Social Environments', *Children's Geographies*, 6(1), 49–61.

Munro, E. (2011) *The Munro Review of Child Protection: Final Report, a Child-Centred System*, Vol. 8062 (London: The Stationery Office).

Powell, M.A. and Smith, A.B. (2009) 'Children's Participation Rights in Research', *Childhood*, 16(1), 124–142.

Putnam, R.D. (2000) 'Bowling Alone: America's Declining Social Capital', in L. Crothers and C. Lockhart (eds.), *Culture and Politics* (New York: Palgrave Macmillan), 223–234.

Sharpe, D. (2009) 'The Value of Young People Doing Research: Where do Young People's Voices Count?', *Research, Policy and Planning: The Journal of the Social Services Research Group*, 27(2), 97–106.

Smith, L. (2010) *Psychology, Poverty, and the End of Social Exclusion: Putting Our Practice to Work* (New York: Teachers College Press).

Törrönen, M. and Vauhkonen, T. (2012) 'Everyone Is Valuable: Participatory Peer Research into Young People Leaving Alternative Care', *Conference: SOS Children's Village*.

Tucker, S. (2012) 'Considerations on the Involvement of Young People as Co-Inquirers in Abuse and Neglect Research', *Journal of Youth Studies*, 16(2).

Index

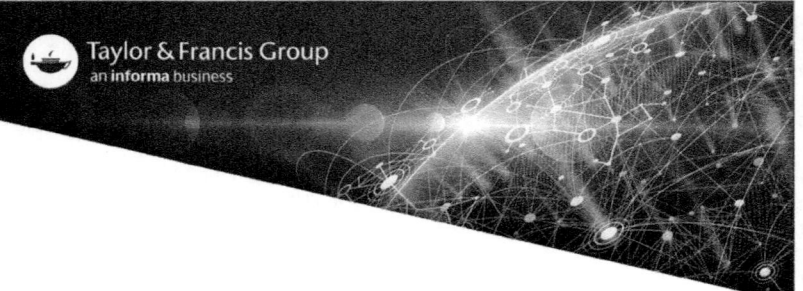